D1562450

Modernization and Revolution

Modernization and Revolution

Dilemmas of Progress
in Late Imperial Russia

ESSAYS IN HONOR OF
ARTHUR P. MENDEL

edited by
EDWARD H. JUDGE
JAMES Y. SIMMS, JR.

with a foreword by
WILLIAM G. ROSENBERG

East European Monographs
Distributed by Columbia University Press, New York
1992

EAST EUROPEAN MONOGRAPHS, NUMBER CCCXXXVI

This book is dedicated

to the memory of

ARTHUR P. MENDEL

(1927-1988)

a superb teacher

a perceptive scholar

a kind and gentle man

CONTENTS

Acknowledgments   ix

FOREWORD   xi
William G. Rosenberg

Contributors   xix

INTRODUCTION   1

THE FAMINE AND THE RADICALS   13
James Y. Simms, Jr.

URBAN GROWTH AND ANTI-SEMITISM
IN RUSSIAN MOLDAVIA   43
Edward H. Judge

RUSSIAN TEACHERS AND PEASANT
REVOLUTION, 1895-1917   59
Scott J. Seregny

PEASANT RESETTLEMENT AND SOCIAL
CONTROL IN LATE IMPERIAL RUSSIA   75
Edward H. Judge

UNSCRAMBLING THE JUMBLED CATALOG:
FEUDALISM AND THE REVOLUTION OF 1905
IN THE WRITINGS OF N. P. PAVLOV-SILVANSKII   95
Thad Radzilowski

NEW THOUGHTS ON THE OLD REGIME
AND THE REVOLUTION OF 1917 IN RUSSIA:
A REVIEW OF RECENT WESTERN LITERATURE   129
Robert W. Thurston

RETHINKING THE ORIGINS OF THE
RASPUTIN LEGEND   169
Mark Kulikowski

MOSCOW, 1917: WORKERS' REVOLUTION,
WORKER CONTROL   187
Diane P. Koenker

ACKNOWLEDGMENTS

As with any collaborative effort, there are a number of persons who contributed in one way or another to each of the articles in this volume. In addition, there are several individuals whose assistance was instrumental in the preparation and completion of the book as a whole. In particular, we would like to express our profound appreciation to our editorial assistants, Rosalind Hingeley and Sharyn Knight. Rosalind spent long hours reading and re-reading the various articles and providing helpful hints and insightful suggestions to the editors and authors. Sharyn typed and re-typed the various articles, making numerous corrections and recommendations and setting the articles in their final form. We are deeply grateful for their patience, tolerance, professionalism, good humor, and skill.

We are also grateful to William G. Rosenberg, Horace W. Dewey, Stephen Fischer-Galati, and a number of others who provided support, assistance, suggestions, and encouragement along the way.

FOREWORD

William G. Rosenberg

Arthur Mendel's premature death from cancer on February 28, 1988 stilled the voice of a splendid human being. Passionate in his commitments, skeptical, and with a deep and wise intelligence, Arthur constantly reached for the essential and was impatient with anything less. He also possessed a finely tuned sense of humor, which leavened his often caustic perspectives. To the end, he could smile wryly at the absurdity of life's many contradictions.

He was born on July 17, 1927, in Chicago, and lived there except for service in the army (1945-47) until graduating from Roosevelt College in 1950. Like most other prominent Russian historians of his generation, he did his graduate work at Harvard University under Michael Karpovich. Between 1953 and 1955, he was a Fulbright scholar in Helsinki. He received his PhD in 1956. Shortly afterwards, he returned for a year to Roosevelt as an assistant professor, and then moved on to the University of Iowa. In 1959, he became an associate professor at New York University.

In New York, in addition to taking a prominent role in NYU's undergraduate program, Arthur gained a prominence which later amused him as a television personality on "The Sunrise Semester." He also saw the publication by Harvard University Press of his first major book, *Dilemmas of Progress in Tsarist Russia* (1961). In 1962, he was invited to come to Ann Arbor as successor to Professor Lobanov-Rostovsky. Four years later, in 1966, he was promoted to full professor. In all respects, Michigan rightly regarded his appointment as one of genuine distinction and great promise.

Arthur's early reputation as a fine scholar and teacher was based both on *Dilemmas of Progress*, a seminal study of legal Marxism and legal Populism, and on his extraordinary abilities in the classroom, where his energy, knowledge and wit captivated even the least able of his students. I first heard him lecture in 1963. Addressing a large undergraduate audience on the complex question of Soviet industrialization strategies in the 1920s, he managed to transport virtually every one of his students into a distant and alien universe, so much so that the end of the hour came and went, causing us both to miss lunch. (Such deprivations are not easily forgotten!)

At Michigan Arthur quickly developed a large and loyal student following. Teaching both the Imperial Russian and Soviet courses from a liberal humanitarian perspective and emphasizing the role of ideas and thinkers in the process of historical change, he rarely failed to use his classroom as a place to argue the dangers of dogmatism and irrationality. Arthur was troubled by much of the youthful utopianism that developed at Michigan and elsewhere during the late 1960s, and equally so by some of the efforts to expand and revise our understanding of the Soviet experience, which he thought (mistakenly in my view) tended to minimize the horrific consequences of a dogma in power. A sense of institutional and professional alienation pulled him toward a fuller exploration of utopian ideologies and outlooks, in all of their complex social and psychological dimensions. Largely giving up his Russian and Soviet teaching for new courses on utopian and apocalyptic thought and behavior, he also became more deeply involved, both personally and intellectually, with the history of the Middle East and especially the experience of Israelis. In 1985 he lectured in Haifa on apocalyptic violence. He also spent much of 1986 in Jerusalem pursuing research on Michael Bakunin. The deeper his convictions, the more important he felt his teaching and research, even if at times he became somewhat impatient with those (like me) who might insist on the merit of views he rejected, especially as they related to Russian and Soviet history. Even after the onset of his illness, students constantly sought him out for training, guidance, and counsel; and many returned to the campus simply to renew a relationship they valued so highly.

Like his teaching, Arthur's scholarship reflected deep personal commitment. When *Dilemmas of Progress* first appeared, the *Slavic Review* saw it providing "a striking example of the quality of engagement". The *American Historical Review* praised its "brilliant insights." A beautifully researched and carefully drawn analysis of the thought and writings of "legal Populists" (especially Mikhailovskii, Vorontsov, and Daniel'son) and "legal Marxists" (Plekhanov, Struve, Berdiaev, and Bulgakov), *Dilemmas of Progress* argues in favor of what Arthur regarded as the humanitarian impulses of Populism as opposed to the dogmatic tendencies of early Russian Marxism, an outlook which, despite its own aversion to many of Lenin's views, he ultimately linked to Stalinism. Mendel's Populists are attractive to him primarily because they struggled to find alternatives to the social brutalities of Western-style industrialization, imposed with some force in the 1890s by Sergei Witte. Mikhailovskii and others were not persuaded that tsarist Russia bore the market capacity to sustain the rapid development of heavy industry, nor the resources to finance it. A process of industrialization forced from above could only lead, in their view, to the further impoverishment and social dislocation of the peasantry, still the overwhelming majority of the population. Russia's comparative impoverishment and its relatively low socio-economic level required a minimalist response to the challenges of industrialization if society as a whole were to avoid social dislocation and revolutionary upheaval. In one of the most interesting sections of the book, Arthur examines with some sympathy contemporary echoes of this approach in modern India. As for Russia, the result of failing to find a humane solution to the "dilemmas of progress" was 1917 and its aftermath.

In contrast to the "Populists" (I use quotation marks, because in my view Arthur's categories were somewhat overdetermined—to use a psychological term he would have appreciated), the "Marxists" cared less about the human deprivations of rapid industrialization than they did about the potential this engendered for radical social and political change.

Marx was an attractive thinker because the *inevitability* of industrial growth posited an equally necessary revolutionary upheaval: the dilemmas of "progress," as measured by late 19th century standards of industrial might, led straight to the end of tsarism. This idealist perspective was for Arthur deeply flawed on at least two counts, both of which he believed Struve and his legal Marxist comrades ultimately came to understand. It denied the central role of human volition in the process of historical change; and it measured "progress" in material terms. It also reflected a youthful impatience and a utopian belief in the efficacy of radical politics, two qualities of mind with which Arthur was to wrestle throughout his career.

Dilemmas of Progress thus helped structure an important debate in Western historiography about the currents of the late imperial period. In opposition to Theodore von Laue, whose volume on Witte appeared shortly afterwards and for whom the tsarist industrializer was a positive, if not heroic, figure, Mendel saw the implicit collusion between Marxists and the state in the 1890s as symptomatic of complementary forms of oppression. Von Laue's Witte was a much more nuanced figure, whose goals for Russia were defined in large part by great power considerations: the fear that without industrial muscle, Russia and its people would suffer a far greater set of degradations than those generated by the necessities of industrial growth. Leopold Haimson and Richard Pipes both took a much broader view of early Russian Marxism. In *The Russian Marxists and the Origins of Bolshevism* (published in 1955), Haimson took a far more sympathetic approach toward what he regarded as the fundamentally humanistic impulses of most Marxists themselves in this period; and Pipes, while he shared Mendel's anti-Marxist critique, responded in his *Social Democrats and the St. Petersburg Labor Movement* (1963) with an argument centering the (malevolent) effects of early Marxism on Lenin, who is almost totally absent from *Dilemmas of Progress*. This debate was soon openly joined, as readers of this volume will surely know, in a famous debate in the *Slavic Review* (No. 4, 1964 and No. 1, 1965), in which Haimson, von Laue, and Mendel sparred on the question of social stability at the end of the old regime and the chances for avoiding revolution, essentially extending the arguments each had made in his book.

The core of the debate centered on the question of whether Russia had, in fact, reached a revolutionary flashpoint in the period just before the outbreak of the first World War as a consequence of the social dislocations of industrial change and the regime's resistance to political liberalization (a necessary corollary to industrial modernization), or whether it was the war itself, rather than the regime's failure to manage industrialization, which led directly to the revolution of 1917. Haimson presented a complex analysis of social alienation and polarization, both within the intelligentsia, between a disillusioned liberal center and a moderate to radical left, and between the intelligentsia as a whole and the Russian *narod*, its alienated and militant workers and peasants. Superimposed on each of these fissures was an additional and comparable alienation from the state. In Haimson's view, this complex pattern of social and political alienation found expression between 1912 and 1914 in the inability, on one hand, of the intelligentsia to reconstruct the broad if loose political coalition that largely characterized the politics of the intelligentsia in 1905, and on the other, in the increasingly independent militance of Russia's industrial proletariat, which rekindled massive strikes, especially during the first six months of 1914. It also forecast the failures of Russian liberalism in 1917, and suggested that Bolshevism, in opposition to the prevailing Western viewpoint, had strong social and structural foundations.

Mendel thought—and continued to believe throughout his career—that Haimson's analysis was little more than a sophisticated variant of the orthodox Soviet view, and that Haimson overdrew the contrast between Western proponents of "stabilization" and "revolution." The issue was not, for him, one of "stability," since he and others fully recognized that the rapid pace of industrialization had indeed led to deep social dislocations. It was, instead, precisely the inability of the regime to respond to these dislocations, especially during the war, and the single-minded determination of the Bolsheviks to seize on worker (and peasant) discontent to further their own narrow political ambitions. Hence it *was* the war that led directly to revolution, especially through the "hideous experiences" (Arthur's words) it forced on the peasantry; and it was Bolshevik *voluntarism*, not embedded structural faults, that explained why October 1917 differed so greatly from October 1905. Constitutional liberalism, otherwise an alternative, was powerless to resist the dogmatic appeal of the radical left and, deprived of its earlier potential for broad support, it dissolved politically in the face of ruthless opponents.

However tempting for someone like me whose research over the years has largely been devoted to the revolutionary period, this is not the place to join these arguments. Many a PhD examination was diverted as the two of us tangled over the political implications of late imperial urban development, the significance of the Stolypin reforms on peasant mentality and culture, or such matters as the nature of relations between Russia's radical and liberal intelligentsia and other population groups, especially Russia's industrial workers. However intense these discussions sometimes became, the perduring essence of Arthur's analysis remained his deep humanitarian sentiments and commitments. What he wanted most to believe about the late imperial period was that progress could be defined in terms of social tolerance and material well-being, and that the very real and very serious dilemmas it engendered could nonetheless be resolved without the horrors of revolutionary upheaval. And his increasing antipathy to the political left over the years, both in historical settings and in more contemporary ones like the university itself, was based in part on the belief that the more intense one's political activism, the less tolerant one became toward the types of compromises that are usually required to solve conflict in a peaceful manner. (Once when a group of student activists seized some administrators' offices at Michigan, and officials convened the faculty to alert them that the state police would probably be called upon to clear the building, Arthur suggested instead that it be dismantled brick by brick if that is what was needed to avoid bloodshed.)

To explore more carefully what he saw as a frequent transition among political activists from "defending freedom to threatening it," as he put it on more than one occasion, Arthur followed *Dilemmas of Progress* with a biography of Michael Bakunin, which was published in 1981. His choice of subject was a good one. No serious biography of the famous Russian emigre radical had been written since E. H. Carr's unsympathetic study of the 1930s; and unlike many other 19th century Russian revolutionaries, Bakunin had left an extensive collection of writings and private papers which were readily available to Western scholars.

Arthur's principal line of enquiry, however, necessarily led him to explore the question of Bakunin's psychology—psychopathology, really—an area of investigation about which most historians feel uneasy. Although his explanation for Bakunin's evolution as a radical rested on a complex set of factors, at its root, in Arthur's view, was a pathology psychoanalytically defined as unresolved Oedipus conflicts and an associated narcissism. This was, in essence, "the root of apocalypse," as the biography was subtitled.

Among psychohistorians and others familiar with the complexities of psychoanalytic explanations, Arthur's new work was extremely well received. An article on Bakunin, Berdyaev and Chaadaev which appeared in *The Psychohistory Review* won that journal's prize for the best essay published in 1984. Other historians had trouble with his approach, however, and like *Dilemmas of Progress* before it, *Bakunin* generated a good deal of controversy. Some rejected his approach out of hand, wrongly assuming that Arthur regarded Bakunin simply as a psychopath, and generally misunderstanding both his argument and his analytic reasoning. Others, including me, accepted his approach and very much appreciated the skill with which he reconstructed Bakunin's psyche, but argued with his implication that psychopathology was a sufficient or even necessary explanation for radical politics.

Perhaps not surprisingly, considering our differences on other historical issues, I failed to make my case with Arthur on this matter as well. Indeed, I felt on more than one occasion that my arguments only reinforced his convictions. In any event, he soon followed the Bakunin book with an exploration of what he called "the vengeance of the knights," a study of Chaadaev, Herzen, Tolstoy, Kropotkin, Leontyev, Berdyaev, and Merezhkovsky, Russia's "aristocratic rebels." His principal contention here was that these and other intellectuals from the landed aristocracy were primarily responsible for the ideology of Russia's radical opposition, "down to and including the Bolsheviks", as he put it in one description of his work. Arthur regarded all of these figures as apocalyptic visionaries who were convinced that only a swift and violent social transformation could achieve their goals. He saw in what he regarded as their "Populist" support of communal traditions and their assumptions about an "implicit alliance" with the peasants an outlook that in other historical contexts would be labelled reactionary or even fascist.

Side by side with this study, Arthur ambitiously conducted an additional and, in his view, complementary exploration of a group of Russian Jewish settlers in Palestine who helped lay the foundations of the kibbutz movement and moderate Israeli socialism. Here, in contrast to Russia's "aristocratic rebels," Arthur saw people attempting to create a form of socialism by means of personal moral regeneration through physical labor, rather than the conquest of political power through class struggle. Their great attraction for him lay in their belief, as he understood it, that "the end should be present in the means," that the force of evil could not produce good ends. This "pharisaic" tradition stood in sharp contrast to the "apocalyptic"; and in attempting to elucidate them both, Arthur was once again determined to make clear what he regarded as history's essential lessons.

It is part of the tragedy of Arthur's early death that he never saw these projects through to publication. Still, the essays of his students included in this volume testify to his deep and admirable commitments, and to his success in encouraging even those whose interpretations he rejected to work through their material as serious and independent scholars. It is a most impressive legacy.

CONTRIBUTORS

EDWARD H. JUDGE is professor of history at Le Moyne College in Syracuse, New York. He is the author of *Plehve: Repression and Reform in Imperial Russia, 1902-1904* (Syracuse, 1983) and *Easter in Kishinev: The Anatomy of a Pogrom* (New York, 1992).

DIANE P. KOENKER is professor of history at the University of Illinois at Urbana-Champaign. She is the author of *Moscow Workers and the 1917 Revolution* (Princeton, 1981) and co-author of *Strikes and Revolution in Russia, 1917* (Princeton, 1989).

MARK KULIKOWSKI is associate professor of history at the State University of New York College at Oswego. He is the author of a number of works in the fields of Russian history, immigration history, and Slavic bibliography.

THADDEUS C. RADZILOWSKI is professor of history at Southwest State University in Marshall, Minnesota. He is the author of *Feudalism, Revolution and History: The Life and Works of N. P. Pavlov-Silvanskii* (Boulder, 1992), and he contributed to and edited (with J. L. Black) "State and Autocracy in Imperial Russian and Soviet Historiography," *Laurentian University Review* 10, no. 1 (November 1977). He has also written extensively on emigration from East Central Europe to North America.

SCOTT J. SEREGNY is associate professor of history at Indiana University in Indianapolis. He is the author of *Russian Teachers and Peasant Revolution: The Politics of Education in 1905* (Bloomington, 1989) and coeditor of *Politics and Society in Provincial Russia: Saratov, 1590-1917* (Columbus, 1989).

JAMES Y. SIMMS, JR. is professor of history at Hampden-Sydney College in Hampden-Sydney, Virginia. He is the author of "The Crisis in Russian Agriculture at the End of the Nineteenth Century: A Different View," *Slavic Review* 36, no. 3 (1977), and other articles on agriculture in late imperial Russia.

ROBERT W. THURSTON is associate professor of history at Miami University in Oxford, Ohio. He is the author of *Liberal City, Conservative State: Moscow and Russia's Urban Crisis, 1906-1914* (New York, 1987) and "The Soviet Family during the 'Great Terror'," *Soviet Studies*, no. 3, 1991.

INTRODUCTION

Among the many legacies of Arthur P. Mendel is the wonderfully appropriate title of his first book, *Dilemmas of Progress in Tsarist Russia*. During the last decades of the tsarist regime such dilemmas were readily apparent, not only to the legal Marxists and legal populists who are the focus of Mendel's book, but also to government officials, public servants, revolutionary activists, members of the liberal intelligentsia, and all Russians who thought seriously about the future of their vast empire. The forces of modernization and revolution were transforming the Russian political, economic and social order into something quite different from what it had been only a few short decades earlier, creating a wealth of opportunities and a host of problems. Each of the articles which make up this volume is concerned in some way with these forces—the problems and opportunities they created, and the impact they had on the people who struggled to deal with them, adapt to them, understand them, and control them.

In the spirit of Arthur Mendel, this collection makes no pretense at presenting a unified interpretation of historical developments in late imperial Russia. Mendel understood clearly the value of diverse viewpoints, and he cherished a good debate. He encouraged and challenged his students to pursue a variety of approaches and ideas, even though they might call into question or contradict his own views and visions. On more than one occasion, in fact, he provided good-natured assistance and strong support to those who were at odds with him on issues and ideas. Professor Simms, in particular, benefited from his open-minded tolerance and willingness to accept interpretations which were in conflict with his own. So it seems only fitting that the works presented here in tribute to Arthur Mendel should reflect a variety of approaches and interpretations.

The first article, "The Famine and the Radicals" by James Y. Simms, Jr., makes a persuasive case that the appropriate place to begin a consideration of modernization and revolution in late imperial Russia is with the crop failure and famine of 1891-1892. According to Simms, the famine is a central event in Russia's economic and industrial history. On one hand, it galvanized the government into action, precipitating the appointment of Sergei Witte as Minister of Finance and the initiation of a massive program of state-sponsored industrial growth and economic reorientation. On the other hand, it helped to reawaken and radicalize the Russian intelligentsia, resulting in a resurgence of the revolutionary movement.

Simms meticulously traces the famine's impact on a whole generation of revolutionary theorists and activists. The thoughts and ideas of Plekhanov, Struve, Martov, Lenin, and Chernov, among others, were profoundly affected by the disastrous harvest of 1891 and the widespread suffering that ensued. More importantly, Simms argues, the famine served as the "catalytic event" which provided the impetus for the dramatic growth and development of Marxism in Russia. Prior to the famine the populists, with their belief that Russia could avoid the development of capitalist relations and create a new order based on peasant agriculture, dominated the revolutionary opposition. The events of 1891-1892, however, raised serious questions about the state of Russian agriculture and the viability of the peasants as a revolutionary force. In the debates that followed, the Marxists, with their disdain for the peasantry and insistence on the necessity of capitalist development, seemed to gain the most. The famine, and the industrialization policies that followed in its wake, helped to bolster the credibility of the Marxist analysis and to attract young revolutionaries to the Marxist side. The famine thus played an instrumental role, both in revitalizing the revolutionary movement and in helping to make Marxism an integral part of that movement.

Radical activism, of course, was by no means the only phenomenon strengthened by the process of modernization. The second article in this collection, Edward H. Judge's "Urban Growth and Anti-Semitism in Russian Moldavia," focuses on the interaction between urbanization and anti-Semitism in Bessarabia province, particularly in its capital city of Kishinev. During the course of the nineteenth century, migration and population growth had transformed this Moldavian provincial town into a diverse metropolis comprised of various nationalities and cultural groups. Meanwhile, in the latter part of the century, government policies designed to "protect" Christian peasants from Jewish "exploitation" had forced large numbers of Jews to reside in cities and towns rather than rural villages.

According to Judge, the result in Kishinev was a volatile situation in which, by 1900, the Jews made up almost half of the population, easily outnumbering both the native Moldavians and the politically dominant Russians. And, despite the fact that Jews tended to dominate the city's industrial, financial and commercial enterprises, as well as the skilled trades, most of the city's Jews were quite poor. This circumstance, combined with the common perception of the Jews as more ambitious, efficient, intelligent and industrious than their Christian counterparts, led to fears that there would be less work and lower pay for Christian artisans and workers. Meanwhile, the anti-Jewish restrictions enforced by the Russian government and the obvious anti-Semitism of leading local officials created the impression that abusive behavior toward Jews was more likely to be rewarded than punished. In this atmosphere, by playing upon religious and cultural antagonisms and by spreading vile slanders and libels, prominent and unscrupulous anti-Semites were able to incite the working-class Christians of Kishinev toward anti-Jewish violence.

If the process of change provided new incentives for the radicals and new opportunities for the anti-Semites, it also provided a host of new challenges for the public servants of the Russian empire. This was especially true of the rural schoolteachers, as depicted by Scott J. Seregny in "Russian Teachers and Peasant Revolution, 1895-1917." The same famine that served as a catalyst for the revival of the revolutionary movement also spurred the rural zemstvos to launch ambitious efforts to improve and extend the education system. The teachers thus became the front line soldiers in the campaign to transform rural Russia by enlightening the peasant masses.

According to Seregny, the period from 1895 to 1905 witnessed not only an upsurge in rural education, sponsored in part by the government, but also an increase among the teachers in political radicalism and activism aimed at transforming the traditional order which supported that government. Summer courses and mutual-aid societies for teachers, in particular, were infiltrated and influenced by liberal and radical opponents of the imperial regime. The heyday of the teachers came during the Revolution of 1905, when they organized their own All-Russian Teachers' Union, helped in the formation of peasant unions, and actively sought to win peasant support for the general objectives of the liberation movement. Hampered at first by peasant perceptions of them as "outsiders" and "gentlefolk," the teachers soon gained a position of status in the village by communicating and explaining the momentous events of war and revolution, and by helping the peasants to draft petitions and organize political activities.

Seregny goes on to point out, however, that the aftermath of the compromised revolution was by no means so encouraging for the rural teachers. The imperial government, recognizing the role played by the teachers in facilitating peasant activism, sought to drastically reduce their influence. The peasant unions were destroyed, the Teachers' Union was abolished, and large numbers of teachers were arrested or dismissed. Government control over the schools was strengthened, and teachers were barred from direct participation in village affairs. As a result, morale declined among the rural teachers, and they in turn lost much of their prestige among the peasantry. And when the new revolution occurred in 1917, the influence of the teachers was minimal.

Ironically, much like the radicals and teachers, government officials found themselves profoundly influenced by the rapidly changing course of events, scrambling to adjust and adapt their policies to the new situations that obtained. In "Peasant Resettlement and Social Control in Late Imperial Russia," Edward H. Judge traces the tortuous history of a single piece of imperial legislation: the Resettlement Law of June 6, 1904. Traditionally, in an effort to maintain public order and social control, the imperial government had sought to limit peasant mobility and keep village residents tied closely to the land. Even after serfdom was abolished in 1861 there were no provisions made for peasants to legally relocate from one area to another. By the 1890s, however, the rapid growth of population, the "crowded" conditions in the central "black-earth" provinces, the construction of the Trans-Siberian Railway, and the widespead illegal migration that continued to occur had compelled the government to ease its restrictions and allow peasants to petition for the right of legal resettlement. But the Ministry of Interior, which feared that too much peasant mobility could undermine social control, continued to resist the notion of large-scale peasant migration.

The impetus for a change in policy, according to Judge, was a series of peasant riots in the central agricultural provinces during spring of 1902. Although the disorders were eventually crushed, the specter of peasant rebellion was frightening enough to compel the Ministry of Interior to abandon its opposition to peasant migration. The crowded conditions in these areas, it appeared, were leading to social unrest. The interests of social control, as well as those of imperial colonization, now seemed to call for a policy of controlled migration which would encourage the poorer peasants from the central provinces to relocate in sparsely populated regions. Thus, for the next two years, ministry officials worked to draft legislation which would encourage and assist the migration of poorer peasants away from crowded areas, while maintaining strict government control over the entire process. In particular, the ministry was determined to support only resettlement from and to certain designated regions. The Ministry of Finance, which favored a less restrictive approach, opposed these provisions but was unable to block them. The resulting law, confirmed by the emperor on June 6, 1904, provided a whole series of incentives and supports for "privileged" resettlers, that is, for poor peasants migrating from certain overcrowded areas to designated target regions.

The irony, as Judge points out, is that the law was destined never to be implemented in its original form. Before its provisions could take effect, the Revolution of 1905 intervened and changed the political landscape. Widespread peasant rebellions made it clear that rural unrest was not confined to the crowded central provinces, and brought to power people who favored unrestricted peasant migration. A special supplement, approved in March of 1906, extended the law's incentives and supports to all peasants who wished to relocate. As a result the Resettlement Law of 1906, designed to control peasant migration and direct it along certain lines, was transformed into a guarantee of state support for any and all peasant migration, and then served as the basis for the vast resettlement movement that subsequently ensued.

The Russian Revolution of 1905, of course, did not just affect the activities of zemstvo teachers and the resettlement policies of state officials. It also had a profound impact on the outlook and understanding of numerous individuals. One whose entire world view was altered dramatically by the events of 1905 was the talented historian Nikolai Pavlovich Pavlov-Silvanskii. In "Unscrambling the Jumbled Catalog: Feudalism and the Revolution of 1905 in the Writings of N. P. Pavlov-Silvanskii," Thad Radzilowski describes the shattering impact of the revolution on this young scholar, and the resulting transformation of his views.

Radzilowski indicates that, in his early career, Pavlov-Silvanskii was both a monarchist and a traditionalist. Despite his controversial work on feudalism, which claimed that Russian feudal institutions had been fundamentally similar to those in the West, he continued to believe that Russian historical development was essentially unique, and that autocratic government was a positive and necessary component of this development. The shocking events of Bloody Sunday, some of which he witnessed, shattered his faith in the monarchy and forced him to reevaluate his attitudes and ideals. Almost overnight he became a liberal, a founding member of the Constitutional Democrats and an active organizer for that political party. His former heroes, "progressive" royal reformers like Grand Duke Konstantine and Peter the Great, he now saw as prominent figures in the development of autocratic oppression, so he transferred his enthusiasm to more radical heroes like the Decembrist Pavel Pestel. More importantly, perhaps, he now saw the historical development of Russia as identical with that of the West, with the events of 1905 corresponding almost exactly to those of 1789 in France and 1848 in central Europe. This new interpretation, of course, had political as well as scholarly implications. If Russia's past mirrored that of the West, apparently so must its future: liberal democratic institutions, it seemed clear, must eventually replace those of patriarchal monarchism. And it also tended to confirm and reinforce Pavlov-Silvanskii's earlier analysis of Russian feudalism: if modern society was developing along western lines, it certainly stood to reason that medieval society would have done the same. In *Feodalizm v drevnei Rusi*, published in 1907, he created a sensation in scholarly circles by extending his new analysis to the entire scope of Russian history, directly attacking the long established notion that Russia was somehow unique in its social, political, and economic development. This analysis was extended in *Feodalizm v udelnoi Rusi*, published posthumously in 1910. As Radzilowski points out, although Pavlov-Silvanskii died of cholera in 1908, his writings and interpretations, influenced so strongly by the dramatic events of 1905, had a profound impact on Russian and Soviet scholars for the next several decades.

Western scholars, too, have been profoundly interested in reinterpretation and re-analysis of historical developments in late Imperial Russia. In "New Thoughts on the Old Regime and the Revolution of 1917 in Russia: A Review of Recent Western Literature," Robert Thurston undertakes the daunting task of summarizing and synthesizing the recent works of Western historians who have studied this period. The result is a perceptive and provocative article that sheds considerable light on the new interpretations and insights and their impact on our understanding of late imperial Russia.

Citing an impressive array of books and studies, Thurston perceives a consensus emerging among Western scholars on some of the central issues involved in the fall of the old regime and the rise of Bolshevism in Russia. The deterioration of the imperial regime, it now seems evident, was due not so much to incompetent leadership (although this no doubt contributed) as it was to inherent contradictions between the theory of autocratic rule and the emerging new realities in Russia. According to Thurston, the research suggests that the very nature and structure of the old order were incompatible with the forces of modernization and westernization. The regime could not hope to adapt itself to the forces of change and simultaneously remain true to the principles of unrestricted absolutism and hereditary social estates.

In discussing recent studies of the workers and peasants, Thurston finds much to applaud. Using a wide variety of methods and sources, modern researchers have managed to pierce the time-worn image of the nameless and faceless "dark masses" whose sufferings and deprivations, combined with the skillful agitation of radical activists, allegedly propelled them toward revolution. Scholars have managed to look inside the villages and factories and discover that, for the most part, peasants and workers were rational actors with a clear idea of what their interests were and how best to protect them. Traditional assumptions about their outlooks and quality of life have been challenged and revised. Although no clear consensus has yet emerged, it has become obvious that the dynamics of village and factory life were far more complex than previously supposed.

The most provocative part of Thurston's essay, and the one that bears most directly upon the legacy and reputation of Arthur P. Mendel, is the part that deals with the impact of the prerevolutionary era on the events of 1917. It could well be, Thurston suggests, that there was an element of prescience in the position taken by Mendel during his famous 1965 exchange with Leopold Haimson in the pages of *Slavic Review*. Recent scholarship seems to indicate that liberals and educated elements were much less isolated from the lower classes than has often been supposed. Perhaps the development of trade unions, the growth of literacy, and the changes in village life could have served as the basis for transition to a more liberal society had Russia remained at peace. If so, the time-honored question of "whither Russia?" on the eve of World War I is still an open issue, not in the sense of "evolution versus revolution," as Mendel and others perceived it, but in the sense of what sort of revolution Russia was heading toward.

The decline and fall of the tsarist regime in Russia has often been ascribed, especially in popular literature, less to the forces of modernization and revolution than to the alleged influence of the notorious Rasputin upon imperial policies and politics in the last few years of the regime. In "Rethinking the Origins of the Rasputin Legend," Mark Kulikowski points out that, despite its fantastic elements, few scholars have sought directly to challenge the veracity of the Rasputin story.

Kulikowski sets out, therefore, to discover the roots and sources of the "Rasputin legend." Interestingly enough, he finds that, with the exception of a few important accounts, not much was published about Rasputin during his lifetime. It was not until after his death that a significant number of articles began to appear, and it was not really until after the February Revolution of 1917 that the legend began to blossom into full bloom. The demise of the old regime, and the corresponding disappearance of its censorship, helped to unleash a flood of sensational articles, pamphlets, and broadsides—and even several books and films—about the escapades and influence of the Siberian "holy man." Many of these were exaggerated and unsubstantiated accounts which focused on the more scandalous aspects of Rasputin's career and made outlandish allegations about his relations with the imperial family and his influence in state affairs. Some of them apparently achieved very wide circulation and reached a broad audience. Enhanced by spurious rumors, some of which were based on Rasputin's own idle boasts, they provided a simple and appealing explanation for momentous events, and helped to create a persistent and enduring legend that captured the popular imagination and continues to influence the reading public today.

The last piece in this volume, Diane P. Koenker's "Moscow 1917: Workers' Revolution, Worker Control," focuses on industrial workers in Moscow during the period between the two revolutions of 1917. It deals primarily with "worker control," the name generally applied to worker attempts to influence and shape the policies and procedures of the factories where they were employed.

The February Revolution of 1917, Koenker asserts, had a major impact on relationships in the workplace. A new, more democratic political order seemed to indicate a new, more democratic managerial system, but the full implications of this transformation were not entirely clear. The workshop thus became "contested terrain," as workers and managers sought to redefine their respective roles in the "balance of power." In a number of enterprises, the workers moved quickly to demand—and in many cases carry out—the removal of certain supervisors and the shortening of the work day. As time went on, the struggle became more acute, and workers were increasingly inclined to go on strike when their demands remained unmet. As often as not, the strikes involved issues of "control" as well as wages: the workers insisted upon things such as employer recognition of their unions and committees, modifications of workplace rules and regulations, and changes in job descriptions. In some instances they demanded that worker committees be given the right to hire and fire employees. And, in a few cases, they even asserted control in the full sense of the word, taking management of the factories into their own hands.

From all this activity, Koenker concludes that the workers of Moscow in 1917 had a somewhat different view of the nature of private property than the factory owners or managers. Ownership to them was a form of public trust that involved certain obligations as well as powers and privileges. If, in their perception, certain managers or owners had betrayed this trust and acted irresponsibly, the workers were inclined to take action either to remove them or to force them to change their ways. Contested notions of property, and the corresponding rights and duties of both owner and employer, were thus part and parcel of the revolutionary struggles of 1917.

What emerges from these essays, then, is an increased appreciation of the complexity and dynamism of the forces affecting Russia in the late imperial period. During these years, almost all aspects of Russian life became, to some extent, "contested terrain." More than that, perhaps, they were in many respects "uncharted terrain," and those who sought to influence events often had little idea where their actions might lead. There were no simple solutions and, as Arthur Mendel himself would insist, there are no simple explanations for the changes that came about. It was a time of challenge and opportunity, but also a time of confrontation, contradiction and confusion, for those who sought to grapple with the forces of modernization and revolution in late imperial Russia.

THE FAMINE AND THE RADICALS

James Y. Simms, Jr.

> The famine, like a terrible fire, spread along the streets
> of the Russian land....
> *Aptekman, "Partiia 'Narodnago Prava.' Vospominaniia"*

> We are convinced that Russia stands on the eve of a
> political revolution....
> *A. I. Bogdanovich, "Nasushchnyi vopros"*

The crop failure and famine of 1891-1892 was one of the most important domestic events in Russian history in the last half of the nineteenth century. It was a tragedy of immense proportions, being one of the most severe crop failures of the entire century and afflicting seventeen provinces of the central black earth and Volga regions of European Russia.[1] An event of such magnitude naturally had a major impact on Russian society; for example, it forced the prohibition of grain exports from Russia in the fall of 1891, brought suffering to millions of peasants, and led to the appointment of Sergei Witte as Minister of Finance. The famine also had a profound impact on Russian society and the intelligentsia, especially within the radical movement, and constitutes a significant point of demarcation in the history of that movement; in essence the famine acted as a catalyst and evoked a resurgence of activity, growth, confidence, and intensity within the ranks of the radicals in the 1890's.[2] One could go so far as to say that the Russian intelligentsia experienced something of a rebirth or reawakening, a revival as a result of the famine.[3] The purpose of this article is to examine the impact of the famine upon the revolutionary movement and its resurgence in the early 1890's.

It seems clear that the crop failure/famine of 1891-1892 greatly disturbed the rather staid public life of Russia in the decade following the assassination of Tsar Alexander II. In July, 1892, in an article concerning Russian cultural life published in the journal *Athenaeum*, Paul Miliukov pointed out that an intellectual renaissance was taking place in Russia. He noted that a transition period had set in; the famine of 1892 "had stirred up the educated classes of Russia, and stimulated them to great efforts, and centered their activities upon a well-defined common object."[4] The journal *Russkoe bogatstvo* said it more poetically, stating that the crop failure in 1891, and especially its consequences, had "stirred up the quiet surface of our life," like a stone thrown into a pond.[5] A fresh enthusiasm infused the public mood and "awakened those who slumbered and encouraged the fallen spirit."[6] Indeed, one observer stated that the famine rocked the intelligentsia.[7] Another contemporary noted that the famine of 1891 liberated the opposition movement from the deadening effects of tsarist oppression of the 1880's.[8] In his study of the revolutionary movement, Professor Norman Naimark states that "no underground organization could have aroused the political consciousness of the Russian intelligentsia the way the famine did."[9]

In terms of the famine and famine relief, there was a great outpouring of sympathy and aid on the part of society. Many of the intelligentsia—conservative and liberal—made monetary donations, sponsored plays, concerts, and lotteries to benefit the starving, and worked in direct famine relief.[10] Hundreds of people, particularly university students, were caught up in a second, and more effective, "movement to the people."[11] Within the universities, the students also made collections for the famine-stricken and donated the money for famine relief.[12] V. G. Korolenko called these youthful humanitarians "new people," and they probably were the largest single group to participate in famine relief.[13]

The excitement generated by the events of 1891 quickened the pulse of the radical movement. The older generation of liberal-radicals pounced upon the issue of the famine as a great opportunity to appeal to the radical young and to begin the overthrow of the tsarist system. In August, 1891, in the emigre newspaper, *Free Russia*, Stepniak wrote:

> We must wish and hope that this calamity may be the beginning of the end, and that the Russian people may give up their dumb patience, and, following the example of other nations, rise and sweep away once and for all a system which is the source of such endless miseries.[14]

Similarly, in January, 1892, there appeared in Russia a proclamation of the Peoples' Will which stated that the tsarist government had brought the country to bankruptcy and ruin, and that now was the time to be organizing the ranks to enable the party to overthrow autocracy at the proper moment.[15]

Statements urging the overthrow of the tsarist system were also published by two of the most respected revolutionaries living abroad—Paul Lavrov and George Plekhanov. In one of his famous essays on the famine, Plekhanov urged the people to introduce reforms—e.g., call a Zemskii Sobor—which would create a new social-political order.[16] Lavrov instructed his fellow Populists to take advantage of the crisis taking place in Russia in order to undermine the state.[17] "Make revolution not charity" was his insistent theme. If a socialist were to fulfill his "duty," his only "duty," he must hasten the fall of capitalism and the triumph of the social revolution.[18] Socialists must overthrow the "vampire" from the body of the Russian people.[19]

The reawakening of society and the subsequent revolutionary upswing actually began at the moment that the government allowed society to take action to ameliorate conditions in the famine district.[20] It is important to emphasize that the famine itself was a very significant factor in the revitalization of the opposition movement. Writing forty years after the event, Struve stated that:

> ...our generation had been greatly impressed by the famine of 1891-92. Those impressions gave birth to that movement of public thought which came to be

known as "legal Marxism." I emphasize the fact that
it was born not from books but from impressions of
life.... The younger generation received such
impressions from the famine of 1891-92.[21]

Probably few radicals and left-leaning liberals assumed
their ideological world-view simply because of the famine,
although some observers argued that a number of students,
having no political bias before going to the village, returned with
a definite revolutionary perspective.[22] The famine was appealing
and vital to the older generation of the opposition movement
because it confirmed their views about the incompetence and
injustice of the tsarist government and reinforced their desire for
reform.   To the already alienated young, the famine gave
credence to the radical arguments against the tsarist system. The
famine gave impetus and force to virtually any schema for reform
because it pointed out how backward Russia was relative to
other European societies. Russia was not India!

Peter Struve was one of that generation of students for
whom the famine was a very significant formative experience. In
1885, at age 15, Struve considered himself a political liberal; by
1888, he had become "by *conviction* only, a Social Democrat."[23]
"By conviction only; for socialism, however it be understood,
never inspired any *emotions* in me, still less a passion."[24]
Apparently it was the famine that engendered the requisite
passion, for in 1908 he wrote that "as far as I am personally
concerned, the hunger of 1891-92 made much more of a Marxist
out of me than the reading of Marx's *Capital*."[25]

The famine also helped shape the revolutionary career of
Iuri Martov. Although Martov was slightly younger than Struve,
he was also alienated from the system prior to the outbreak of
the famine and prior to his admission to the University of St.
Petersburg.[26] The famine gave this young student an issue to
focus on, and in December of 1891, he gave his first public
speech in which he predicted that the famine would lead to
spontaneous peasant riots, which in turn would end in a march
on the cities.   The task of young radicals, he said, was to
organize a strong revolutionary party "united with workers and

soldiers, and in a fitting moment, when the state will be disorganized, to perform a revolution...in order to overthrow autocracy and seize power."[27] But after the spontaneous and uncontrolled cholera riots in the summer of 1892, Martov turned away from what he termed "my naive riot period"[28] and concluded that Russia was not ready for a mass revolution.[29]

Martov relates that he was greatly influenced by the writings of Plekhanov and Akselrod pertaining to the famine. These writings caused him to read a French translation of *Capital*, which changed his entire approach to the question of revolution. He states, "to me it suddenly became clear how superficial and groundless up to that time was the whole of my revolutionism and how subjective political romanticism is dwarfed before such philosophical and sociological heights, to which Marxism rises."[30] This perspective ultimately led in December of 1892 to the formation of the Petersburg Emancipation of Labor Group, a group whose name emphasized the ideological connection of Martov and his circle with the Social Democrats in Geneva.[31] Clearly the famine of 1891 played a significant role in shaping Martov's political and radical philosophy.

Similarly, P. B. Akselrod stressed the importance of the famine and Plekhanov's ideas about the famine on the younger generation of emigres. Akselrod attended a speech on the famine given by Plekhanov in the winter of 1891 in Zurich[32] in which, according to Akselrod, Plekhanov so devastated his opponents that he acquired a number of converts to Social Democracy, and to the revolutionary movement in general.[33]

Another major Social Democratic revolutionary who was greatly influenced by the famine of 1891-92 was Vladimir Il'ich Ul'ianov (Lenin). There is little doubt that Lenin accepted and espoused narodovol'tsy ideas in the 1880's.[34] It is unclear at what point, between 1889 (when he first read *Capital*) and 1892, that Lenin accepted Marxist doctrine, although we do know that on occasion he was very critical in debates of some aspects of the Populist viewpoint.[35] Some historians argue that prior to 1890, no evidence exists that he leaned toward the Social Democratic faction which was developing along the Volga. In fact, it is argued that at that time he shared none of Marx's admiration for capitalism's historic accomplishments.[36] Since autobiographical materials on this stage of his career are sparse, it remains a matter of speculation precisely when he decided to adopt the ideas of Marx and Plekhanov concerning the social and economic development of Russia.[37]

Professor Naimark states in his book *Terrorists and Social Democrats* that Lenin became committed to Marxism as a young lawyer in Samara in 1892-93,[38] a date given by Lenin himself as the start of his revolutionary career.[39] If Lenin was teetering in his commitment to Populism and flirting with Marxism prior to the famine, and was a fully committed Marxist after that calamitous event, then one could conclude that the famine was an important factor in altering his revolutionary world-view. After the events of 1891-92 convinced Lenin that all was not well in the Russian village, he began a systematic study of agriculture based on Zemstvo statistics. He concluded that a form of class differentiation was indeed emerging in the countryside, which supported the contention that capitalism was developing in Russia. Thus it was probably at this time that Lenin became a Marxist and severed his association with the *narodovol'tsy*.[40] By the end of 1892, he was reported to have composed three articles attacking the view of Vorontsov, a major Populist writer.[41] More substantial works followed, and from 1893 to 1900, he was a severe and unflinching critic of Populism and an advocate of the Marxist challenge to the Populist views of the economic development of Russia.[42]

In terms of numbers and historical prominence, the famine seems to have had a greater impact on the growth and influence of the Social Democratic movement than on the Populist, especially among the younger generation of radicals. Nonetheless, the Populists too felt the imprint of the famine, as Victor Chernov, the subsequent leader of the Socialist Revolutionary Party, related in his memoirs. Like Lenin, Chernov was from the Volga region, in his case Saratov in the heart of the famine district. He attended the Saratov gymnasium and formed friendships with a number of students who were arrested with him in 1892—Keller, Likhtrammer, Epifanov, and

Iakovlev.[43] Undoubtedly, these young men were also affected by the famine.

Chernov states that after finishing his formal education in 1891, he went home with a diploma in one hand and a revolutionary proclamation entitled "The First Letter to the Starving Peasants" in the other.[44] In the summer of 1892, young Chernov was a keen observer of the cholera riots and the young radicals who wanted to shift the direction of these outbursts from the doctors to politics. As a matter of fact, the crowds in their anger did on occasion attack police stations. But these attacks were incidental to the fear, hostility, and frustration of the peasants coping with the cholera epidemic. By and large the students were unable "to take possession" of the peasant movement, and thus the young radicals emerged from their efforts tired, stunned, and prepared for a "scoldling" from the older generation.[45] In the meantime, Chernov left Saratov, and in 1892 began to study law at Moscow University where he quickly became a leading figure in a group of narodovol'tsy.[46] This circle of Populists subsequently radicalized some of the larger student organizations and began to use their meetings to discuss topics relevant to the revolutionary movement, such as the applicability of terror and the revolutionary potential of the peasantry.[47]

While the famine failed to produce a massive peasant uprising against the government, and appeals for an immediate overthrow of the tsarist system went unheeded by society at large, it did engender greater activity on the part of the opposition movement.[48] There was a considerable increase in the writings—books, articles, brochures, studies—about the economic life of Russia, and, apropos of these developments, in early 1892 Mikhailovskii and some of his friends assumed control of and revitalized the famous Populist journal *Russkoe bogatstvo*.[49] Thus the famine was also a catalyst in the resurgence of revolutionary Populism.[50]

The Populists reacted more decisively and quickly to the famine than did the Social Democrats by forming new political circles; the last extensive organization of Populist circles had essentially vanished under police repression by the end of 1890.[51]

Discussions for the formation of a new political society of Populists began in October of 1891, with intense debate over the type of society it should be. Out of these debates and discussions was formed the Group of Narodovol'tsy. The Group was particularly interested in operating a printing press to propagate its ideas, but was concerned that no professional writers were members of the circle.[52] However, that concern was eventually resolved.

On January 1, 1892, the members set about quite haphazardly to print their first two brochures. The first, entitled "Free World," was written by Mikhailovskii. This proclamation was a critical, but in terms of oppositional literature relatively bland, account of government efforts to deal with the calamity, as well as a condemnation of the languid response of society to the famine. It did call for elected representatives and new leadership in the government.[53] The other proclamation was entitled "From a Group of Populists," written by A. A. Fedulov. This writer saw the famine as a propitious moment for action against the state. Young revolutionaries were urged to unite with the old revolutionaries and join in the struggle with autocracy bequeathed to them from the past.[54]

Whether these leaflets had any long term impact is questionable. The fact that publications like *Moskovskii vedomosti, Vestnik Evropy* and Populist leaflets printed abroad refer to these proclamations would suggest that they had considerable circulation in Russian society. Mikhailovskii ended his relationship with the Group of Narodovol'tsy early in the spring of 1892, largely due to disagreements over his writings for the Group and the emergence of the more moderate People's Rights Party. While the Group may have been more radical than the People's Rights Party, it was nonetheless concerned to disabuse the public of its belief in the association of terrorism with Populism.[55]

In February, 1892, the Group received an offer from Nikolai Astyrev, a statistician and prominent radical writer, to use the the famine as an occasion to publish material designed to appeal to the peasantry. The Group responded by printing a series of brochures in the latter part of the month. The first brochure of 1,000 copies was entitled "Program of the People's Will," and it tended to downplay the Populist component of the program and emphasize that they were socialists. The second publication was the famous pamphlet drafted by Astyrev--"The First Letter to the Starving Peasants," 1800 copies; this is the revolutionary pamphlet particularly referred to by Chernov in his memoirs about the famine. It was written in simple, popular language designed for peasants to read. It also proved to be the last letter written by Astyrev because he was arrested in April, 1892. A third pamphlet in this series "Letter to the Young," 500 copies, was drafted by A. A. Fedulov. This was an ardent appeal to organize under the banner of the People's Will.[56]

After this spurt of mid-winter publishing activity, the Group began to prepare for another "publishing campaign" in the summer of 1892.[57] Their publishing schedule was quite sporadic because they were moving their printing operations from one apartment to another, apparently in order to avoid arrest and confiscation by the authorities.[58] A. A. Fedulov was again called forth to organize and write two of the three articles of the publication "Letuchii Leaflet of the Group of Narodovol'tsy."[59] Despite the easing of famine conditions by the spring of 1892, the activities of the Group continued. Although for almost a year there were no new publications by the Group because of a lack of printing materials, in April, 1893, the Group began work on issue no. 2 of the "Letuchii Leaflet." However, a scare from the police and the disruption of their printing schedule delayed the issue until July.[60]

In the "Leaflet," the Group seemed to be staking out the revolutionary middle ground between the Populists--with their emphasis on the peasant, peasant society, and the uniqueness of Russia's development-- and the Social Democrats, who espoused an unshakeable belief in scientific socialism. The Group took a pragmatic approach and argued that aspects of Russia's development vis-a-vis the peasant were peculiar to Russia, while on the other hand, it accepted the gradual evolution of capitalism in the countryside. The Group believed that they held the "just right" position within the opposition/liberation movement in that (1) they were willing to ally with the liberals and also were willing to use terror when necessary, and (2) they favored the development of socialism among both workers and peasants. The "Leaflet" stated the Group's claim to be heir to the long years of the revolutionary movement.[61] These, however, were the last leaflets published by the Group. In April, 1894, the tsarist police carried out a series of arrests and essentially closed down the press; any remnants of the printing operation that survived this police crackdown were caught in new wave of arrests in 1896.[62]

The narodovol'tsy produced a second and more prominent organization at Saratov, roughly contemporary with the Group of Narodovol'tsy.[63] The primary figure in this new Populist organization was Mark Natanson, one of the founders of the Land and Liberty party in the 1870's.[64] Upon returning from exile in 1890, Natanson joined with liberals in Saratov and established contacts with other Populists who had returned from exile to lay a foundation for a new, more broadly based radical movement.[65] His group turned away from the more radical Populist program of the 1870's and was adamantly against the use of terror as a means to achieve its revolutionary ends.[66] At this time, however, this radical circle in Saratov was largely a society for intellectual debate of the "accursed questions" of Russian society.[67]

The famine of 1891-92 galvanized Natanson and friends into expanding their efforts, and early in 1892, Natanson's organization reached out to other radical circles in cities throughout European Russia—Moscow, St. Petersburg, Orel, Saratov, Perm, Khar'kov. By spring, Natanson had established personal contact with Mikhailovskii, seeking his support for the group.[68] Natanson, in traveling to St. Petersburg to see Mikhailovskii, already had in mind the publication of journal which would call for constitutional-democratic reform of Russian society.[69] In addition to Mikhailovskii, among the prominent people associated with Natanson's movement were the radicals O. V. Aptekman and N. S. Tiutchev, as well as members of the intelligentsia such as V. G. Korolenko and N. F. Annenskii. Mikhailovskii, Korolenko, and Annenskii agreed to work on a new journal for Natanson, but did not actually join the illegal party.[70] The journal itself never came to fruition.[71] When it met in Saratov in the late summer of 1893, Natanson's group became a party in its own right known as the Party of the People's Rights.[72]

The People's Rights Party represented a new direction for the Populists, a direction engendered by the failure of the Populist movement up to that time as reflected in the decimation of the party at the end of the 70's, the decade of small deeds in the 80's, and the lack of peasant response to the famine.[73] The decision to deemphasize terror as an acceptable means to an end was a result of the party's determination to follow a new path to reform, i.e., it would become preoccupied with achieving political and personal freedom.[74] It stressed that the people had political as well as social and economic rights.[75] In fact, the party espoused the same basic principle that Mikhailovskii had long espoused, which was that the opposition movement should concentrate on the political struggle; this emphasis probably explains Mikhailovskii's willingness to associate with Natanson's circle rather than the Group of Narodovol'tsy.[76] Egorov described the members of the party as "followers of revolutionary constitutionalism,"[77] but they remained socialists nonetheless.[38] It was their view that the emergence of socialism would not be possible without the establishment of political freedom.[79]

When the party was formed in the summer of 1893, it adopted a program,[80] and in February of 1894, the party published its program called the "Manifesto of the Party of People's Rights." In the spring, it also issued a brochure "The Vital Question," written by A. I. Bogdanovich.[81] The party's ideas as expressed in the brochure and particularly in the "Manifesto" constituted a unique approach within the Populist movement for reform, based on a political platform, of the tsarist regime.[82] First, the party was unique in its proclamation not only because it made the establishment of political liberty its primary goal, but also because it delineated a different means to establish that goal. The organization of public opinion was to be the primary weapon in the struggle with autocracy.[83] Second, the party was the first group within the opposition movement to question the institution of the tsar, repudiating the idea that the tsar could solve the problems of Russia and that only the bureaucracy was the enemy. The People's Rights Party believed that autocracy could be more effectively destroyed by political action rather than by bombs.[84] The following quotations from the brochure and the program are illustrative:

> It is time for us to wake up. It is time to shake off the yoke of the decayed ideas of populism, culture-bearing (*Kulturnichestvo*) and the propagation of small deeds. It is time also to get rid of the condescending worship of the mythical 'people' (*narod*)....Life itself calls us...to the struggle for political liberty, which was never hostile to anything but absolutism. For absolutism it spells death, for the people—*conditio sine qua non* for public life. And as far as socialism is concerned, political freedom and socialism are not only not incompatible but are, on the contrary, complementary and mutually dependent....*Political freedom is not only the first step towards the achievement of socialism, but also the conditio sine qua non for its existence.*[85]

> Since there is not and cannot be a hope that the government will willingly enter upon the path indicated, there is one course remaining for the people: to oppose the force of *organized public opinion* to the inertia of the government and the narrow dynastic interests of autocracy....The party has set itself the task of uniting all oppositional elements in the country and of organizing an active force which should...attain the overthrow of autocracy and secure for everyone the rights of citizen and man. These rights include:
>> representative government on the basis of universal suffrage;
>> freedom of religious belief;
>> independence of the courts of justice;
>> freedom of meeting and association
>> inviolability of the individual and of his rights as a man;

the right of self-determination for all the
nationalities entering into (the) composition
(of Russia).[86]

As the selection from the brochure indicates, Natanson and friends were not severing their ties with populism and socialism. Political freedom was to be in part the means to achieve socialism and thereby improve the well-being of the people. Mikhailovskii and the Program itself stated that the people not only had political rights but economic and social rights as well.[87] "Popular right includes in itself the conception of the right of the people to political freedom and the conception of its right to secure its material needs upon the basis of national production."[88] Similarly, Aptekman stated that "the members of the People's Rights party are socialists...if you will—socialists-populists, but without the Populists' prejudices and fear of political freedom of the populist-utopians of the 70's."[89] Naimark has pointed out that even the Populist weapon of terrorism was not totally discarded by the new party, which is further evidence of the party's link to its Populist heritage.[90] On the other hand, there would seem to be a weakening of these ties in the failure of the program to comment on (1) Russia's uniqueness as regards the development of socialism, (2) the peasant commune, and (3) the probability of a peasant revolution.[91]

Both prior and subsequent to the formation of the party and the publication of its program, Natanson, Tiutchev and others hoped to expand the membership of the party and traveled throughout Russia seeking converts.[92] In addition to the original party center under the leadership of Natanson, Tiutchev, and V. O. Aptekman, and given credibility among radicals and liberals by the association of Mikhailovskii, Annenskii, and Korolenko, two other radical circles gravitated toward the People's Rights Party. The more important of these groups, which were essentially absorbed by the new Populist Party, was the Riazanov circle. This circle was formed by A. I. Riazanov after the circle formed by N. M. Astyrev, of the Group of Narodovol'tsy faction, was destroyed by arrests in spring of 1892.

The Riazanov Circle was noted for its flexibility and openness, and Populists—such as the young Victor Chernov—and Marxists—such as Riazanov himself, and S. N. Prokopovich and E. D. Kuskova, who were in a stage of transition to Marxism from Populism—were members. This particular circle was in very close contact with liberals in Tver and Moscow. When the People's Rights Party was founded in the summer of 1893, the circle ceased to exist; the Populist members joined the People's Rights and the Marxists went their own way.[93]

The third basic component that merged to form the Peoples' Rights Party involved radicals and others who had no particular affiliation with a given circle. A. I. Bogdanovich, the author of "The Vital Question," V. Ia. (Iakovlev) Bogucharskii, a historian, and V. V. Khizhniakov, a leading figure in the Free Economic Society of St. Petersburg in the early 1900's, were part of this third component. Bogucharskii, Khizhniakov, Kuskova, and Prokopovich were to become leaders of the Union of Liberation.[94]

In terms of the subsequent history of the radical movement, possibly the most important member of the People's Rights Party was Victor Chernov. Chernov was persuaded to join the party by one of the older generation of radicals, P. F. Nikolaev. As a party member, Chernov participated in an effort to distribute indoctrination leaflets to the peasants, such as the "Letters to Starving Peasants."[95] Writing about this period late in his life, Chernov stated that the young radicals of the day were basically attracted either to Marxism or the People's Rights Party.[96] It would seem that it was in part their response to the famine and their expectations of peasant revolt that helped the young decide which faction to choose. Chernov argued that the young radicals, who thrust themselves into the village hoping to incite revolution at the time of the famine, were psychologically prepared for indoctrination and conversion to Marxism. On the other hand, the other element of young radicals, who were better acquainted with the peasant, who did not expect an immediate revolution, and who were prepared to cultivate the peasant patiently, stubbornly resisted Marxism and tended to join the People's Rights Party.[97] Quite possibly Chernov is reading into history a more sophisticated view of peasants by young Populist radicals than they actually had. It would appear they too were disappointed by the relatively passive reaction of peasants to the famine, an assessment which led many Populists to affiliate with the People's Rights Party.[98] This frustration and the desire to develop a new approach for reform were aptly expressed by Korolenko who said that "before these 'ignorant and barbaric masses' could be of any use to the revolution, it would be necessary to educate them and 'to awaken in them the self-awareness of citizens.'"[99]

Unfortunately for the new party, the tsarist police crushed this faction with extensive arrests of its leadership in April, 1894.[100] Cognizant of the existence of this party from its inception, the government decided to act a few months after the publication of the "Manifesto" and the brochure (which from the government's viewpoint had made the party more dangerous)[101] by striking simultaneously in five cities across Russia—Khar'kov, Moscow, St. Petersburg, Smolensk, where their printing press was located, and Orel, the party's headquarters. Chernov, Natanson, and Tiutchev were among the fifty-plus party members arrested.[102] On that same night, the police also arrested some sixty members of the Group of Narodovol'tsy, effectively destroying both factions at one time.[103]

Like Victor Chernov, the People's Rights Party was far more significant to the subsequent history of the opposition to the government than it was to events in the early 1890's. The Peoples' Rights Party provided both ideas and leadership to the liberation movement which emerged at the turn of the century, and also had close ties to the developing Socialist Revolutionary and Kadet Parties.[104] Contacts established in the party lasted into the future.[105] Indeed, "among the five representatives of the radical intelligentsia on the board of the first elected Council of the Union of Liberation, four (Annenskii, Bogucharskii, Peshekhonov and Prokopovich) were former members or supporters of the People's Rights Party."[106]

The Russian famine of 1891-92 had its greatest impact on the development of the Marxist, or Social Democratic, faction of the Russian opposition movement. While Russian Marxism had emerged in the 1880's, both at home and abroad, it had attracted relatively little attention, and Populism remained the predominant ideology among Russian radicals. The famine was the catalytic event that helped the Social Democratic Party become a major ideological competitor with the Populists and, in terms of numbers, fostered the dramatic growth of the party.[107] Given the more pessimistic approach of the Marxists to reform in Russia and to the development of socialism than that espoused by the Populists, i.e., that a society must pass through the exploitation of capitalism before reaching the socialist stage, the Marxists needed "historical shocks" like the famine to attract members of the intelligentsia to their movement. Similarly, the failure of the peasants to respond more aggressively to the famine seemed to support the Marxist view that the peasants were a backward social force, which tended to confirm the Marxist assessment of Russian conditions.[108]

Writing twenty years after the famine, Iurii Martov acknowledged the significance of the famine as a turning point in the growth and influence of the Russian Social Democrats.[109] As noted above, Plekhanov published two long essays in 1892 in response to the famine—"The All-Russian Devastation" and "The Tasks of the Socialists in the Struggle with Famine." While these essays had little immediate impact on the revolutionary class itself—the proletariat—they did have a direct impact on some of the young intelligentsia.[110] That notwithstanding, it was still the event more than the analysis that proved decisive in the minds of the young. "The famine of 1891-92, which so emphasized the decomposition of the peasant economy and social helplessness of the village, made the broad circle of radical intelligentsia psychologically able to adopt the propaganda of the Marxist."[111] The demise of the Peoples' Rights Party further accentuated the shift of large numbers of the young intelligentsia to the Marxist side,[112] and by the mid 1890's, the Russian Social Democratic Party had become, for the time being, the more dynamic element in the revolutionary movement.

With the renewed vibrancy within Russian society, and especially in the opposition movement, an intense controversy ensued between the Marxists and Populists concerning the meaning and significance of the famine and the future course of the Russian economy.[113] Debate and discussion had already existed between these groups in the 1880's after Plekhanov founded the Emancipation of Labor Group in 1883. The debates at that time had tended to focus on viability of the peasant commune—the Populists considered it the basic building block of the future socialist order, while the Marxists viewed the commune as a remnant of an outmoded economic historical stage. The commune, according to the Marxists (i.e., Plekhanov), had to be destroyed if the true development of capitalism were to take place.[114] This debate was essentially between Marxists living abroad and Populists within Russia. In his book on the radical movement of the 1880's, Naimark has persuasively established that ordinary Populists and Marxists within the country tended to downplay ideological differences and formed a united front against the government.[115]

In the context of the Marxist-Populist debate of the 1890's, the famine of 1891-92 played a significant role because it sharply focused the country's attention on agriculture and the economy, and thereby gave vent to the real ideological differences between the Marxists and Populists with regard to the appropriate path for Russia. As any student of history might expect, both the Populists and Marxists considered the famine incontrovertible substantiation of their respective analysis of the current state and evolution of the Russian economy. The dispute was revealed largely in the legal literature of the day and thus had broad public exposure and circulation. Given the legal nature of the publications, the participants became known as legal Marxists and legal Populists.[116]

The Populists considered the famine of 1891-92 as proof of their analysis and prophesies concerning the Russian economy, made in the 1880's. In their opinion, the development of a capitalist economy and governmental fiscal policies had impoverished the peasant, and the famine was *prima facie* proof of their position. Since the peasantry was impoverished, and thus obviously unable to serve as a market for a capitalist system, capitalism on the western model could not possibly develop in Russia. This general interpretation was held by leading Populists, in particular Vorontsov and Nikolai-on.[117] After the famine, Vorontsov, Nikolai-on and Mikhailovskii entered into a general attack on the Marxist position, in part through the pages of the *Russkoe bogatstvo.*[118]

In 1893, N. F. Danielson (Nikolai-on) enlarged and republished his famous study of the Russian economy, *Outlines of Our Post-Reform National Economy*, originally printed in 1880. Without question, this work was one of the most forceful statements of the Populist position. All during the 1880's, Nikolai-on had gathered additional data designed to prove the utter insanity of the government's policies, as well as the unsuitability of capitalism for Russia.[119] The famine seemingly confirmed for him the viability of his interpretation, especially that the advent of capitalism was a detriment to Russia.[120]

The famine of 1891-92 was a primary consideration in prompting him to republish his work. Nikolai-on argued that some scholars wished to avoid unpleasant facts like the famine, but the famine forced Russia to study these unpleasant facts because of its tragic impact—its high cost in money, the ruination of tens of thousands of farmers, and a general lowering of the economic viability of the population.[121]

Nikolai-on's book had a great impact on the intelligentsia, both Populist and Marxist. It has been called the most important theoretical work of all Populist literature.[122] The Marxists, who were well aware of Nikolai-on's expertise in Marxist thought, were particularly stung by his work, and began an assault on his ideas. In turn, Nikolai-on responded to his critics in a number of long articles. The essential ideas of the book are repeated in two essays printed in the *Russkoe bogatstvo* in 1894 and 1895, and he again emphasized the significance of the famine as proof of the deterioration of Russian agriculture under the impact of the spread of capitalism.[123]

Similarly, other Populists in the 1890's, such as V. P. Vorontsov, S. Yuzhakov, and N. A. Karyshev viewed the famine as evidence for their general view of the distress in the agrarian sector, a reflection of the destitution and exhaustion of the Russian peasant, which in turn inhibited the formation of a domestic market, a prerequisite for the full development of capitalism in Russia.[124] Thus, for the Populists, the famine of 1891-92 offered proof of the agricultural crisis which indicated the improbability of the development of capitalism for Russia. The Marxists, on the other hand, drew a completely different conclusion from the famine and began to challenge the Populists. It was in the years immediately after the famine that "Social Democracy in Russia became transformed from a secret doctrine into a distinct movement."[125]

In the early 1890's, the Populists clearly had the upper hand in their clash with the upstart Marxists because only the Populists had access to the legal press—not just in books but also in journals such as *Novoe slovo* and *Russkoe bogatstvo*.[126] In a very real sense, the legal Populists held dominance over the educated public. This situation changed abruptly in 1894, when the monopoly of the legal press was weakened as the censor accepted two books for publication presenting Marxist views of conditions in Russia and attacking the Populist assessment: Struve's *Critical Notes on the Question of Russia's Economic Development,* and Plekhanov's *On the Question of Developing a Monistic View of History* (published under the pseudonym "Beltov").[127] These publications were the first major shots in the rather bitter Marxist-Populist debate which appeared in the pages of the legal press.

The debate actually began in 1892, when Struve very quietly published his first articles in Germany and began criticizing the Populist perspective. On reading some of this material, Nikolai-on sniped at Struve, who, in turn, criticized Nikolai-on.[128] These initial discussions occurred primarily under the impetus of the famine and dealt with agriculture.[129] Similarly, the famine and the discussion of the famine found in the writings of A. I. Skvortsov were the motivation for the publication of Struve's monograph.[130] This work, printed at his own expense, instantly made Struve a significant figure within the intelligentsia.[131] He stated "my book, published in September, 1894, had a very great success, and within a few weeks turned me from a 'promising' young student, hardly known to anyone outside a very limited circle of the Petersburg intelligentsia, into a well-known writer who at once became 'the principle representative...of legal Marxism' of that period, at least according to Lenin."[132] Struve viewed the famine of 1891-92 not as proof that capitalism was impossible or futile for Russia, but proof that capitalism was a necessary development for Russia in order to prevent such tragedies in the future. According to Struve, the misfortunes that had befallen Russia were a result of her backwardness and heritage of serfdom and not due to the rise of capitalism.[133] In his view, capitalism had already begun to be established in the countryside, as evidenced by the growth of a money economy and differentiation among the peasantry.[134] Struve was sympathetic to the suffering of the masses caught up in the agrarian crisis, but he felt that the cause of their suffering was "lack of culture," and the only remedy was more capitalism, not less.[135]

Struve, in 1894, was responding to the same tragedy that had spurred Nikolai-on to publish his views on the economy, but Struve arrived at a completely different hypothesis concerning the economic future of Russia. The famine demonstrated that indeed agriculture was in the throes of differentiation and that capitalism was in the ascendency.[136] Struve had negated the Populist theory of Russia's "original economic development" and asserted "that Russia had long ago set out on the path of capitalist development."[137] The Populists were outraged at his assertions, on the one hand because he viewed the famine as a regrettable episode in the evolution of progress in Russia, and on the other hand because he recommended that Russia acknowledge her backwardness and throw in her lot with capitalism.[138]

The development of an intense debate between the Marxists and the Populists marked the full flowering of Marxism in Russia. Much of this was due to the publication of Struve's book and other legal Marxist publications.[139] According to Theodore Dan, young Marxists worked very diligently at gathering data, statistics, etc., and passionately attacked the Populists.[10] To this extent, the Populists lost the struggle for the younger intelligentsia, who became convinced that the Marxist world-view and the benefits of capitalism for Russia were closer to reality than the hypothesis held by the Populists.[141]

Lenin, being a recent convert, was another young Social Democrat who came into public view through his writings of the 1890's—motivated at least in part by the famine of 1891-92. In these writings, he was critical of both Struve and the Populists.[142] Lenin undertook a study of Russian agriculture and its relationship to the development of capitalism in Russia, and published his views in 1893 in the work *On the So-Called Question of Markets*, which he later expanded into *The Development of Capitalism in Russia* in 1899. While Lenin might quarrel with the philosophical approach of Struve, he would seem basically to agree that capitalism was already well on its way in Russia. In his essay of 1893, he argued that poverty in the countryside actually fosters the growth of a market economy, whereas differentiation of the peasantry signals the existence of a bourgeoisie and a proletariat among the peasants. The same phenomenon was also evident in the destruction of the small scale handicraft industry. "The existence of these two polarizing trends among our petty producers clearly shows that capitalism and mass impoverishment, far from precluding, actually condition each other, and irrefutably proves that capitalism is already the main background of the economic life of Russia."[143]

The Marxist-Populist debate over the possibility of capitalism gradually ended in the late 1890's with the publication of Tugan-Baranovskii's work *The Russian Factory* and Lenin's *The Development of Capitalism in Russia*. There was no longer any argument because the capitalist stage had arrived.[144] The Marxist view of the early 1890's was proven correct, and the Social Democrats gathered in the harvest of the young intelligentsia.[145] What is remarkable about this victory is the fact that it took the intelligentsia so long to finally accept it. "It took the magnificent development of the nineties to open the skulls of the intelligentsia to the comprehension of a process that had been going on for almost four decades."[146] It should be pointed out, however, that by the turn of the century, Populism was beginning to make a comeback vis-a-vis Marxism.[147]

The Russian Famine of 1891-92 had an important impact on the opposition movement in the last decade of the nineteenth century. In a very real sense, the famine energized and revitalized Russian society—the government, the bureaucracy, the intellectuals, the students, and all the citizens who contributed to famine relief—after the so-called "depressing decade" of the

1880's.[148] The famine also energized and revitalized the opposition movement, which had staggered through a disillusioning and dispiriting decade after the extensive crackdown on the radicals in 1881. In this regard, the famine evoked an enthusiastic response from students, many of whom joined the ranks of the radicals. For the younger generation of radicals, as well as their elders, the famine sanctified their alienation from the system, appealed to their biases, and verified the radical assessment of the corruption and incompetence of the tsarist government, of the embarrassing backwardness of society, and of the necessity for reform. Finally, the famine became the focus of the Marxist-Populist debate, which accentuated the differences in the two movements far more then had been the case in the 1880's. The Marxists and Populists disagreed over the implications of the famine and used it as evidence to support different assessments of conditions in Russia; as a result of this disagreement, the Marxists attracted the majority of the young intelligentsia in the 1890's primarily because their analysis of conditions more accurately reflected reality. The famine thus not only brought a renewed sense of urgency and meaning to the revolutionary movement, it also helped to make the Marxists a major component of that movement and gave the radicals an alternative program of reform to that proffered by the Populists.

NOTES

1. [A. S. Ermolov], *Neurozhai i narodnoe bedstvie* (St. Petersburg, 1892), 18; *Entsiklopedicheskii slovar'*, 9 (St. Petersburg: Efron and Brokhaus, 1893): 104; U.S., Congress, *The Miscellaneous Documents of the House of Representatives*, 52nd Cong., lst Sess., 1891-92, "Grain Crops of the World," 37: 172-74; U.S., Congress, *The Miscellaneous Documents of the House of Representatives*, 52nd Cong., lst Sess., 1891-92, "The Russian Farm Products in 1891," 38: 321-322; Alfred Vendrikh, *Otchet po upravleniia perevozkami* (St. Petersburg: Ministerstvo Putei Soobshcheniia, 1896), 2; Charles E. Smith, "The

Famine in Russia," *The North American Review* 154 (May, 1892): 542;
U.S., Department of State, *Russia, Diplomatic Dispatches of Charles
Emory Smith*, vol. 42, no. 142 (January 11, 1892); U.S., Department of
State, *Papers Relating to the Foreign Relations of the United States*, no.
120 (October 22, 1891), 746.

    The enormity of the calamity is exemplified by the fact that the
tsarist government expended 196,000,000 r., providing famine relief to
13,000,000 of the approximately 35,000,000 inhabitants in the stricken
region. See: Smith, "Famine in Russia," 542; William Barnes Steveni,
*Europe's Great Calamity: The Russian Famine; An Appeal for the
Russian Peasant* (London: F. Griffiths, 1922), 2,6; Vendrikh, 2; M. W.
Kovalevsky, *La Russie a la fin au 19e siecle*, an official publication of
the Ministry of Finance (Paris: Paul Dupont, 1900), 786. *The
Statesman's Yearbook*, ed. J. Scott Keltie (London, 1894), 873, states
that the tsarist government spent 162,000,000 r. for famine relief in
1891 and 87,474,219 r. in 1892. See also Richard Robbins, *Famine in
Russia, 1891-1892* (New York: Columbia University Press, 1975), pp.
168, 187, where he indicates that approximately 11,800,000 received
aid, and p. 151, where he states that 150,000,000 r. were spent on
famine relief.

    2. To argue that the famine induced a resurgence of and
revitalized the revolutionary movement does not mean to imply that
the radical movement in the 1880's had atrophied or was insignificant
per se. Indeed, Norman Naimark, in his excellent study of the
opposition movement in the decade of the 1880's, has demonstrated
conclusively that much was going on among the radicals, i.e., intense
and vibrant discussions concerning policy and tactics continued, efforts
were made to connect the disparate radical elements throughout
Russia, especially by the Populists, and a Marxist faction began to
develop within Russia itself. See, Norman Naimark, *Terrorists and
Social Democrats* (Cambridge, Mass.: Harvard University Press, 1983).

    Derek Offord's work on this subject is essentially in agreement
with Naimark. He argues that the radicals of the 1880's not only
preserved the existence of the opposition movement but also
strengthened it in many ways, so that in the following decade the
revolutionarty movement did not have to start from the very beginning
in terms of ideas and organization; it had a solid base on which to
build. See Derek Offord, *The Russian Revolutionary Movement in the
1880's* (Cambridge: Cambridge University Press, 1896), 161-170.
Nevertheless, the famine, by creating a crisis, clearly invigorated the

revolutionary movement and thereby brought many new converts to the revolutionary cause.

3. A. Egorov (Martov), "Zarozhdenie politicheskikh partii i ikh deiatel'nost'," in *Obshchestvennoe dvizhenie v Rossii v nachale xx-go veka*, 4 vols, ed. L. Martov, P. Maslov, and A. Potresov (St. Petersburg: 1909), 1: 375; A. Potresov, "Evoliutsiia obshcheştvenno-politicheskoi mysli v predrevoliutsionuiu epokhu," in *Obshchestvennoe dvizhenie v Rossii v nachale xx-go veka*, 4 vols., ed. L. Martov, P. Maslov, and A. Potresov (St. Petersburg, 1909) 1:538; N. Cherevanin, "Dvizhenie intelligentsia," in *Obshchestvennoe dvizhenie v Rossii v nachale xx-go veka*, 4 vols., ed. L. Martov, P. Maslov, and A. Potresov (St. Petersburg, 1909),1: 268-69.

4. Paul Miliukov, "Russia," *Athenaeum* (July 2, 1892), 25.

5. "Kronika vnutrennei zhizni," *Russkoe bogatstvo* 2 (February, 1892): 108.

6. A. Argunov, "Iz proshlogo partii sotsialistov-revoliutsionerov," *Byloe* 10 (October, 1907): 101. See also O. V. Aptekman, "Partiia 'Narodnago Prava.' Vospominaniia." *Byloe* 19 (July, 1907): 189, who noted that the famine gave a decisive jolt to the Saratov circle that subsequently founded the People's Rights Party. For more on the awakening of society, see pp. 182-3, 192.

7. D. Kol'tsov, "Rabochie v 1890-1904 gg," in *Obshchestvennoe dvizhenie v Rossii v nachale xx-go veka*, 4 vols., ed. L. Martov, P. Maslov, and A. Potresov (St. Petersburg, 1909), 1: 187.

8. Potresov, 539-40.

9. Naimark, 232.

10. I. Gofitter, "Vodka ili khleb," *Russkoe bogatstvo* 10 (October, 1891): 180; P. L. Korf, "Poezdka v neurozhainyia mestnosti Kursk Gubernii," *Trudy imperatorskago vol'nago ekonomicheskago obshchestva* no. 4 (July-August, 1892), 116-17; Ivan Sergeevskii, *Golod v Rossii: so vvedeniem i noslesloviem P. Lavrov* (Geneva: Published by the Society of Old Populists, 1892), 23; V. A. Obolensky, *Ocherki minuvshago* (Belgrad, 1931), 198; "Kronika vnutrennei zhizni," *Russkoe bogatstvo* 2 (February, 1892): 26.

11. Obolensky, 198, 229; A. A. Kornilov, *Sem mesiatsev sredy golodaiushchikh krest'ian* (Moscow: D. I. Inosemtsev, Arbat, and D. Karinskii, 1893), 89; Iu. O. Martov, *Zapiski sotsialdemokrata* (Berlin: A. I. Grschebin, 1922), 86; Donald W. Treadgold, *Lenin and his Rivals* (New York: Frederick A. Praeger, 1955), 3, 7, 8; P. Miliukov, "Russia," *Athenaeum* (July 2, 1892), 25; P. Miliukov, *Russia and its Crisis* (New York: Collier Books, 1962), 237; Potresov, 539; Cherevanin, 269.

12. Obolensky, 200; V. A. Maklakov, *Iz vospominanii* (New York: 1954), 146-50.

13. V. Korolenko, *V golodnyi god: nabliudeniia razmyshleniia, i zametki* (Petrograd: Tipographiia Pervoi Trudovoi Arteli, 1915), 348; Kornilov, 89.

14. *Free Russia*, 2 (August 1891): 4.

15. Ibid., 3 (September 1892): 10.

16. G. V. Plekhanov, "Vserossiiskoe razorenie," *Sotsial demokrat* 4 (Geneva: 1892): 100-101.

17. Sergeevskii, 3.

18. Ibid., 6.

19. Ibid., 39-40.

20. Maklakov, 154.

21. Peter B. Struve, "My Contacts and Conflicts with Lenin," *The Slavonic and East European Review* 12 (April, 1934): 585-586.

22. M. S. Aleksandrov, "Gruppa narodovol'tsev," *Byloe* 11 (November, 1906): 14; Cherevanin, 269.

23. Struve, "My Contacts and Conflicts with Lenin," 575-577. Italics in the original.

24. Ibid., 577. Italics in the original.

25. P. Struve, "Na raznye temy," *Russkaia Mysl* 3, pt. 2 (March, 1908): 211.

26. Leopold H. Haimson, *The Russian Marxists and the Origins of Bolshevism* (Cambridge, Mass.: Harvard University Press, 1955), 65-66; Israel Getzler, *Martov* (Melbourne, Australia: Cambridge at the University Press, 1967), 11.

27. Martov, 94

28. Ibid., 137.

29. Ibid.; Samuel Baron, *Plekhanov: The Father of Russian Marxism* (Stanford, Calif.: Stanford University Press, 1963), 142-43.

30. Martov, 137.

31. Getzler, 16.

32. P. B. Akselrod, *Etiudy i vospominaniia* (Leningrad: State Publishing House, 1925), 20.

34. Richard Pipes, *Struve: Liberal on the Left 1870-1905* (Cambridge, Mass.: Harvard University Press, 1970), 129; Robert Service, *Lenin: A Political Life*, vol. 1 (Bloomington: Indiana University Press, 1985): 44; Naimark, 187.

35. Pipes, 129; Service, 44-45. See also, V. V. Moskvin, "Nachalo rabochego dvizhenie i rasprostranenie marksizma v Rossii (1883-1894), *Voprosy istorii KPSS* 10 (1984): 110.

36. Pipes, 129.

37. Service, 44-45; Pipes, 129.

38. Naimark, 187; Esther Kingston-Mann, *Lenin and the Problem of Marxist Peasant Revolution* (New York: Oxford University Press, 1983), 42.

39. Service, 45.

40. Pipes, 129-30; see also Baron, 143.

41. Service, 47.

42. Kingston-Mann, 42 ff.

43. Victor M. Chernov, "K istorii partii Narodnago Prava," *Krasnyi arkhiv* 1 (1922): 282.

44. Chernov, *Zapiski socialista revoliutsionera* (Berlin: Z. I. Grzhebina, 1922), 92.

45. Ibid., 95-96.

46. Maureen Perrie, *The Agrarian Policy of the Russian Socialist-Revolutionary Party* (Cambridge: Cambridge University Press, 1976), 14.

47. Allan K. Wildman, *The Making of a Worker's Revolution* (Chicago: The University of Chicago Press, 1967), 12.

48. Argunov, 101-102.

49. Potresov, 540-41; James H. Billington, *Mikhailovsky and Russian Populism* (Oxford: At the Clarendon Press, 1958), 157.

50. Perrie, 7.

51. Aleksandrov, 6; Naimark, 232.

52. Aleksandrov, 14-15.

53. Ibid., 16-17.

54. Ibid., 17-18.

55. Ibid., 18-19.

56. Ibid., 19-20.

57. Ibid., 20.

58. Ibid., 15.

59. Ibid., 20-21.

60. Ibid., 21.

61. Naimark, 234-35.

62. Aleksandrov, 21.

63. Naimark, 235; Billington, 157.

64. Egorov, 373; Aptekman, 187; Naimark, 235; Wildman, 11.

65. Aptekman, 187-88; Egorov, 373; Naimark, 235-36; Billington, 157-58.

66. Aptekman, 187, 190; Billington, 157.

67. Aptekman, 188.

68. Aptekman, 189; Egorov, 374; Billington, 158.
69. Aptekman, 189.
70. Ibid., 189, 193, 196, 199, 200, 201; Egorov, 374; Naimark, 235-36; Shmuel Galai, *The Liberation Movement in Russia 1900-1905* (Cambridge: At the University Press, 1973), 60.
71. Billington, 158; Naimark, 236.
72. Aptekman, 190, 196, 198; Egorov, 373; Galai, 59; Bilington, 158; Naimark, 236.
73. Galai, 59-60.
74. Aptekman, 190, 195-97; Galai, 59; see also Egorov, 373-374.
75. Billington, 159; Aptekman, 197.
76. Billington, 158. See also Aptekman, who states (p. 200) that A. I. Bogdanovich sought Mikhailovskii's advice concerning his article "Vital Question," which emphasized the need for political reform.
77. Egorov, 373.
78. Aptekman, 190, 201; Galai, 63.
79. Aptekman, 201.
80. Aptekman, 196.; Galai, 64; Naimark, 236.
81. Egorov, 373-74; Galai, 65; Naimark, 237.
82. Argunov, 101-102.
83. Galai, 64; Aptekman, 196.
84. Billington, 159.
85. Cited in Galai, 63-64; see also Aptekman, 201.
86. Cited in Galai, 64-65; see also Aptekman, 197.
87. Aptekman, 201; Billington, 159; Naimark, 236.
88. Cited in Billington, 159.
89. Aptekman, 201.
90. Naimark, 236.
91. Ibid.
92. Aptekman, 198, 199, 202.
93. Galai, 60-61.
94. Ibid., 61-62.
95. Chernov, *Zapiski*, 156-57.
96. Ibid., 158.
97. Ibid.
98. Galai, 59; Naimark, 237; see also Wildman, 14-15.
99. Cited in Galai, 63.
100. Aptekman, 204-5; Egorov, 374; Billington, 159; Galai, 65.
101. Galai, 65.
102. Aptekman, 205; Chernov, "K istorii partii Narodnago Prava," 282; Galai, 65.

103. Naimark, 237; Galai, 65; Billington, 159.
104. Galai, 59. Naimark, 237.
105. Galai, 59.
106. Ibid., 65.
107. Wildman, 14.
108. Philip Pomper, *The Russian Revolutionary Intelligentsia* (Arlington Heights, Ill.: AHM Publishing Corporation, 1970), 156-58.
109. Egorov, 375.
110. Egorov, 375; Struve, "My Contacts and Conflicts with Lenin," 577.
111. Egorov, 375.
112. Egorov, 374, 378; Galai, 66.
113. The debate between the Marxists and the Populists has been discussed at considerable length by a number of historians. In particular, see Arthur P. Mendel, *Dilemmas of Progress in Tsarist Russia* (Cambridge, Mass.: Harvard University Press, 1967); Alexander Gerschenkron, "The Problem of Economic Development in Russian Intellectual History of the Nineteenth Century," in *Continuity and Change in Russian and Soviet Thought*, ed. E. J. Simmons (Cambridge, Mass.: Harvard University Press, 1955), 11-39; Solomon M. Schwarz, "Populism and Early Russian Marxism on Ways of Economic Development of Russia," in *Continuity and Change in Russian and Soviet Thought*, ed. E. J. Simmons (Cambridge, Mass.: Harvard University Press, 1955), 40-62; Richard Wortman, *The Crisis of Russian Populism* (Cambridge: At the University Press, 1967); Richard Pipes, *Social Democracy and the St. Petersburg Labor Movement, 1885-1897* (Cambridge, Mass.: Harvard University Press, 1963); Haimson, *The Russia Marxists and the Origin of Bolshevism*; Pipes, *Struve*; Billington, *Mikhailovsky*; Wildman, 18-25; Galai, 66 ff.
114. Hugh Seton-Watson, *The Russian Empire, 1801-1917* (Oxford: At the Clarendon Press, 1967), 512; Kingston-Mann, 33-35; Billington, 164.
115. Naimark, 184, 240. The existence of the Riazanov Circle in Moscow in 1892, made up of Marxists and Populists, supports Naimark's view. Galai, 60-61.
116. See Wildman, 14.
117. Billington, 164; Schwarz, 43; Pipes, *Struve*, 60-61.
118. Billington, 164-67.
119. Pipes, *Struve*, 79-80.
120. Nikolai-on, "Apologiia vlasti deneg, kak priznak vremeni," *Russkoe bogatstvo* 1 (January, 1895): 155-56; Billington, 164.

121. Nikolai-on, *Ocherki nashego poreformennago khoziaistva* (St. Petersburg: A. Bepke, 1893), xiv, xv; see p. 257 for more on the role of the famine as a catalyst in spurring studies on agriculture.
122. Schwarz, 46-47.
123. Nikolai-on, "Nechto ob usloviiakh nashego khoziaistvennago razvitie," *Russkoe bogatstvo* 4 (April, 1894): 1; Nikolai-on, *Russkoe bogatstvo* 6 (June, 1894): 117; Nikolai-on, *Russkoe bogatstvo* 1 (January, 1895): 155, 185.
124. Schwarz, 45-47; Wortman, 160-69; Mendel, 43-47; S. Yuzhakov, "Voprosy ekonomicheskago razvitie v Rossii," *Russkoe bogatstvo* 12 (December, 1893): 203-204. See also Billington, 164-71, for Mikhailovskii's role in the debate, and Wildman, 22.
125. Pipes, *Struve*, 79.
126. Wildman, 18, 19, 24.
127. Schwarz, 56, Wildman, 18-19.
128. Richard Kindersley, *The First Russian Revisionists* (Oxford: Clarendon Press, 1962), 42-43, Wildman, 18-19.
129. Kindersley, 42.
130. Pipes, *Struve*, 60; Struve, "My Contacts and Conflicts with Lenin," 581.
131. Wildman, 21.
132. Struve, "My Contacts and Conflicts with Lenin," 581.
133. P. B. Struve, *Kriticheskie zametki k voprosu ob ekonomicheskom razvitie Rossii* (St. Petersburg: I. N. Skorokhovdova, 1894), 9: 287-88.
134. Ibid., 115-16, 138-39, 238, 240-45.
135. Ibid., 287-88.
136. Pipes, *Struve*, 61.
137. Struve, "My Contacts and Conflicts with Lenin," 581.
138. Pipes, *Struve*, 94; Billington, 165; Schwarz, 56-57.
139. Baron, 144-45.
140. Theodore Dan, *The Origins of Bolshevism*, ed. and trans. Joel Carmichael (New York: Harper and Row, 1964), 190-92. Dan stresses that it was the famine of 1891-92 which turned Social Democracy from a minor faction into a significant opposition movement, 188-89.
141. Haimson, 51.
142. For a more detailed discussion, see chapter 3 of James Y. Simms, Jr., "The Impact of the Russian Famine of 1891-92: A New Perspective" (Ph.D. diss., University of Michigan, 1976).

143. V. I. Lenin, "On the So-Called Market Question," *Collected Works*, Vol. I (Moscow: Foreign Language Publishing House, 1963): 109. For the evidence Lenin used to prove this thesis, see 111, 125.

144. Schwarz, 60-62.

145. Billington, 171; Galai, 68, 72; Wildman, 26.

146. Gerschenkron, 100.

147. Galai, 71-72; Wildman, 26.

148. This was certainly the view of many of the radicals who lived through the 1880's. See, for example, Aleksandrov (p. 1), who stated in 1906 that "the end of the 80's of the past century is one of the most gloomy, the most, it seems, hopeless and dismal periods of modern history." Aptekman (pp. 179 and 185) in 1907 referred to the 80's as a period of "darkness" over the fatherland and those "nightmarish" years. Ivannov-Razumnik, in his study of revolutionary thought, argued that the decade of the 80's is a void. V. Ivannov-Razumnik, *Istorii Russkoi obshchestvennoi mysli*, 4th ed. (St. Petersburg: M. M. Stasulevich, 1914), 235.

URBAN GROWTH AND ANTI-SEMITISM IN RUSSIAN MOLDAVIA

Edward H. Judge

Among the changes taking place in Russia during the late imperial period, the unprecedented growth of the cities and towns may well have had the most far-reaching impact. The growth of industry and commerce and the influx of tens of thousands of impoverished peasants helped to create conditions of social dislocation, economic oppression, and civil unrest. These in turn helped set the stage and provide the impetus for the great revolutions of 1905 and 1917. But urban growth also had other implications which were a bit less obvious and dramatic. In the expanding cities, large numbers of persons of diverse ethnic and cultural backgrounds were brought together for the first time in close and regular contact. This was especially true in the western border provinces, where government policies and economic concerns compelled thousands of Jewish people to settle in urban centers. This phenomenon, in turn, helped contribute to the conditions which set the stage for the anti-Jewish pogroms of the late imperial period.

One area where the connection between urban growth and anti-Semitism was most apparent was the province of Bessarabia, the Russian-controlled portion of the region known as Moldavia. At the beginning of the twentieth century, this area was little more than an obscure border province of the vast Russian empire. Situated in a distant corner of the tsar's domain, it was far from the great centers of political power and economic influence. As a rule, therefore, it attracted little attention in the outside world. In April of 1903, however, an event occurred in Kishinev, the capital city of Bessarabia, which focused worldwide attention on the problem of anti-Semitism in Russian Moldavia.

On Easter Sunday, April 6 of 1903, groups of Christian townspeople assembled in a large square in the southeastern part of town. Before long they began moving out along nearby streets and throwing rocks through the windows of Jewish shops. Meeting little resistance from the local police, they became increasingly violent. By the following evening, when military troops finally quelled the disorder, forty-three Jews had been killed, six more had been mortally wounded, scores of others had been injured, and vast numbers of shops and homes had been damaged or destroyed.[1] This was the infamous Kishinev pogrom, one of the most important and most notorious of the anti-Jewish riots that afflicted late imperial Russia.

Early reports on the pogrom seemed to implicate the Russian government. The rioters themselves apparently thought they were carrying out the will of the tsar. The authorities and police had done little to discourage them, and had seemed instead to be sympathetic. The local newspaper, published by a rabid anti-Semite with high connections in Saint Petersburg, had done its best to provoke anti-Jewish fears. And the minister of interior, according to various accounts, had warned the provincial governor of the impending disorders, advising against forceful intervention. To many observers, the evidence seemed to suggest that the pogrom had been planned by the central government itself and carried out by its local agents.[2] Several historians, in fact, concluded that the Kishinev massacre was part of a larger state policy designed to combat revolutionary discontent by directing popular anger against the Jews.[3]

Later scholarship, however, cast doubt on this interpretation, noting that there was little evidence of a conscious state policy of pogrom-instigation at this time. Imperial officials, it is true, were guilty of fostering Russian chauvinism and imposing legal restrictions on Jews. But, given their general determination to maintain order and prevent civic turmoil, it was unlikely that they were actively seeking to incite violent rioting among the lower classes.[4]

Whether or not the Russian government played a conscious role in engineering the Kishinev massacre, the fact is that this pogrom could not have taken place unless tensions and antagonisms already existed between the city's Jewish residents and their Christian neighbors. Some of these tensions, no doubt, were exacerbated by the anti-Semitic attitudes of important Russian officials,[5] and by the incendiary behavior of prominent local instigators. But many of them were rooted in the social, economic, demographic and cultural conditions which had developed in Russian Moldavia during the preceding half-century.

Russian Moldavia was located in the extreme southwestern portion of the Russian empire, along the Rumanian border and the shore of the Black Sea. It was a pleasant land whose fertile soil and temperate climate supported farms, orchards and vineyards, which in turn provided the livelihood for many of its two million inhabitants. Kishinev, its capital, sat in the center of the province, in a hilly region dotted with gardens and vineyards. Some forty miles to the west was the River Pruth, which ran along the Rumanian border; to the east, about half that distance away, lay the Dnester River and the empire's Ukrainian provinces.

Historically and culturally, the region had been part of the Rumanian principality of Moldavia, and its natives had largely derived their traditions, language, customs, and characteristics from this association. From the sixteenth through nineteenth centuries, however, the Rumanian principalities had come under Turkish sway. Then, in 1812, as the result of a Russo-Turkish War, the easternmost part of Moldavia was ceded to the Russians. Eastern Moldavia—which the Russians chose to call Bessarabia—became part of the tsarist empire.[6]

In 1812, at the time of the Russian annexation, there were fewer than half a million people living in eastern Moldavia. There were no cities to speak of: even the largest towns had fewer than 10,000 residents. And the bulk of the people—at least two-thirds of the population—were Moldavians. The rest appear to have been mainly Ruthenians, Bulgarians, Germans, and Jews.[7]

Although there were fewer than 5,000 Jewish families living in the region when the Russians took over, anti-Jewish sentiment was by no means unknown. Over the centuries, political authorities had occasionally subjected the Jews to repression and persecution, while Orthodox Church leaders had at times condemned them as heretics and forbidden Christians to associate with them. The Moldavians themselves, and occasional groups of outside invaders, had sporadically committed acts of harassment and violence against the Jews. In the eighteenth century, on several occasions, Moldavian Jews had been accused of murdering Christian children for ritual purposes, and local Christian clergy had apparently helped spread these libels. Jews had been abused and plundered, and some even killed, before the real culprits were exposed. Despite these scattered incidents, however, the level of anti-Jewish violence seems to have been lower in Moldavia than in neighboring Wallachia and Ukraine.[8]

In the long run, the Russian annexation of 1812 was to have enormous consequences for eastern Moldavia and its Jews. At first, distracted by the Napoleonic wars and anxious to portray their takeover as a liberation, the Russians had treated their new territory as an autonomous region. Eventually, however, they had begun to incorporate it into the empire's political and economic system. Russian laws, language, currency, and administrative practices were imposed, and migration of peoples from other parts of the empire was encouraged. Russian Moldavia became part of the "Pale of Jewish Settlement," the fifteen-province area where Jews were legally allowed to reside.

During the first half of the nineteenth century, substantial numbers of Russians, Ukrainians, Jews, Bulgarians and Germans moved to Russian Moldavia, some of them encouraged by government policy, others attracted by economic opportunities. Partly due to this influx of outsiders, the region's population not only doubled, it also began to change. The old Moldavian nobility lost much of its influence, and new groups—especially Russians, Ukrainians, and Jews—came to play an increasingly important role in the area's political and economic life. In 1856, at the end of the Crimean War, there were approximately one million persons living in Russian Moldavia. About 55% of these were Moldavians, while Russians and Ukrainians accounted for another 23%. Jews now made up about 8% of the population, while the rest was comprised of Germans, Bulgarians, Gypsies, Gagaus, and others.[9]

The second half of the nineteenth century brought further dramatic changes. In 1873, eastern Moldavia was formally incorporated as a full-fledged Russian province, known as "Bessarabia." In the 1880s and 1890s, attempts to "russify" the province intensified, while urbanization and industrial growth began to make their mark. The villages and rural areas remained predominantly Moldavian, but the region's growing cities became multi-national and multi-cultural enclaves.

The Jewish population in particular grew by leaps and bounds. In 1856, as noted above, the region's 80,000 Jews represented about eight percent of its one million inhabitants. During the next four decades, while the overall population doubled, the Jewish community nearly tripled in size. By 1897, according to that year's census, there were over 220,000 Jews in the province. More importantly, the Jews now comprised nearly twelve percent of the population. Their accelerating rate of natural increase, common to many groups in the nineteenth century, was augmented by extensive immigration from elsewhere in the tsarist empire. Consequently, the Jewish community in Bessarabia was growing half again as quickly as the rest of the population.[10]

The remarkable growth in the number of Jews was most noticeable in cities and towns. At first the Russian government had allowed Jews to reside in rural villages and had even encouraged the formation of Jewish agricultural colonies in Russian Moldavia. By the late nineteenth century, however, this situation had changed. The notorious "May Laws" of 1882 forbade Jews from purchasing land and settling in the villages throughout the "Pale of Settlement." Many of the Jewish farming settlements were closed down, and scores of Jews were expelled from peasant villages. In 1897, only about seven percent of Bessarabia's Jews were engaged in agriculture. Three-quarters of all Jews now lived in cities and towns, and most made their living in commerce, craftsmanship or industry. Most significantly, they tended to dominate these areas. Jewish people made up fully 37% of the province's urban population, and a significant portion of the region's commerce was now in Jewish hands.[11]

Nowhere was this more evident than in the provincial capital. Like the region itself, Kishinev had grown enormously in the course of the nineteenth century. In 1812, at the time of the Russian annexation, it had been an obscure provincial town with fewer than 7,000 residents. Because of its central location, however, the Russians soon made it their headquarters. This not only brought prominence and prestige, it also provided incentive for improving the town's appearance, accessibility, architecture, and public works. Meanwhile, Kishinev was developing into an important commercial and manufacturing center, handling much of the fruit and grain train and the processing of food and food by-products for the region. By 1900, it was a modern, bustling metropolis with a religiously and ethnically diverse population of well over 100,000.[12]

The Jews, meanwhile, had become the city's largest and fastest growing nationality group. In the 1860s, according to various estimates, Kishinev's 18,000 Jews made up about 20% of the city's 90,000 residents. By 1897, based on census data, their numbers had risen to 50,000, and they now comprised about 45% of the populace. If these figures are at all credible, they chart a remarkable phenomenon: in the last third of the nineteenth century, Kishinev's Jewish community had nearly tripled, while the city's non-Jewish population had slightly declined. Most of the growth seems to have come from immigration: in 1897, nearly 30% of all Kishinev residents had been born outside of Bessarabia province, mostly in other areas of the Pale of Jewish Settlement. Some Jews apparently were attracted to Kishinev because of the favorable climate, the expanding economy, and (prior to the 1890s) the relatively mild enforcement of anti-Jewish legislation. Others, no doubt, were forced to move to the city by the May Laws of 1882 and further government moves to prohibit Jewish rural residence.[13]

In economic terms, the Jews were even more influential than their numbers would indicate. The majority of Kishinev's commercial, financial and industrial enterprises, including three-fourths of the city's factories, were in Jewish hands. Jewish-owned businesses included flour-mills, wineries, tobacco-processing plants, credit and loan agencies, trading companies, and the like. The skilled trades, especially sewing, tailoring, shoemaking, and cabinetmaking, were likewise dominated by Jews. By general reputation, Jewish businesses were better organized than others, their prices were more competitive, and their merchandise was often superior. Karl Schmidt, the city's longtime mayor, was candid enough to admit that the city owed its prosperity largely to the Jews.[14]

This economic strength, however, had brought neither prosperity nor peace to the Jewish community. Although some Jews were quite prosperous, the bulk of them were poor, and many were almost destitute. The large number of artisans had created a fierce competition which kept prices, and hence profits, rather low. Poorer still were the unskilled Jewish workers, whose wages afforded only a bare subsistence. Worst off were the unemployed, who lived by the charity of their fellows—by 1900 there were over 2,000 Jewish families seeking such aid, and their numbers were growing steadily. In social and cultural terms, moreover, the Jews were set apart. They were, for the most part, a traditionalist lot who dressed in distinctive garb, discouraged intermarriage with non-Jews, strictly observed their religious and dietary laws, and kept their social life within their own community. They even ran their own schools, orphanage, hospital, and welfare institutions. On one hand, this brought them a higher level of education, a lower death-rate, and lower levels of drunkenness and crime, than the general population. On the other hand, it seems to have reinforced the fears, suspicions, and resentments of many of their non-Jewish neighbors.[15]

In the early twentieth century, Kishinev was divided into several communities. Along Aleksandrov Street, the town's main thoroughfare, stretching to the south and west atop the city heights, was "upper Kishinev," the newer party of town. Here the streets were broad, straight, paved and tree-lined, and the buildings—which included schools, theaters, churches, offices, and residences of the well-to-do—were made of stone. North of Aleksandrov Street was the older or "lower" section of town, rising gradually from the River Byk along the sloping hillside. It was comprised of narrow, winding, unpaved streets, muddy in spring and dusty in summer, and crowded with single-story wooden shanties that served as the shops, homes, and workplaces for the city's poor. Here was located the Jewish sector, as well as polyglot ethnic communities made up of Ukrainians, Greeks,

Armenians, Poles, Germans, Serbs, Bulgarians, Gypsies, and others. The most important nationalities, however, were the Russians and the Moldavians.[16]

According to the 1897 census, there were about 29,000 Russians in Kishinev, comprising some 27% of its 108,000 residents. These figures may be high: critics of the census claim it exaggerates the number of Russians.[17] Nevertheless, it is clear that substantial numbers of Russians had migrated to eastern Moldavia during the preceding century. Some had come seeking freedom: in the early nineteenth century, in order to attract Russian settlers, the tsarist government had refrained from extending serfdom to Russian Moldavia. Others, apparently, had been attracted by the economic activities a city like Kishinev seemed to offer. The most influential among the Russians, however, were the several thousand administrators, civil servants, and military officers who made up something of a "governing class" in Kishinev. Russians dominated the provincial administration, the police establishment, and the military garrison, all of which were headquartered in or near the city. They often tended to be somewhat contemptuous of other Kishinev residents—condescending to the native Moldavians and hostile toward the rest.[18]

The Jews, in particular, were targets of Russian antipathy. Their large numbers, cultural achievements, and economic accomplishments made them a potential threat and thus increased the determination of tsarist officials to limit Jewish influence. Anti-Jewish laws were strictly enforced: Jews were forbidden to vote in city elections, they could serve on the city council only if appointed by the authorities, and even then they could comprise no more than 10% of its members. Certain restrictions were carried to extremes: since Jews were forbidden to move to rural areas, for example, Kishinev officials would not let them work at the stone quarries seven miles out of town. To make matters worse, Russian administrators tended to sympathize with those who mistreated Jews, to ignore Jewish grievances, to look the other way when Jews were harassed or abused, and to condone the anti-Semitic activities of the local press. It is little wonder, then, that a number of Jewish intellectuals and youths—deprived of an outlet for their political energies and oppressed by various laws and deprivations—had begun joining revolutionary groups. Nor is it surprising that these actions would further alarm the Russian authorities, confirming their fears about the Jewish "menace," and reinforcing their view of the Jews as dangerous, unreliable, and undesirable aliens.[19]

The Moldavian people, the "natives" of Russian Moldavia, had neither the political power of the Russians nor the economic influence of the Jews. Furthermore, they were becoming a minority in their own land. In 1812, at the time of the Russian annexation, Moldavians had made up over two-thirds of the area's population, but by 1897, according to that year's census, they were down to 48%. Their problem was even worse in the cities: in Kishinev, according to this same census, the natives accounted for only 18% of the townsfolk, even though they made up 63% of the people in the surrounding county. Some sources, however, question the census, asserting that in 1900 the Moldavians still made up a substantial majority of the province as a whole. In Kishinev itself, however, it is clear that the natives were outnumbered.[20]

Furthermore, their influence in the capital was weak. They were, for the most part, peasants and former peasants from the surrounding countryside who tended to be employed mainly as farmers, gardeners, manual laborers, and servants. Their male literacy rate (about 18%) was much lower than that of the city's Russians (42%) and Jews (51%).[21] Politically and militarily, they were under the control of the Russians, who dominated the higher ranks of the civil and armed services. Economically, they were also dependent on "outsiders," especially the Jews, who played such a prominent role in the city's commerce.

To some observers, the subservient status of the Moldavians seemed quite consistent with their national character. By stereotype they were a kindly and simple folk, good-natured and courteous, uneducated and carefree, and even a bit lazy. In political affairs they were regarded as unsophisticated, unambitious, and obedient—although they sometimes displayed an impulsive violent streak. In financial matters they were reputedly naive, uncompetitive, and easily swindled, with a tendency to mismanage their affairs and live beyond their means.[22]

There is evidence, however, that by 1903 many Moldavians were becoming increasingly unhappy with their situation. A few were joining the revolutionary movement, which had begun to grow rapidly in the late 1890s, making inroads among the city's workers and young people. By 1902, the local social democrats were printing an illegal newspaper and organizing strike movements. Although the socialist movement, like so much else in Kishinev, was dominated by Russians and Jews, some Moldavians were starting to get involved. Meanwhile, Rumanian nationalism was also becoming a force. With the emergence of an independent Rumania in the 1860s, Russian Moldavia had become something of an *irredenta*: by nationalist logic, based on historical, cultural and ethnic affinities, it should rightfully be part of Rumania, not Russia. In the 1890s, tsarist attempts to "russify" Bessarabia province had served to heighten nationalist tensions. By the early twentieth century, Rumania was beginning to align itself with Russia's Austro-German adversaries, and clandestine Rumanian nationalist groups were beginning to form in Russian Moldavia. As yet, only small numbers of persons were involved, and most Moldavian aspirations were expressed in cultural, not political, terms. Still, it is apparent that nationalist sentiments were beginning to make an impact even before the emergence of a genuine separatist movement in 1905.[23]

Anti-Semitism, too, was a prominent factor among the Moldavians. The periodic episodes of intolerance, persecution, blood libel and atrocity, which had taken place over the centuries, provided ample evidence of anti-Jewish prejudice within the Rumanian culture. Although the Moldavians had generally managed to live in peace with their Jewish neighbors, in times of economic or political stress it had not been unusual for authorities and common people to turn against the Jews. Like other cities in south Russia, for instance, Kishinev had experienced anti-Jewish disturbances in 1881, in the wake of the assassination of Tsar Alexander II. The disorders were not serious, but they did show that anti-Jewish sentiments were present among the Moldavians, and that such sentiments could lead to violence during situations of stress.[24]

On top of this, by the late nineteenth century, the traditional fears and prejudices in Russian Moldavia were being compounded by the rapid increase in the size of the Jewish community. The economic influence of prominent Jews aroused concerns about Jewish domination while, ironically, the growth in numbers of impoverished Jews led to fears that there would be lower wages and fewer jobs for working class Moldavians. And Rumanian nationalist sentiment, which had emerged earlier in the nineteenth century, also incorporated an anti-Semitic strain, as evidenced by the systematic repression of Jews in the new Rumanian state.[25]

Anti-Semitism, for the Moldavians, was a relatively safe pursuit. It was dangerous for them to be socialists or nationalists; these were illegal and seditious activities that involved risky defiance of the Russian authorities. Jew-hatred, however, was fairly respectable, encouraged by the Russian government and condoned by the Orthodox Church. This was one sentiment that Moldavians could share with Russians, and prominent persons could share with the lower classes. For Russians and Moldavians alike, anti-Semitism could be patriotic, politically acceptable, religiously tolerable, and—for those who felt the strain of financial competition—perhaps even economically beneficial.

To make matters worse, the smoldering fires of anti-Semitism were actively stoked by opportunistic individuals who saw gain for themselves in such activity. By the turn of the century *Bessarabets*, the province's main newspaper, had become a beacon of anti-Jewish propaganda in the hands of its publisher, Pavolachi Krushevan. Diatribes against the Jews were standard fare in this gazette, and apocryphal stories of Jewish crimes, conspiracies, and rituals appeared regularly in its pages.[26] Other Kishinev luminaries, meanwhile, helped to fan the flames. Georgii Pronin, a Christian contractor who had lost business to Jewish competitors, lent money to Krushevan's newspaper, published anti-Jewish articles and poems within its pages, and acted as a self-styled "protector" of Christian workers against the Jewish "threat." He was joined in these activities by A. I. Stepanov, the head of a local organization of Christian artisans.[27]

V. G. Ustrugov, the province's vice-governor and *de facto* administrator of Bessarabia, made harassment of the Jews a cornerstone of his policy, while using his position to protect those who baited the Jews.[28] And even the Orthodox metropolitan, Bishop Iakov, refused to use his influence to stop the spread of vicious anti-Semitic rumors.[29]

By the early twentieth century, then, anti-Semitism in Russian Moldavia was a potent and palpable force. It was rooted, as elsewhere, in cultural differences, religious prejudices, and economic competition. It was nurtured, in the late nineteenth century, by the spread of nationalism among both Russians and Moldavians. It was encouraged by prominent individuals, who spread anti-Jewish libels and provoked anti-Jewish sentiments among the Christian masses. And it was fostered by Russian officials, who set the tone for bigotry by their own anti-Semitic behavior.

Urban growth was not the cause of anti-Semitism in Russian Moldavia; indeed, this sentiment had existed in Moldavia long before the region's cities had begun to grow. But the forces of urbanization and population growth did help create the climate which fostered tensions between Christians and Jews in Kishinev. For one thing, they brought large numbers of persons with diverse culture backgrounds into a relatively small area, compelling them to live in close proximity with one another. This was particularly true of working class families, the ones most vulnerable to economic frustration and susceptible to rumors, agitation, and provocation. For another thing, they brought large numbers of Jews, driven by government policies and economic considerations, into the city. Some gained positions of economic prominence, controlling much of the city's commerce, and paving the way for accusations about "Jewish exploitation." Many others were compelled by destitution to work for very low wages, thus giving rise to fears that they were taking jobs away from Christian workers. Unscrupulous persons thus found it relatively easy to exploit the fears of working-class Christians, instilling in them the impression that anti-Jewish activity was acceptable, and even desirable. This impression was encouraged by local agitators, fostered by Kishinev's anti-Semitic newspaper, and enhanced by the blatant anti-Semitism of many local officials. In this atmosphere, in spring of 1903, new libels about a Jewish ritual murder and persistent rumors about a secret tsarist order to beat the Jews were readily believed by the Kishinev townsfolk, and the stage was set for the violent Easter pogrom.

NOTES

For a more thorough treatment of the issues and developments discussed in this article, see chapters 2 and 3 of Edward H. Judge, *Easter in Kishinev: The Anatomy of a Pogrom* (New York: New York University Press, 1992).

1. *Novoe vremia*, April 11, 1903, 1; April 29, 1903, 1; *New York Times*, 6 June 1903, 3; S. M. Dubnov and G. Ia. Krasnyi-Admoni, eds., *Materialy dlia istorii antievreiskikh pogromov*, 2 vols. (Petrograd: Tipografiia "Kadima," 1919; Moscow: Gosudarstvennoe izdatel'stvo, 1923), 1:134-147, 151-166, 333-335, 339-342; M. B. Slutskii, *V skorbnye dni: Kishinevskii pogrom 1903 goda* (Kishinev: Tipografiia M. Averbukha, 1930), 1-6. The final death toll included 49 Jews and 2 Christians. D. Volchonsky, "The First Pogrom of the XX Century" [Hebrew], *He'-Avar* 20 (1973): 139.

2. *The Times* (London), 6 May 1903, 7; 18 May 1903, 5; 19 May 1903, 3; 20 May 1903, 7; 27 May 1903, 6; *New York Times*, 24 April 1903, 6; 14 May 1903, 5, 8; 15 May 1903, 2; 16 May 1903; 1, 3; 22 May 1903, 1; 31 May 1903, 5; G. B. Sliozberg, *Dela minuvshikh dnei*, 3 vols. (Paris: Imprimerie Pascal, 1933-1934), 3:63-64; S. M. Dubnov, *A History of the Jews in Russia and Poland*, 3 vols. (Philadelphia: Jewish Publication Society of America, 1916-1920), 3:72-74, 76-78.

3. Dubnov, *History*, 3:68-71; Louis Greenberg, *The Jews in Russia* (2 vols., New Haven, Yale University Press, 1944, 1951), 2:50-52; E. Semenoff, *The Russian Government and the Massacres* (London: John Murray, 1907), xviii, xix; Sliozberg, 3:64.

4. See Hans Rogger, "The Jewish Policy of Late Tsarism: A Reappraisal," *Weiner Library Bulletin* 25 (1971): 42-51; Eliyahu Feldman, "Plehve and the Kishinev Pogrom of 1903" [Hebrew] *He-'Avar* 17 (1970): 137-150; Shlomo Lambroza, "Plehve, Kishinev and the Jewish Question: A Reappraisal," *Nationalities Papers* 23, no. 2 (1981): 117-127; Lambroza, "The Tsarist Government and the Pogroms

of 1903-06," *Modern Judaism* 7, no. 3 (1987): 287-296; Edward H. Judge, *Plehve: Repression and Reform in Imperial Russia, 1902-1904* (Syracuse: Syracuse University Press, 1983), 93-101.

5. For discussions of official Russian anti-Semitism see G. Krasnyi-Admoni, "Staryi rezhim i pogromy," in Dubnov and Krasnyi-Admoni, eds., *Materialy*, 1:xvi-xxxii; Rogger, *Jewish Policies and Right-Wing Politics in Imperial Russia* (Berkeley: University of California Press, 1986), 25-39, 56-112, 113-175; Heinz-Deitrich Lowe, *Antisemitismus und reaktionare Utopie* (Hamburg: Hoffman und Campe, 1978), 40-68; L. M. Aizenberg, "Vidy pravitel'stva v evreiskom voprose," *Evreiskaia letopis'* 1 (1923): 37-51; 2 (1923): 73-86.

6. George F. Jewsbury, *The Russian Annexation of Bessarabia, 1774-1828* (New York: East European Monographs, 1976), 7-54.

7. Jewsbury, 57, 67; A. Zashchuk, *Materialy dlia geografii i statistiki Rossii: Bessarabskaia oblast'* (Saint Petersburg: n.p., 1862), 10-11, 147-148, 151-181.

8. Zashchuk, 171-172; S. Zelenchuk, *Naselenie Bessarabii i podnestrov'ia v XIX v.* (Kishinev: "Shtiintsa," 1979), 63-64, 158; *Encyclopedia Judaica* 14:386-387; 4:704; *Jewish Encyclopediia* 10:512-513.

9. Jewsbury, 66-67; *Pervaia vseobshchaia perepis' naselenie rossiiskoe imperii, 1897*, vol. 3, *Bessarabskaia guberniia* (Saint Petersburg: Izdanie tsentral'nago statisticheskago komiteta ministerstva vnutrennikh del, 1905), xi, 74-93; Zelenchuk, 148-160; *Istoriia Kishineva*, comp. Kishinevskii gosudarstvennyi universitet kafedra istorii SSSR (Kishinev: "Kartia Moldoveniaske," 1966), 47-50, 99-101.

10. Zelenchuk, 64, 158, 203-206; *Encyclopedia Judaica* 4:704.

11. Zelenchuk, 201-207; *Encyclopedia Judaica* 4:705-706.

12. *Istoriia Kishineva*, 49, 83-87, 101; A. S. Konstantinov, *Kishinev: ekonomicheskii ocherk* (Kishinev: "Kartia Moldoveniaske," 1966), 12-13, 18-21.

13. *Pervaia vseobshchaia perepis'*, 3:3, 36-39, 178-179; Zelenchuk, 203-206; Zashchuk, 171-173; *Evreiskaia Entsiklopediia* 9:504-505; *Encyclopedia Judaica* 10:1063-64.

14. *Jewish Encyclopedia* 7:512; *Encyclopedia Judaica* 10:1063-64; *Pervaia vseobshchaia perepis'*, 3: 178-179; S. D. Urusov, *Memoirs of a Russian Governor* (London and New York: Harper and Brothers, 1908), 158-165; Michael Davitt, *Within the Pale* (New York: A. S. Barnes, 1903), 155-156, 162-163, 181.

15. *Jewish Encyclopedia* 7:512; *Encyclopedia Judaica* 10:1063-64; *Evreiskaia Entsiklopediia* 9:504-505; Urusov, 33-34, 147-148, 153-154.

Urban Growth and Anti-semitism in Russian Moldavia 57

16. Konstantinov, 22-23; Davitt, 158-159; Urusov, 96-97; *Istoriia Kishineva*, 49, 101.

17. *Pervaia vseobshchaia perepis'*, 3:228-231; Zelenchuk, 154; Anthony Babel, *La Bessarabie* (Paris: Librairie Felix Alcan, 1926), 229-231; Andrei Popovici, *The Political Status of Bessarabia* (Washington: Ransdell, Inc., 1931), 84-88.

18. *Pervaia vseobshchaia perepis'*, 3:178-179; Jewsbury, 67-68; *Istoriia Kishineva*, 99-101; Zelenchuk, 171-178; Urusov, 25, 37-38, 59-61.

19. *Polnoe sobranie zakonov rossiiskoe imperii*, 3rd ed., 33 vols. (Saint Petersburg: Gosudarstvennaia tipografiia, 1885-1916), 12, no. 8708 (June 11, 1892); *Jewish Encyclopedia* 7:512; Henry J. Tobias, *The Jewish Bund in Russia* (Stanford: Stanford University Press, 1972), 2-10.

20. Zelenchuk, 154, 158; *Pervaia vseobshchaia perepis'*, 3:2-3, 178-179; Babel, 229-231; Popovici, 84-88.

21. *Pervaia vseobshchaia perepis'*, 3:112-119, 178-179; Zelenchuk, 168-171; *Istoriia Kishineva*, 49.

22. Urusov, 19, 25, 100-101, 112, 161-162; Davitt, 93-94.

23. *Istoriia Kishineva*, 133-144; Popovici, 105-117.

24. Dubnov and Krasnyi-Admoni, eds., *Materialy*, 2:183-185, 531; I. Michael Aronson, *Troubled Waters: The Origins of the 1881 Anti-Jewish Pogroms in Russia* (Pittsburg: University of Pittsburgh Press, 1990) 59, 110.

25. Urusov, 147-148; E. Schwarzfeld, "The Jews of Roumania," *American Jewish Year Book* 5662 (1901/2), 28-54; 63-84; Stephen Fischer-Galati, "Romanian Nationalism," in *Nationalism in Eastern Europe*, ed. Peter Sugar and Ivo Lederer (Seattle: University of Washington Press, 1969), 385-386; Babel, 220-221; *Bessarabets*, 22 March 1903, 1; 4 November 1903, 2.

26. Slutskii, 43-45; Davitt, 97-99; *Bessarabets*, 4 January 1903, 2-3; 14 January 1903, 3; 16 January 1903, 3; 24 January 1903, 2; 27 January 1903, 2; 29 January 1903, 3; 8 February 1903, 2; 9 February 1903, 3; 11 February 1903, 2; 13 February 1903, 3; 14 February 1903, 3; 19 February 1903, 2; 20 February 1903, 3; 27 February 1903, 2; 9 March 1903, 3; 11 March 1903, 2; 19 March 1903, 3.

27. Slutskii, 46-48; Urusov, 47-49; *Bessarabets*, 17 April 1903, 3; 21 April 1903, 3; 27 January 1904, 3.

28. Davitt, 97-99, 137; Slutzkii, 52-53; Urusov, 28-34, 145-146, 157-158.

29. Slutskii, 2-3.

RUSSIAN TEACHERS AND PEASANT REVOLUTION, 1895-1917

Scott J. Seregny

The historian of late Imperial Russia is confronted with two images of the rural teacher. The first is that of the "zemstvo rabbit," timid, vulnerable and oblivious to wider professional concerns or the burning social and political issues of the day. The type was characterized by the following traits: 1) extreme material insecurity, reflected in high turnover and flight from the profession; 2) low status and subordinate administrative position (with no right of appeal in disciplinary matters); 3) isolation from both educated society and other teachers; 4) meager formal education aggravated by cultural deprivation on the job, little access to reading material, and few means for professional association; 5) social and cultural isolation within the peasant community, with status as an "outsider" stemming from social origin, feminization and peasant suspicion of carriers of secular and alien culture. In short, teachers faced an array of social and institutional impediments to both professional solidarity and influence among the population. Many of these traits, of course, are part of the sociology of teaching as a profession.[1] In Russia they were hypertrophied.

The second image is quite different: the teacher as inveterate populist agitator, providing a vital link between revolutionary groups in the cities and the peasantry. The first view is firmly anchored in zemstvo statistical studies which yield a collective profile of the profession over a long time period.[2] It is reinforced by memoirs, literary portrayals and, in part, what we know about peasant attitudes toward schooling.[3] The second view derives from police reports (and arrests), beginning with the

"To the People" movement of the 1870s and continuing through the Revolution of 1905, as well as from memoir accounts.[4]

Both types existed. "Zemstvo rabbits," often barely equipped to teach the three "R's," let alone engage in wider activity, were probably a majority at any given time. Radicals were clearly more than a product of the imaginations of overly-suspicious police. Yet both generalizations are essentially static and flawed, failing to account for the dynamics of the teachers' movement. The period 1895-1905 saw an unprecedented upsurge of professional and political activism among rural teachers, profoundly shaped by their interactions with state, society and peasantry. This essay will provide a brief overview of this formative period, concentrating on teachers' roles in rural political mobilization during 1905.

The 1890s marked a critical juncture in Russian rural development. Devastating famine and cholera exposed the backwardness of rural society and lent a special urgency to the task of enlightening the "dark masses." Zemstvos launched an impressive campaign to extend the school network and recruit new teachers while popular education stirred the imagination of educated society.[5] Tied to this campaign was a flurry of efforts to galvanize the torpid teaching "caste," generally perceived to be in acute crisis, as reflected in plummeting qualifications, low morale, and headlong flight by male teachers into posts with the new state liquor monopoly.[6]

The new orientation affected teachers in fundamental ways. Society envisioned the humble village pedagogues as the advance cadres in a protean effort to transform peasant Russia. As the Viatka zemstvo put it, teachers should do much more than teach children; they should exert a real influence on the population at large, countering the influence of clerics, integrating peasant society with the dominant culture, explaining "the significance of major natural phenomena and public (*obshchestvennye*) events."[7] The more sanguine among zemstvo activists saw teachers playing a pivotal role in rural political enlightenment, nothing less than the rearing of literate citizens at a time when constitutional reform was thought to be imminent. Revolutionary parties, such as the Socialist-Revolutionaries, targeted teachers as potential cadres in the village.[8] This was all heady stuff. Nevertheless, whether liberal or radical in tone, a new professional ethos was rapidly taking shape. More important, it was effectively conveyed and internalized by teachers after 1895 when, under zemstvo auspices and conditional government support, efforts were made to address teachers' pressing needs in the areas of association and cultural rehabilitation. These included: 1) summer courses and local professional congresses, both of signal importance in combatting recidivism and fostering a sense of corporate solidarity; 2) mutual-aid societies, the only permanent organization permitted by the regime; 3) efforts to bring reading material to rural teachers.[9]

The impact of these efforts (peaking in 1902-03) on the profession—and only at this point can one really speak of a professional identity—was substantial. Thousands participated in the summer courses, and their recorded impressions leave no doubt that the experience worked a sea-change in teachers' consciousness, measured in a renewed commitment to teaching, solidarity, and a militant embrace of the mission to transform peasant society.[10] That this professional identity was rapidly politicized there is also little doubt. Evidence that liberal opponents of the autocracy and groups like the SRs utilized summer courses and mutual-aid societies to make contact with teachers—and through them try to penetrate the village—is ample.[11]

More fundamental in the politicization of the nascent teachers' movement was the ambivalent and vacillating policy of the government toward the profession. On the one hand the state had made a limited commitment to public education, though given its industrialization priorities it was unable to allocate sufficient funds to augment teachers' salaries and the like. On the other hand the government was concerned with security, namely the potential threat schooling and teachers might pose to the traditional social order: peasant monarchism, deference and religiosity. Hence its approach to the profession had always been restrictive and often repressive: school inspectors wielded considerable police powers; professional and even intimate social gatherings of teachers at various times were banned; rural teachers were not permitted to read material cleared by censorship for the general urban population.[12] The state was clearly perceived as helping to perpetuate teachers' isolation and cultural deprivation.

Given the inherent tension in official education policy, its approach was also inconsistent. When in the wake of agrarian disorders in 1902 official attitudes tilted toward preoccupation with security, the promising developments of recent years were cut short. The years 1903-04 saw a steady erosion of the legal means for professional association, part of a futile effort to quarantine the countryside from political opposition mounting in the cities.[13]   In light of rising expectations and increased solidarity, the result for many teachers was a high level of frustration, reflected in organized political opposition.

The onset of revolution in early 1905 accelerated these developments. On the basis of the modest mutual-aid societies and links forged during the previous decade, 13,000 teachers formed an All-Russian Teachers' Union committed to the end of the autocracy and a constitution and civil rights as the only guarantees of professional autonomy. Teachers thereby joined their voices to a national Liberation chorus that would, along with mounting labor protest and agrarian unrest, compel the regime to concede the Manifesto of October 17, 1905.[14] The real significance of teachers' mobilization, and potentially their most important contribution, would lie in efforts to garner peasant support for the wider political goals of liberal society by means of political enlightenment and organization in the countryside.

There was a certain urgency to such efforts. The liberal opposition was concerned with the problem of peasant monarchism and afraid that the autocracy might effectively appeal to a loyal *narod* against the urban opposition. (If a constitution were to be won the attitude of the peasant majority would be crucial.) More ominously, there was concern, shared by some on the left, that peasant activism, beginning already in February 1905, might be wholly destructive and indiscriminate, a spontaneous *bunt* directed not only against gentry property and officialdom, but also against "culture" (schools, zemstvo clinics) and the intelligentsia, often lumped together in the peasant mind, along with traditional privileged and exploiting categories, as "gentlefolk." Both concerns were underscored by a wave of anti-intelligentsia agitation affecting various locales in late 1904 and early 1905, which was clearly inspired by clerical and official supporters of the regime. Teachers and other rural intelligenty were branded as "antichrists" or "hirelings of the Japanese" (with whom Russia was then at war); in some instances threats turned to violence. In Saratov province a drunken peasant mob looted a school, boasting that "for the murder of a teacher they would receive only thanks from the authorities and would have to answer for it less than for killing a frog."[15]

With such experiences fresh in mind, organizing teachers placed the issue of political enlightenment at the top of their agenda. At meetings of mutual-aid societies in the spring of 1905, adherents of the Teachers' Union called upon their fellows to bring the "liberation movement" to the village:

> Agrarian rebellions indicate disaffection among the *narod*, but regrettably the latter does not yet comprehend the whole significance of the present moment; within it is still in command a "dark force," this "black hundred" which impedes us, the intelligentsia, from merging with the peasantry. You, comrades, must penetrate the popular masses, enlighten and transform them, bridge the deep gulf between the educated and ignorant classes.[16]

Similar pleas were echoed by liberal zemstvo activists and others.[17] Teachers were summoned to play a more active political role in the village. What were the prospects?

The anti-intelligentsia agitation of early 1905 underscored problems in teacher-community relations. Teachers were "outsiders" within the peasant commune, both legally and socially. Though a large percentage of male teachers were drawn from the peasant "estate," many came from other backgrounds. In a world that was patriarchal, most teachers were young, unmarried and female. As an occupation, teaching did not necessarily command prestige: peasant attitudes about the value of schooling were still ambivalent; intellectual labor was not held in high regard; and the teacher's dependence on the commune for heat, light and other necessities often bred contempt and resentment among peasants who felt that zemstvo taxes, which supported the schools, fell disproportionately on their shoulders. Longevity in a given locale, crucial in acquiring a measure of influence, was the exception rather than the rule.[18] Peasants had a keen appreciation of power relations in the countryside, and the teacher's extreme subordinate administrative position did nothing to enhance prestige. (In contrast to French teachers under the Third Republic, Russian teachers did not enjoy the unqualified support of the state.) All of this would seem to militate against teachers achieving authority, the status of local "notables. " In the French context such status was based on the provision of concrete services to the local community beyond instructing children.[19] Cooperatives, adult courses and similar services were at the experimental stage in Russia. However, as they impinged upon the village, the revolutionary events of 1905 themselves cast teachers in new roles.

The early months of 1905 registered an unprecedented peasant interest in national events, which, according to zemstvo surveys, was reflected in high levels of subscriptions to newspapers: "such reading has increased ten-fold and it is not rare for an entire village to pool money for a subscription, with the paper passed from house to house and eventually reduced to shreds."[20] Initially fueled by thirst for news from the front, interest was sustained throughout the year by tumultuous domestic events; Bloody Sunday, workers' strikes and news of agrarian disturbances deluged the village. Events demanded interpretation, arcane political concepts (many derived from foreign sources) demanded explication, and, in many instances, the printed word required literate decoders. Not surprisingly, peasants turned to literate villagers, clerics and often to teachers for assistance.[21] A certain G. N. Vozkov, from Odessa district, related his experience: "In my village are many soldiers' wives who came to me with newpapers imploring, 'Read, for God's sake, how things are going at the front; perhaps my husband has already been killed and if so I must know.'" Vozkov read to peasants about the Russian defeats at Mukden and Tsushima

Straits. The land captain, striving to bolster patriotic support for the war, tried to persuade the peasants that all such news was a lie: "but then the peasants went to a neighboring village where the news was confirmed and trust in the teacher was solidified."[22] From that point peasants were receptive to teachers' arguments that the reasons for Russian defeats lay with a corrupt bureaucracy, fettered public opinion, educational backwardness and the like. Such analyses proved more persuasive than the conspiracy theories circulated earlier in the year linking the intelligentsia with Japanese gold.

Peasant interest in broader issues was also stimulated by the government's hesitant attempts to provide a an outlet for rural grievances and, hopefully, tap a reservoir of peasant monarchist support. A decree of February 18, 1905 granted peasant communes the right of direct appeal to the tsar, an alluring prospect for Russia's peasantry, generating 60,000 communal *cahiers* during the spring.[23] Above all, these *prigovory* addressed economic issues (such as land hunger); yet they also echoed the political demands of educated society: democratization of education, civil freedoms, an end to the war, controls over police and officials, reform of local zemstvo government, and even a constitution.[24] Rural teachers played a visible role in this petition campaign. Official decrees seemed to provide legal basis for such political enlightenment, and there was considerable peasant demand that teachers provide such services; for example, they were asked to explain exactly what a "constitution" was and what benefits peasants might derive from it. Petitions were commonly drafted by teachers at the request of communes, but official claims that rural intelligenty somehow hoodwinked peasants into signing such documents are belied by what we know of teacher-peasant relations. A process of political education was underway and teachers, under pressure "from below," helped facilitate it. As a result, their authority in the village had never been stronger.[25]

To summarize, a number of factors worked to propel teachers into politics in 1905: their own professional aspirations, promptings from their liberal patrons in the zemstvos, and peasant demand. The logical outcome of this process of political enlightenment was political organization, most notably the formation of peasant unions. As yet little studied, the peasant union movement succeeded, in a remarkably short time, in organizing tens of thousands of peasants around a program that included radical land reform (expropriation of gentry lands through legislative means) and democratic political changes. In terms of tactics the peasant unions, for the most part, eschewed agrarian violence and land seizures in favor of boycotts, agricultural strikes and non-payment of taxes.[26]

Aside from its program, which included democratization of education, reform of local self-government and constitutional transformation, the tactics of the Peasant Union appealed to teachers. Teachers distrusted spontaneous peasant activism, fearing that an elemental jacquerie might sweep all "culture" away with the landlord's estate. The peasant unions promised to steer the peasant movement into peaceful channels, supportive of the broader goals of the intelligentsia. Such support became doubly urgent after promulgation of the October Manifesto, when teachers faced government repression and a sharp shift to the right on the part of their zemstvo employers. Peasant ignorance and suspicion were still potent after October. In Bronnitsy district (Moscow) a teacher attempted to convene peasants in the school to explain the October "freedoms." "I had no idea," he later recalled, "that the dark *narod*, under provocation, had gathered to subject me to a 'strike' (*ustroit' mne 'zabastovku'*), that is beat me and, possibly kill me."[27] This was by no means an isolated incident.

For these reasons teachers and other rural intelligenty supported a "conscious," organized peasant movement. The Teachers' Union and its local chapters endorsed the peasant unions, and there was a close correlation between membership in teachers' professional organizations and activism on behalf of peasant unions.[28] All information on local peasant unions, including arrests and trials of organizers, indicates that rural teachers played a prominent role.[29] In fact, their prominence was utilized by conservative gentry and government officials in their contention that these rural political organizations were essentially non-peasant in character and aims, an assertion belied by the facts. In general the period after October 17 was one of intensive involvement by teachers in rural political mobilization. The manifesto itself seemed to sanction such activity, and peasant pressure, spurred by the upcoming elections to the Duma and expectations of sweeping reforms, was often intense. A member of a teachers' union group in Petersburg province described the situation.

> After October 17 one began to notice a special upsurge; our group began to arrange meetings to elucidate the freedoms of October 17, organized workers and peasants, explained the tasks of the Peasant Union and attitude toward the Duma. The population was extremely pleased with these gatherings; deputations would come for teachers from 20-30 versts away, the peasants listened avidly, the teacher became a genuine friend of the *narod*.[30]

A Ministry of Education official, trying to defend teachers against police charges of revolutionary agitation, reasoned that the village teacher was quite naturally sought out by peasants, given the fact that "government manifestoes contain ideas which are new and incomprehensible for rural dwellers, who are at the same time bombarded by revolutionary leaflets. Teachers cannot possibly avoid the basic questions occasioned by the reforms."[31]

Despite instances of continued peasant hostility after October 1905, as in Bronnitsy, it is clear that in many more cases teacher-community relations improved during the course of the 1905 Revolution. Dramatic proof of this was provided by the elections to the First Duma which convened in April 1906. Despite the fact that the electoral law barred the majority of rural teachers (those not of the peasant "estate" and women) from participation, a good number of teachers' candidacies were put forward by the peasantry, and a number of teachers of peasant origin were elected to Russia's first modern national assembly.[32] Elections to the Second Duma returned a slightly larger number (38) of teachers.[33] Peasants selected such rural intelligenty to represent them in St. Petersburg for several reasons: many were of peasant origin and knew the village firsthand, and they possessed literacy skills and the political savvy to defend peasant interests in competition with other groups (e.g., the gentry) in a national forum. Most important—and this stands out in teachers' statements at various congresses during this period—teachers were perceived by peasants as having their interests at heart. Intelligenty, who in the course of 1905 (or earlier) had demonstrated their support for popular interests, often at considerable risk, would not betray them.

The Revolution of 1905 stands as a high water mark in political activism among Russia's rural teachers and in their influence in the village. Propelled by their own professional interests and pressure from below, many of these "zemstvo rabbits" enlisted as vocal opponents of the autocracy, immersed themselves in rural politics, and, in the process, achieved a measure of "notability" in peasant affairs. Most of these gains, however, appear to have been erased quite rapidly.

The government, once it reasserted control in late 1905, cast a suspicious eye upon activist teachers and other rural intelligenty. Despite the efforts of Peasant Union agitators, agrarian disturbances flared up in various provinces in November-December 1905, and officials tended to construe all political efforts, including simple discussion of the tsar's own manifestoes, as open "incitement to agrarian riots." There was little discrimination between violence and essentially peaceful, organized tactics; accordingly, the peasant unions were crushed. The government was loath to see peasant demands for radical land reform and sweeping democratization of institutions given political focus and underpinned by mass organization. Reading official reports, one has the sense that the tsarist regime preferred to confront traditional forms of peasant protest (agrarian revolts, no matter how destructive) with traditional methods of containment (armed pacification).[34]

The result was a massive purge (arrests, dismissals) of teaching personnel in 1906-07. Given their relative isolation in the countryside, administrative subordination, and weak organizational networks, teachers were particularly vulnerable. The rightward shift among their former patrons in the zemstvos meant that little support was forthcoming from their employers, and peasant attempts to shield teachers, given the absence of community control over schools, were ultimately ineffective.[35] It is likely that at least twenty thousand teachers—in other words roughly one-third of the primary school teachers under the jurisdiction of the Ministry of Education—lost their jobs. No doubt a higher proportion of zemstvo teachers found themselves out of work.[36] No other social or professional group sustained such losses in 1905-07. Teachers' professional organizations were dealt a shattering blow: the Teachers' Union was proscribed, and even the modest mutual-aid societies had only *begun* to recover by the eve of World War I.[37] The consequences were significant. In the short-term schools remained empty until new teachers could be recruited. Repression left lasting scars on the collective psyche of the profession, which remained until the demise of the tsarist order. Contemporaries bemoaned a sharp decline in "public spirit" among teachers after 1907, and an activist of 1905 described the period between the two revolutions in these words: "Twelve years of systematic persecution... the constant position of teachers under a 'Damocles sword' irrevocably altered the physiognomy of the schoolteacher, and from a hopeful public activist (*optimist-obshchestvennik*) rendered him passive, cowardly, isolated in his bear's corner."[38]

The government did its best to reinforce teachers' isolation, particularly from the peasantry. As a result of Stolypin's *coup d'etat* of June 7, 1907 and official decrees, most teachers were disenfranchised and removed from the Duma electoral process.[39] State control over schools was strengthened through increases in the staff and powers of school inspectors. Some of these officials issued circulars warning teachers that they would be harshly disciplined if they appeared at village assemblies (*skhody*) or other peasant meetings.[40] In 1914, under the stewardship of the ultra-conservative Kasso, the Ministry published a circular barring teachers from participation in any organizations other than their own mutual-aid societies, a move that was interpreted in the field as prohibiting their involvement in the burgeoning rural cooperative movement and similar endeavors.[41] These were precisely the types of activities through which teachers in France and other countries had carved out a position of local authority.

Changes in the composition of teaching personnel during this period also appear to have affected teachers' status in the village. Feminization was a natural process, but there is strong evidence that government repression tended to accelerate it. During 1906-07 males were purged from the teaching profession in disproportionate numbers. This may have been a result of greater activism during the 1905 Revolution, but it also reflected official consensus that women would prove more docile candidates.[42] During the war years military conscription, from which primary school teachers were not exempt, further accelerated the process. Many of the new recruits were graduates of clerical institutions (the "diocesan schools") , and aside from meager educational credentials, contemporaries agreed that these "priests' daughters" (*popovskie dochenki*) tended to typify the inert "zemstvo rabbit" type.[43]

In light of these developments it is scarcely surprising that rural teachers appear to have exercised little influence in rural politics during 1917. A Provisional Government survey in the spring of 1917 noted that peasants tended to avoid the election of teachers and other intelligenty to new *volost'* committees and other bodies. As the report put it: "Male teachers, and especially female teachers, who had been vigilantly isolated from the peasants by the old regime, lack any link with the population and enjoy no authority."[44] This stands in marked contrast with the 1905 experience. In evaluating this turn of events it is necessary to note that the political situation in 1917 was much more polarized than had been the case twelve years earlier. Peasants were gravely disillusioned with the prospect of orderly, gradual reform and patience had been exhausted by the war. As members of the resurrected Teachers' Union sadly admitted, class lines were sharply drawn and, more often than not, teachers were regarded by peasants not only as "outsiders," but as "bourgeois" enemies of popular interests.[44]

In modern, literate societies, where the overriding and often sole function of schoolteachers is the instruction of children, the profession's status is generally low. As the sociologist J. A. Jackson notes, low status inevitably accrues to "teachers in primary schools to which *everyone* goes to learn *what everyone* knows."[46] Pre-revolutionary Russia was not such a society. Indeed, the basic issues of peasant schooling and rural modernization were still unresolved. In this context teachers, potentially, could play significant roles. Much depended on their own perception of their function in society. This perception, as well as concrete opportunities for action, was shaped to a large extent by external forces: state, society, and peasantry. As such, teachers' status was not immutable. Neither stereotype—the "zemstvo rabbit" or the "political activist"—can adequately convey the dynamics and complexities of the teachers' place in rural Russia during a period of rapid change.

NOTES

1. T. Leggatt, "Teaching as a Profession," in J. A. Jackson, ed., *Professions and Professionalization* (Cambridge, 1970), 153-178; Amitai Etzioni, ed., *The Semi-Professions and their Organization* (New York, 1969), especially the preface.

2. Useful are the results of a survey conducted by the Moscow Committee of Literacy in 1894-95 and published in part under the general title "K voprosu o polozhenii uchashchikh v narodnoi shkole," in *Russkaia mysl'*, no. 6, section 2 (1897): 82-94; no. 12, section 2 (1897): 61-78; no. 9, section 2 (1898): 189-212. Much of this material is conveniently summarized in L. N. Blinov, "Narodnyi uchitel'' v Rossii," in kn. D. I. Shakhovskoi, ed., *Vseobshchee obrazovanie v Rossii* (Moscow, 1902), 63-84. For a good survey of the problem, see Ben Eklof, "The Village and the Outsider: The Rural Teacher in Russia, 1864-1914," *Slavic and European Education Review*, no. 1 (1979): 1-19.

3. See Ben Eklof, "Peasant Sloth Reconsidered: Strategies of Education and Learning before the Revolution," *Journal of Social History* 14, no. 3 (1981): 355-380, and especially Eklof, *Russian Peasant Schools: Officialdom, Village Culture and Popular Pedagogy, 1861-1914* (Berkeley, 1986).

4. E. G. Kornilov, "Zemskie uchitelia v revoliutsionnom dvizhenii 70-kh gg. XIX v.," *Uchenye zapiski Moskovskogo gosudarstvennogo*

pedagogicheskogo instituta im. V. I. Lenina 439 (Moscow, 1971): 132; Minister of the Interior V. K. Plehve repeatedly made this charge: *Osvobozhdenie*, no. 11/35 (November 12/25, 1903): 194-95.

5. See Allen Sinel, "The Campaign for Universal Primary Education in Russia, 1890-1904," *Jahrbucher fur Geschichte Osteuropas*, 30, no. 4 (1982): 481-507; on the zemstvo campaign, see B. B. Veselovskii, *Istoriia zemstva za sorok let*, 4 vols. (Saint Petersburg, 1909-11), I. There were 10,300 zemstvo teachers in the thirty-four zemstvo provinces of European Russia in 1880 (about 70% of all rural schools). By 1903 there were over 27,000 zemstvo teachers.

6. "Khronika vnutrennei zhizni," *Russkoe bogatstvo*, no. 4, section 2 (1900): 186-88.

7. Tsentral'nyi gosudarstvennyi istoricheskii arkhiv (TsGIA), f. 733, op. 173, d. 127, *ll*. 4-74ob.

8. See Scott J. Seregny, *Russian Teachers and Peasant Revolution: The Politics of Education in 1905* (Bloomington, Ind., 1989), 84-98.

9. On these developments, see Seregny, *Russian Teachers*, chapters 3 and 4.

10. V. Denisov, "Znachenie uchitel'skikh kursov po otzyvam zemskikh uchitelei," *Obrazovanie*, no. 7, section 2 (1904): 42-47.

11. Seregny, *Russian Teachers*, 84-88.

12. L. D. Briukhatov, "Nuzhdy russkago uchitelia," *Russkiia vedomosti*, no. 265, 3. On government policies generally, see Seregny, *Russian Teachers*, chapter 2.

13. Zemstvos sponsored 11 courses in 1898, 12 in 1899, 18 in 1900 and 22 in 1901; 18 were held in 1902, but only 7 were sanctioned in 1903 and 4 in 1904: A. A. Loktin, "Uchitel'skie kursy i s"ezdy, " *Vestnik vospitaniia*, no. 6, section 2 (1904): 77-78.

14. For a brief survey of the union, see Ronald H. Hayashida, "The Unionization of Russian Teachers, 1905-1908: An Interest Group Under the Autocracy, " *Slavic and European Education Review*, no. 2 (1981): 1-16.

15. *Russkiia vedomosti*, no. 91, 4 April 1905, 3.

16. TsGIA, f. 733, op. 173, d. 56, *l*. 280ob-281.

17. E. D. Chermenskii, *Burzhuaziia i tsarizm v pervoi russkoi revoliutsii*, 2nd ed. (Moscow, 1970), 90-95.

18. See Eklof, "The Village and the Outsider," 1-19 and Seregny, *Russian Teachers*, 13-16, 146-147.

19. Barnett Singer, "The Teacher as Notable in Brittany, 1880-1914, " *French Historical Studies* 9 (1976): 635-659, and Eugen Weber, *Peasants into Frenchmen* (Stanford, 1976), 317-318.
20. K. Vorob'ev, "Narodnye otzyvy o tsenzure, " *Russkiia vedomosti*, no. 182, 8 July 1905, 2; "Gazeta v derevne," in *Statisticheskii ezhegodnik Moskovskoi gubernii za 1906* (Moscow, 1907), part 1, 209-19.
21. Studies indicate that literacy rates were not high among village officials. A study in Kazan province in 1904 determined that only 18.2% of village elders were literate: *Vestnik vospitaniia*, no. 4, section 2 (1905): 78. Thus, recourse was made to local "outsiders" like teachers.
22. *Syn otechestva*, no. 91, 2 June 1905, 4.
23. Chermenskii, *Burzhuaziia*, 57, 60-61.
24. K. V. Sivkov, "Krest'ianskie prigovory 1905 goda, " *Russkaia mysl'*, no. 4, section 2 (1907): 24-48.
25. A well-documented case can be found in I. G. Drozdov, "Petitsii Novozybkovskikh krest'ian v 1905 g.," *Proletarskaia revoliutsiia*, no. 11 (1925): 124-151.
26. The best treatment is E. I. Kiriukhina, "Vserossiiskii krest'ianskii soiuz v 1905 g.," *Istoricheskie zapiski* 50 (1955): 95-141; also Scott J. Seregny, "A Different Type of Peasant Movement: The Peasant Unions in the Russian Revolution of 1905," *Slavic Review*, 47, no. 1 (1988): 51-67 and idem, "Peasants and Politics: Peasant Unions during the 1905 Revolution," in Esther Kingston-Mann and Timothy Mixter, eds., *Peasant Economy, Culture and Politics in European Russia, 1800-1917* (Princeton, N.J., 1991): 341-377.
27. S. I. Kudriavtsev, "Uchitel' i naselenie Bronnitskogo uezda v 1905 godu (vospominaniia)," Tsentral'nyi gosudarstvennyi arkhiv oktiabrskoi revoliutsii (TsGAOR), f. 6862, op. 1, d. 84, *ll*. 205-20ob.
28. *Russkoe slovo*, no. 295, 9 November 1905, 3-4 (regional teachers' union congress in Moscow)
29. A Soviet historian provides incomplete data on the backgrounds of Peasant Union agitators at the local level; see E. I. Kiriukhina, "Mestnye organizatsii Vserossiiskogo Krest'ianskogo Soiuza v 1905 godu, "*Uchenye zapiski Kirovskogo pedagogicheskogo instituta*, 10 (1956): 138).

Peasants	Rural intelligentsia	Others
Peasants 30	Teachers 43	Students 9
Kulaks 3	Doctors 13	Socialist
Village elders 5	Rural clerks *(pisari)* 7	Revolutionaries 6
Volost elders 4	Clerics 2	Social Democrats 5

30. *Protokoly vtorogo delegatskago s"ezda Vserossiiskago Soiuza uchitelei i deiatelei po narodnomu obrazovaniiu 26-29 dekabria 1905 goda* (Saint Petersburg, 1906), 8.
31. TsGAOR, f. DP, OO (1905), d. 999, ch. 1, t. III, *l.* 6-9.
32. B. V., "Pedagogicheskii mir i Gosudarstvennaia Duma," *Russkaia shkola*, no. 4 (1906), 123-138; Terence Emmons, *The Formation of Political Parties and the First National Elections in Russia* (Cambridge, MA, 1983), 349.
33. "Narodnye uchitelia-izbranniki naroda," *Narodnyi uchitel'*, no. 8 (1907), 14-19.
34. Seregny, *Russian Teachers*, 184-187, 197-201.
35. *Russkiia vedomosti*, no. 144, 3 June 1906, 4; *Saratovskii dnevnik*, no. 36, 15 February 1906, 3-4.
36. N. Iordanskii, "Voprosy tekushchei zhizni: krizis intelligentsii," *Sovremennyi mir*, no. 2, section 2 (1908): 84
37. P. Zhulev, "Uchitel'skie obshchestva vzaimopomoshchi," *Russkaia shkola*, no. 1 (1912): 1-20.
38. I. Stepnoi [I. S. Samokhvalov], "Zhivotvoriashchii dukh," *Dlia narodnago uchitelia*, no. 5 (1915), 4; Iv. Sergeini, "Ternistym putem (K 20 letiiu uchitel'skogo prof. ob"edineniia)," TsGAOR, f. 6862, op. 1, d. 74, *l.* 36-37.
39. *Vestnik vospitaniia*, no. 1, section 2 (1907): 83-85.
40. A. A. Parshinskii, "Uchitel'stvo za gody pervoi revoliutsii i reaktsii," *Otrazhenie pervoi russkoi revoliutsii v S.-Dvinskoi gubernii* (Velikii Ustiug, 1926): 78-79.
41. I. Zhilkin, "Provintsial'noe obozrenie," *Vestnik Evropy*, no. 5 (1914): 376-77. In his diary in late 1910 the Third Duma deputy I. S. Kliuzhev mentions a recent secret circular issued by the Ministry of Interior to the effect that rural teachers be removed from the field of adult education entirely: TsGIA, f. 669, op. 1, d. 4.
42. TsGIA, f. 733, op. 201, d. 46, *l.* 13-28.
43. Parshinskii, "Uchitel'stvo," 79; TsGAOR, f. 6862, op. 1, d. 87, *l.* 18.
44. *Krasnyi arkhiv*, no. 2/15 (1926): 42.
45. N. V. Chekhov, "Russkii uchitel' i revoliutsii," *Narodnyi uchitel'*, no. 5-6 (1918): 3-5; E. Vakhterova, "Iz zhizni," *Uchitel'*, no. 1 (1918): 29-31.
46. J. A. Jackson, "Professions and Professionalization: Editorial Introduction," in Jackson, ed., *Professions*, 14.

PEASANT RESETTLEMENT AND SOCIAL CONTROL IN LATE IMPERIAL RUSSIA

Edward H. Judge

In the early years of the twentieth century, the attitude of the imperial Russian government toward peasant resettlement underwent a rather significant change. For centuries, peasant migration had been viewed as a potentially disruptive force that was inconsistent with social stability and social control. As a result, Russian governments had generally sought to restrict or prevent peasant movement. By the late nineteenth century, however, it was no longer evident that such restrictions actually served the best interests of the imperial regime. On one hand, the empire encompassed vast expanses of sparsely-populated territory; on the other hand, there was growing concern about peasant "land-hunger" in the central "black earth" provinces.[1] By 1902, it was beginning to look as if the inability of peasants to secure adequate land could eventually pose a threat to the existing social order. The interests of economic welfare, imperial security, and overall social stability seemed to call for a new resettlement policy.

The tsarist government, not surprisingly, had little experience to draw upon in devising a resettlement policy. During the centuries of serfdom, peasant serfs had been bound by law to the soil and prohibited from moving to new lands. An effort had been made during the 1830s to provide some mobility for the neediest state peasants—those who were not under control of a private landowner. This "Kiselev resettlement" did achieve some modest success: some 320,000 peasants relocated between 1831 and 1836 alone.[2] But, ironically enough, the abolition of serfdom in 1861 brought an end to this period of legal migration.

The authors of the Emancipation Act, anxious to prevent widespread dislocation and to protect the cheap labor supply of large landowners, made no provision for peasant mobility. In 1866, when state peasants were brought under the same legal order as their newly-liberated peers, almost all possibility of legal resettlement vanished.[3]

It reappeared in the 1880s, mainly as the result of government efforts to get control of the illegal resettlement that continued to take place. Between 1860 and 1885, according to official estimates, approximately 300,000 peasants illegally migrated to Siberia and the steppes.[4] Laws of 1881 and 1889, attempting to deal with this phenomenon, allowed peasants from the most crowded areas to petition the Ministries of Interior and State Domains for the right to relocate. Persons attempting to migrate without such permission could be returned to their original locale and subjected to administrative punishment. Certain lands in Siberia and the steppes were set aside for resettlement purposes, and legal resettlers were provided with temporary tax exemptions to ease their transition.[5] This was as far as the government of Alexander III had been willing to go.

In 1892, however, a dynamic new force appeared on the resettlement scene. Sergei Iul'evich Witte, brilliant, impetuous, energetic and impatient, was appointed minister of finance. Convinced that Russia's ultimate survival required rapid economic growth, and backed by the firm support of Alexander III, Witte embarked on a series of programs designed to transform his backward, agrarian country into a modern industrial state. Such a rapid, wholesale transformation involved a great deal of risk to political stability and social order, as Witte well understood; still, he reasoned, the risks of continued economic stagnation were even greater. A cornerstone of his program was the 5,400 mile Trans-Siberian railway, designed to unlock Russia's natural resources, to provide access to new markets and, incidentally, to facilitate the colonization of Russia's hinterlands.[6]

The construction of the Trans-Siberian line gave a strong impetus to peasant resettlement. The enormous difficulties, hardships and uncertainties involved in moving to Siberia were reduced dramatically by railway transport. In addition, the

Siberian Railway Committee, established in 1893 to administer the railroad and its adjacent lands, took an active interest in colonization. Tracts of land were reserved for new settlers, and large annual sums were allocated to ease the burdens and costs of resettlement. Migrating families were encouraged to send scouts ahead to inspect suitable parcels, and "resettlement stations" were set up along the railway line to provide food, information, and advice. By 1896, certain provincial authorities were given the right to approve resettlement requests without consulting the ministries. The result of all this was a striking increase in peasant migrations: according to government figures, 1,115,000 peasants moved to Siberia in the decade 1893-1902, as compared with roughly 300,000 between 1860 and 1884, and 260,000 during the period from 1885 to 1893.[7]

Despite these increases, the new resettlement policy was hardly an overwhelming success. For one thing, only about two-thirds of the settlers relocated successfully; many returned to their former provinces. For another thing, over a third of the new migrants came from provinces where there was no land-hunger. Meanwhile, the rapid growth of population made resettlement efforts appear decidedly meager: in the last quarter of the nineteenth century, while perhaps a million peasants successfully relocated, the population grew by more than twenty million.[8] Resettlement may have been helping colonization, but it was doing relatively little to alleviate land-hunger.

Furthermore, powerful conservative interests continued to oppose the very concept of large-scale peasant resettlement. Large landowners were concerned that significant migration might deplete their supply of cheap labor and drive down land values. They were supported, in general, by the Ministry of Interior, which feared that rapid economic change and too much peasant mobility might give rise to political unrest.[9] On several occasions, in 1892-1894 and again in 1896-1897, this ministry simply refused to grant any requests for resettlement. On other occasions, it took the position that migration could be permitted, but only under the strictest government supervision and control. This attitude gave rise, in 1896, to the formation of a Resettlement Administration, within the Ministry of Interior, to monitor all aspects of internal colonization.[10] Clearly, there could be no extensive resettlement without this ministry's support.

Early in the twentieth century, however, the attitude of the Ministry of Interior changed. The major catalyst was a series of peasant disorders which rocked the central agricultural provinces in the spring of 1902. For several weeks, bands of hungry peasants roamed the countryside, looting and destroying the estates of large landowners. The rebellion was finally crushed, with the aid of Cossack troops, but the spectre of peasant revolt frightened the government and weakened conservative arguments against resettlement. For one thing, it became abundantly clear that peasant land-hunger was not in the best interests of noble landowners, whatever one might say about cheap labor and high land values. For another thing, the dangers inherent in large-scale migration were suddenly overshadowed by the prospect of peasant rebellion in "overcrowded" areas. Peasant land-hunger appeared to have reached crisis proportions and, in a very real sense, the *lack* of peasant mobility was becoming a threat to effective social control.[11]

Meanwhile, just as these disorders were being suppressed, a change occurred in the leadership of the Ministry of Interior. On April 2, 1902, Minister D. S. Sipiagin was assassinated; two days later Viacheslav Konstantinovich Plehve was appointed in his stead. The new minister, a former police director and assistant minister of interior, was as thoroughly conservative as any of his predecessors. But he was also, like Witte, a man of talent, intelligence, self-confidence and energy.[12] A quick trip to the troubled provinces convinced him that shortages of land and food had made these areas fertile ground for revolutionary agitation. His overriding mandates were to destroy the revolutionary movement and restore order; to accomplish these, he concluded, he must find a way to alleviate peasant land-hunger.[13]

According to Plehve, it was on his trip to the riot-torn areas that he first began to consider the possibilities of peasant resettlement as a means of social control. One of the local governors, apparently, persuaded him that extensive migration was necessary to relieve the crowded conditions among the local peasants.[14]   Plehve may also have been influenced by A. V. Krivoshein, a talented and ambitious young official who had served as Assistant Director of the Resettlement Administration since 1896. At any rate, Plehve soon promoted him to Director and enlisted his collaboration in formulating a new resettlement policy.[15]

Within the Ministry of Interior, then, a new approach to peasant migration gradually began to emerge. In the autumn of 1902, a circular letter was sent out to the governors, requesting their recommendations.[16] By November, Plehve's feelings on the subject had crystallized enough for him to declare publicly that peasant resettlement, and the supportive activity of the Peasant Land Bank, were "the two strongest levers in the hands of the state for bringing serious improvement to the peasant land tenure situation."[17] In December, during a major policy speech on the one-hundredth anniversary of the Ministry of Interior, he praised the Siberian Railway Committee's work in directing resettlement affairs. It was necessary, he proclaimed, to go even further in this direction.[18]

Meanwhile the minister of finance, perhaps anticipating a challenge to his position, was also speaking out on the resettlement issue. Returning in October 1902 from a long journey across Siberia on the nearly-completed railway, Witte filed a report describing the possibilities for peasant migration in the most glowing terms. Praising the work of the Siberian Railway Committee, he called for a further expansion of peasant migration, in order both to alleviate land-hunger in the central provinces and to colonize the vast expanses of Siberia. "There will be no lack of persons wishing to resettle in Siberia. . . ," he wrote. "Meanwhile, the quickest possible colonization of our Asiatic properties represents a matter of primary state significance, both economically and politically."[19]

By the end of 1902, then, both Plehve and Witte were on record as favoring an expanded resettlement program. It might have been expected that this apparent convergence of opinion would lead directly to the enactment of such a program. After all, Plehve's ministry and the interests it represented had been the major opponents of large scale peasant migration. Now the ministry was supporting such a concept; indeed, Plehve was offering it as a cornerstone of his solution to Russia's peasant problem. Unfortunately, however, the issue was complicated by a bitter rivalry between Witte and Plehve. And, as it turned out, their attitudes toward resettlement were substantially different, despite the superficial similarity.

The major difference in the two approaches was over the extent of state control. Witte and his supporters, interested primarily in colonization and economic growth, favored the passive policy which had hitherto been pursued. The government *permitted* resettlement—in some ways it *encouraged* and *assisted* resettlement—but it did not really attempt to control *who* should migrate, and *where* they should migrate from. Plehve and his colleagues, concerned above all with social control, proposed to change all this and give the government a more active and dominant role. Henceforth, they insisted, the state should control the entire process: it should decide which peasants should migrate, where they should migrate from, and where they should settle. In so doing, the government could establish, within each province, the pattern and mix of population most suitable to its political interests, and to the interests of social stability.[20] It was no accident that, although both men had praised the Siberian Railway Committee, Witte had pointed to increased numbers of settlers while Plehve had emphasized organization and control.[21]

The conflict over resettlement also took place against the backdrop of a thorough government review of its agrarian policies, launched by Tsar Nicholas II early in 1902. The work on this question had been divided from the beginning. Witte had been named chairman of a Special Conference on the Needs of Agricultural Industry, an extra-ministerial body charged with improving Russian agriculture. The Ministry of Interior, meanwhile, had been commissioned to institute a reexamination and revision of all legislation concerning the peasantry.[22] The seeds of future conflict were contained in this split mandate, as Witte immediately realized: any attempt to improve agriculture must necessarily deal with the legal status of the peasants and the legal organization of rural life. And one could scarcely deny that an issue like peasant migration, although technically a matter of legislative regulation, could have a profound impact on Russian agriculture.[23]

The first major clash on this issue came within the framework of a reexamination of the policies of the Peasant Land Bank. This bank had been founded in 1883 as a credit institution designed to help peasants expand their land holdings; it operated under the direct supervision of the Ministry of Finance. Since more peasant migration currently occurred through purchase of private parcels than through settlement on vacant state lands, the Peasant Bank played an important role in the overall resettlement process.[24] In December of 1902, Witte received permission from the tsar to set up a special inter-ministerial commission on the direction and boundaries of Peasant Bank activity. Perhaps, as one of Plehve's minions later suggested, he was trying to steal a march on the Ministry of Interior and "secure the dominating role in the revision of peasant legislation."[25]

At any rate, the commission seems to have been taken quite seriously by both ministers. Its makeup was weighted in favor of Finance: a total of twelve members came from this ministry and the Peasant Bank, as against only four from Interior and two from the Ministry of Agriculture. The chairman, Prince A. D. Obolensky, was an assistant minister of finance. This did not, however, prevent Plehve from making an effort to influence the commission's work. He selected a strong delegation from his ministry, including Resettlement Director Krivoshein and Land Section Chief V. I. Gurko, a key figure in the ministry's peasant reform project. He instructed them to keep him informed, and to consult him on all important questions.[26] Then, on January 28, 1903, five days after the commission's first session, he submitted a long official letter to Witte, outlining his views on Peasant Bank operations as they related to peasant resettlement.[27]

Plehve's letter was highly critical of bank policies. The Peasant Bank operated in two ways: it acquired land for resale to the peasants, or it lent them money to purchase land directly. Unfortunately, according to Plehve, little effort was made to coordinate its activities with the best interests of the state. As a credit institution, the bank made loans only to those who could be expected not to default, and it acquired land indiscriminately, wherever it became available. In Plehve's opinion, these policies only served to undermine social control. For one thing, they excluded the poorer peasants—those most likely to become involved in violent disturbances—from buying land. For another, by allowing too much of the nobles' land to be sold to peasants, they diluted the stabilizing influence of the landed nobility in certain provinces. The large scale transfer of land, he argued, was too important to be left to chance on the open market. Assistance must be given, not to wealthier peasants who wished to purchase land from local nobles, but to poorer peasants who were willing to resettle in underpopulated areas.[28]

Plehve proposed, then, that the Peasant Bank should turn its efforts from purchasing noble lands to resettlement of peasants in outlying areas. It should cease making loans in regions where its actions might contribute to instability. Instead, it should concentrate its land-acquiring operations primarily in areas such as the western provinces and the Caucasus, where an increased proportion of native Russians was desirable for political stability. The minimum size of land parcels handled by the Bank should be decreased, so that more land plots would be available to poorer peasant families. Special "home ownership loans" (to be handled, incidentally, by the Ministry of Interior) should be issued to needy peasant settlers. Bank policy should be conducted "according to a program set up each year by agreement between the ministers of finance and interior, based on whatever steps are necessary to show aid to the neediest village residents."[29]

The minister of interior was proposing, in effect, that the Peasant Land Bank become an instrument of social control. By helping to move the neediest and most disaffected peasants to less crowded regions, it would serve to stabilize the situation in the areas of land-hunger. And by carefully regulating its loan and procurement policies, the bank could serve as a lever for adjusting the ratio of classes and nationalities in each province so as to increase political stability. Plehve's proposals, if implemented, would also have had an important side effect: they would have increased the influence of the Ministry of Interior in affairs of the Peasant Bank.

The views of the Ministry of Interior were amplified within the commission by Resettlement Director Krivoshein. The Bank's own statistics, he argued, showed that its operations were not serving the best interests of the state. Resettlement of Russians in the Caucasus, and in the western provinces, had been virtually non-existent, while the land-hunger problem in the central provinces was growing more acute. Meanwhile, the Bank continued to assist the relocation of peasants in provinces where no land-hunger existed. Some way had to be found to coordinate the Bank's activity with the political concerns of the state, and with the actions of the Resettlement Administration.[30]

It is hardly surprising that the Commission, dominated as it was by the Ministry of Finance, did not take kindly to the proposals of Plehve and Krivoshein. The commission met seven times in the first three months of 1903, then twice more to consider Plehve's letter separately. According to one participant, the commission meetings were filled with violent debates between representatives from Interior and Finance.[31] The vote on almost every issue split along ministerial lines. A Ministry of Interior proposal to allow peasant allotted land as collateral for loans was defeated, as was a plan to lower the minimum size of plots that peasants could acquire through the bank. Krivoshein's proposal for closer correlation between the Bank and the Resettlement Administration was shunted off to a subcommittee. Least remarkable of all, Plehve's proposals to give the Ministry of Interior a more active voice in determining Bank policy were watered down beyond recognition: the ministry would be permitted to "make comments" on the Bank's annual report before it went to the State Council.[32]

The Obolensky commission, therefore, failed to recommend any significant changes in the operations or philosophy of the Bank. The commission's majority, led by Obolensky, voted time after time to preserve the integrity of the Bank as a purely financial institution, and to reject efforts to make it an instrument of social regulation. If the commission accomplished anything, it was merely to clarify the issues and to exacerbate the Witte-Plehve feud.

Witte's victory over Plehve, however, was only a partial one. While the ambitions of the Ministry of Interior were being frustrated in the Obolensky Commission, they were receiving a boost from the Siberian Railway Committee. At a meeting of January 15, 1903, Emperor Nicholas II had requested examination of various proposals for transferring peasants from the crowded central provinces to outlying regions—regions which were not sufficiently "secure" from a military and political standpoint. In response to this request the Ministry of Interior compiled several proposals on resettlement. These were then turned over, in spring of 1903, to a special "Preparatory Commission" within the Railway Committee. Following preliminary discussion, they were submitted to the full committee on June 18, 1903.[33]

This development provided the Ministry of Interior with a new forum for its resettlement ideas. In expounding these proposals to the committee on June 18, Minister Plehve called for a "special privileged order of resettlement" to assist land-hungry peasants from the central provinces. The government, he added, should restrict its assistance to those whose relocation conformed to its own political aims; and the Peasant Land Bank should be compelled to act in conformity.[34] In order to discuss these proposals more fully, it was decided to form a Special Conference on Resettlement under the chairmanship of A. N. Kulomzin, the managing secretary of the Siberian Railway Committee. The Conference would also include the ministers of finance, agriculture, and interior.[35]

Although the Special Conference on Resettlement did not actually meet until January of 1904, its character and tone were influenced greatly by events which occurred the preceding summer. On August 15, 1903 Sergei Witte, the most capable and effective proponent of unrestricted peasant migration, was dismissed from his post as minister of finance. This was a significant victory for the minister of interior, removing his most influential rival and establishing Plehve's unquestioned preeminence among the ministers. The new minister of finance, E. D. Pleske, lacked his predecessor's ability, energy and cunning; moreover, it soon developed that he was terminally ill. By the time the Resettlement Conference finally met, the Finance Ministry was under the interim direction of assistant minister Romanov, who clearly was not in a strong position to challenge the minister of interior's ascendancy over peasant affairs.[36]

Plehve, meanwhile, was moving to take the initiative in resettlement policy reform. As a preparation for the Special Conference, late in the summer of 1903 he and Resettlement Director Krivoshein made a tour of peasant settlement areas in Western Siberia.[37] More significantly, the minister ordered Krivoshein and his colleagues to "compile a memorandum which could serve as material for the work of the conference."[38] The memorandum, as it turned out, was designed to provide more than simply material: it included, besides a broad overview of resettlement affairs, a series of arguments, interpretations and suggestions which amounted to a proposal for a revision of resettlement legislation. It was followed, in fact, by formal legislative proposals designed to replace the existing legislation on resettlement.[39]

The argument put forth in this new memorandum was in fact very similar to the one used by Plehve in criticizing the Peasant Bank. The Siberian Railway Committee had indeed done much for resettlement, but the resulting patterns of migration did not correspond with the government's political interests. Thus, for example, large-scale movement had occurred not only from areas of land-hunger, but also from regions where there was plenty of land—and even from places, like Western Siberia, which were themselves targets for settlement. Meanwhile, no significant migration had taken place to such politically significant border areas as the Caucasus, Turkestan, and the Maritime Provinces of the Far East. Furthermore, a fairly significant number of the migrants (110,000 in the preceding five years) had come from the Western border provinces, thus decreasing the ratio of native-Russians to non-Russian nationalities. Even in the "land-hunger" provinces, the movement had not been beneficial, since under the existing set-up only the wealthier peasants had the means and motivation to relocate. As a result, the borderlands were being deprived of the more politically reliable Russian element, and the central provinces were losing some of their most prosperous and stable residents. In short, current practices were actually detrimental to the government's goals of political stability and social control.[40]

To correct this situation, then, the memorandum made a number of specific proposals. Henceforth, it insisted, settlers should be divided into two categories. Those whose relocation served the aims of the governnment would be considered "privileged"; the rest would be classed as "voluntary." Only those who were moving from the poorest villages in the most crowded provinces, or those who were moving to locales needing colonization, would be eligible for state aid. The determination of which villages and locales would qualify would be made jointly by the ministers of finance, interior and agriculture. Every feasible assistance would be given to the "privileged" settlers—free transportation, tax exemptions, loans, and military deferrals—in order to insure their successful relocation. In addition, such settlers would be fully compensated for the land they left behind, to which end the government should issue loans to village societies so they could purchase the land of departing members. Finally, a series of government agencies would be established to assist and supervise these peasants in their new areas of settlement.[41] These proposals, and others like them, were fully incorporated into the draft laws appended to the text of the memorandum.[42]

By drafting such specific proposals and actual legislative acts, the Ministry of Interior was able to structure the work of the Special Conference on Resettlement. When the Kulomzin Conference finally met, on January 30, 1904, the Resettlement Administration memorandum was accepted as a basis for discussion.[43] Not all of its proposals, however, went unchallenged. The minister of agriculture, for instance, objected to a proposal which would have unified all resettlement activities under the control of the Ministry of Interior: this, he felt, would violate his own ministry's legal mandate to manage state-owned lands.[44] The acting minister of finance opposed the notion of granting tax exemptions, and he insisted that military deferments should be extended to *all* settlers, not just those who qualified as "privileged."[45] In the end, however, these objections were overcome. The conference simply sidestepped the first issue, instructing the ministers of interior and agriculture to settle any jurisdictional disputes between themselves. The tax exemption and military deferment issues were decided in favor of the minister of interior. The emperor approved the work of the conference on February 19, 1904—the forty-third anniversary of the emancipation of the serfs—and ordered it submitted to the State Council for legislative consideration.[46]

The results of the Special Conference represented a victory for the Ministry of Interior; still, further obstacles remained. One of these was presented by the new minister of finance, V. N. Kokovtsov, who took office in February, 1904. A few weeks after his appointment, Kokovtsov wrote a long letter to conference chairman Kulomzin, taking issue with certain provisions in the draft legislation which would have denied "voluntary" resettlers the right to choose their own land. Even if the government did not wish to assist these persons, he argued, it was wrong to leave them "solely at the mercy of the administrative channels of the Ministry of Interior" for assignment of land parcels.[47] In a letter of his own, Plehve responded that to allow them free selection might deplete the supply of first-rate land available to "privileged" settlers, and thus contradict the "basic notion of the law." Nevertheless, the issue was settled by compromise, with Plehve agreeing to allow voluntary settlers to select their own land, while quietly reserving the best lands for privileged settlers from the areas of land-hunger.[48]

The State Council, which considered these proposals in April and May, represented the final hurdle for the new resettlement law. Several members, led by State Secretary Polovtsov, objected to the proposals as detrimental to colonization. For colonization purposes, they argued, the sturdier and more prosperous peasants, not the weaker elements, were needed. Besides, as Polovtsov noted in a separate letter to Kulomzin, the proposals designated only the Causasus, Turkestan and the Far East as areas of "privileged" resettlement; but colonization of Siberia and the Steppes was also important.[49] In his response before the State Council, Plehve brushed aside these objections, saying they came from persons who were opposed in principle to government intervention in economic life, a conviction he could not share. He insisted that the alleviation of land-hunger was as important a goal as colonization, and that the government could and must try to regulate resettlement so as to achieve both goals. On one issue, however, the minister of interior did give ground: he admitted that the law, if worded too precisely, might tie the government's hands. He opted, then, for a less precise formulation which would give resettlement officials a greater degree of flexibility.[50] Since these officials were under the supervision of his ministry, this prospect could hardly displease him.

The only other serious objection was raised by a group of State Council members, including an assistant minister of finance, who opposed the provision that "privileged" resettlers would be compensated by their fellow villagers for the lands they left behind. This arrangement, they argued, would place too heavy a burden on the rest of the village. To delete this stipulation, however, would have robbed the legislation of one of its major thrusts: the desire to make it easier for the poorest peasants to leave the central provinces. The Ministry of Interior refused to compromise, and the proposal to delete was defeated handily.[51] This proved to be the last obstacle: the measure was approved by the State Council on May 24, and formally confirmed into law by Emperor Nicholas II on June 6, 1904.[52]

The Resettlement Law of June 6, 1904 was destined to become a very important piece of legislation. In its original form, it represented an attempt by the government to facilitate and control the process of peasant migration. It stipulated that the ministers of interior, finance and agriculture—and in some cases the minister of war—should designate certain areas as overcrowded, and others as colonization targets. Only those peasants who were moving out of one of the former areas, or into one of the latter, would be entitled to state assistance. Such settlers would also be compensated for the land they left behind, by either the village community or the individual acquiring the land. They would further be entitled to reduced railway rates and a five-year exemption from certain forms of taxation. Males over 18 would be granted a three-year postponement of their military obligation. Internal migration, hitherto limited to those who could afford it, would now be available to even the poorest peasant families.[53]

The new law represented a rather significant shift in the government's attitude toward peasant agriculture. For one thing, peasant migration was no longer seen as a threat to social stability—as long as it could be controlled. Instead, it was now advanced as a stabilizing force which could, if properly supervised, serve to enhance social control. For another thing, the wealthier peasants were no longer seen as "just about the worst and most harmful element of the population."[54] The law sought to restore political stability and economic well being in the central provinces by encouraging the poorer peasants to move away.[55] The implication, at least, was that social control and economic prosperity in these areas could best be preserved by relying on the more prosperous elements.

The resettlement law also revealed a subtle change in the government's attitude toward the peasant commune. The commune had generally been associated with social stability, and efforts to weaken or abolish it had run into strong resistance. In one way, the new law continued this tradition, by providing a means to relieve land-hunger without sacrificing the communes.[56] In another way, however, it effectively encouraged certain peasants to leave their communes, and it provided loans and assistance for those who opted to do so. It even required that they be compensated by their former communes for the lands they left behind. And it did not ordain that they set up new communes when they arrived at their destination: settlers were allowed to decide, by majority vote, between communal and hereditary tenure.[57]

The main thrust of the law, however, was its concern for social control. Resettlement was now to be encouraged, but only to enhance stability. By relieving land-hunger in the central provinces, and by helping to colonize the border areas, it was hoped that both could be made more stable. Most significantly, by careful and selective granting of privileges, it was intended to place the whole resettlement process under the direction and supervision of the government—and in particular the Ministry of Interior. The law, as it stood, represented a creative attempt by conservative state officials to adjust to new realities, to satisfy basic needs and, in so doing, to gain a greater measure of control over the Russian peasant situation.

In the end, thanks to rapidly changing circumstances, the actual effects of the resettlement law were rather different than its framers had intended. The law itself was not immediately implemented, since the Russo-Japanese War of 1904-1905 brought a temporary suspension of resettlement activity. By the time the war ended, Russia was in revolution. Only in 1906 did things calm down enough for the government again to take up resettlement—and by this time things had changed dramatically. Plehve, the law's sponsor, had long since been assassinated, Krivoshein's Resettlement Administration had been transferred to the Ministry of Agriculture, and the new post of prime minister was occupied by none other than Sergei Witte. Furthermore, the revolution of 1905 had witnessed large-scale rebellions in numerous provinces, not just in those of the land-hungry "center" as occurred in 1902. The implication was not lost on the government: if the new resettlement rules were going to restore stability they would have to be applied, not just in the central provinces, but in all provinces of European Russia.[58]

As a result, when the law finally did go into effect, its implementation was very much broader than originally anticipated. A special supplement, drafted by the Resettlement Administration and approved by the emperor on March 10, 1906, extended the law's privileges and exemptions to all peasant resettlers, regardless of where they came from or where they settled. This change substantially altered the nature of the entire law. What had begun as an attempt to direct and supervise peasant migration, so it would conform to certain political goals of the state, had turned into a government guarantee of the right of peasants to resettle at state expense. Over the next several years, millions of peasants would avail themselves of this opportunity. The Resettlement Law of June 6, 1904, as supplemented by the provisions of March 10, 1906, became the basis for the large-scale internal migration that occurred during the years of the Stolypin land reforms.[59]

NOTES

1. The actual severity of this crisis is not beyond question: see James Y. Simms, Jr., "The Crisis of Russian Agriculture at the End of the Nineteenth Century: A Different View," *Slavic Review* 36 (1977): 377-398.

2. Tsentral'nyi gosudarstvennyi arkhiv oktiabrskoi revoliutsii (TsGAOR), f. 586 (V. K. Pleve), op. 1, d. 404, *ll*. 2-4.

3. TsGAOR f. 586, op. 1, d. 404, *l*. 5.

4. Ibid.

5. Ibid., *ll*. 6-7.

6. For Witte's views and policies see Theodore H. von Laue, ed., "A Secret Memorandum of Sergei Witte on the Industrialization of Imperial Russia," *Journal of Modern History* 26 (1954): 64-74 and von Laue, *Sergei Witte and the Industrialization of Russia* (New York and London, 1963), 71-119.

7. TsGAOR f. 586, op. 1, d. 404, *ll*. 10-12.

8. Ibid., *ll*. 16-17.

9. S. Iu. Witte, *Vospominaniia: Detstvo, Tsarstvovaniia Aleksandra II i Aleksandra III, 1849-1894* (Berlin, 1923), 399-400.

10. TsGAOR f. 586, op. 1, d. 404, *ll*. 9-11.

11. For the 1902 peasant riots and the government's response see L. I. Emeliakh, "Krest'iansko dvizhenie v Poltavskoi i Khar'kovskoi guberniakh v 1902g.," *Istoricheskie zapiski* 38 (1951): 154-175; M. S. Simonova, "Politika tzarizma v krest'ianskom voprose nakanune revoliutsii 1905-1907gg.," *Istoricheskie zapiski* 75 (1965): 212-215; D. N. Liubimov, "Russkaia smuta nachala deviatisotykh godov, 1902-1906 gg." (unpublished manuscript in the archives of the Hoover Institution, Stanford, California) 10-12; *Novoe vremia*, 29 April 1902, 2.

12. For the character and abilities of Plehve see Edward H. Judge, *Plehve: Repression and Reform in Imperial Russia, 1902-1904* (Syracuse, 1983) 32-37; D. N. Liubimov, *Pamiati V. K. Pleve* (Saint Petersburg, 1904), 20, 38, 46, 50; V. I. Gurko, *Features and Figures of the Past*, trans. Laura Matveev (Stanford, 1939), 47, 107-111; A. V. Pogozhev, "Iz vospominanii o V. K. fon-Pleve," *Vestnik Evropy* 46 (1911): 263-265.

13. Tsentral'nyi gosudarstvennyi istoricheskii arkhiv (TsGIA), f. 1273, op. 1, d. 443, *ll.* 2, 629; Liubimov, "Russkaia smuta," 10-12; *Novoe vremia*, 18 April 1902, 4; 21 April 1902, 5; Gurko, 114, 122.

14. TsGIA f. 1273, op. 1, d. 443, *l.* 2. See also V. A. Stepynin, "Iz istorii pereselencheskoi politiki samoderzhaviia v nachale XX veka," *Istoricheskie zapiski* 75 (1965): 162.

15. K. A. Krivoshein, *A. V. Krivoshein (1857-1921gg.): Ego znachenie v istorii Russii nachala XX veka* (Paris, 1973) 15; Gurko 192-197; *Novoe vremia*, 22 May 1902, 1.

16. *Novoe vremia*, 27 October 1902, 3.

17. TsGIA f. 1233, op. 1, d. 23, ll. 44-45. See also Simonova, 216.

18. Liubimov, *Pamiati Pleve*, 47; *Novoe vremia*, 30 December 1902, 3.

19. Krivoshein, 119.

20. TsGAOR f. 586, op. 1, d. 404, *l.* 28; TsGIA f. 1273, op. 1, d. 443, *l.* 2; TsGIA f. 592, op. 44, d. 422, *ll.* 21-22; "Agrarnaia programma g. f.-Pleve," *Osvobozhdenie* 20/21 (18 April/1 May 1903): 349-350.

21. Krivoshein 118-119; *Novoe vremia*, 30 December 1902, 3.

22. G. G. Savich, ed., *Novyi gosudarstvenny stroi Rossii: spravochnaia kniga* (Saint Petersburg, 1907), 1; *Novoe vremia*, 15 January 1902, 2.

23. A. A. Polovtsov, "Dnevnik," *Krasnyi arkhiv* 3 (1923): 114-116; Gurko, 205-207.

24. TsGIA f. 592, op. 44, d. 422, *l.* 84.

25. Ibid., *l.* 89; Gurko 211-212.

26. TsGIA f. 592, op. 44, d. 422, *l.* 89; Gurko 212.

27. TsGIA f. 592, op. 44, d. 422, *l.* 91; "Agrarnaia programma g. f.-Pleve," 349-350.

28. "Agrarnaia programma g. f.-Pleve," 349-350.

29. Ibid., 350-352.

30. TsGIA f. 592, op. 44, d. 422, *ll.* 83-97, 99.

31. Gurko, 213-214

32. TsGIA f. 592, op. 44, d. 422, *ll.* 93, 96, 100, 101, 103, 106.

33. TsGIA f. 1273, op. 1, d. 443, *ll.* 5, 6, 496. See also Stepynin, 162.

34. TsGIA f. 1273, op. 1, d. 443, *ll.* 496-497.

35. Ibid., *ll.* 2, 497.

36. S. Iu. Witte, *Vospominaniia: Tsarstvovaniia Nikolaia II*, 2 vols. (Berlin: "Slovo," 1922), 1: 218-219; A. N. Kuropatkin, "Dnevnik,"

Krasnyi arkhiv 2 (1922): 55, 60-61; Gurko, 225-226; TsGIA f. 1273, op. 1, d. 443, *ll.* 416, 496.

37. Gurko, 193; Krivoshein, 121.
38. TsGIA f. 1273, op. 1, d. 443, *l.* 5.
39. Ibid., *ll.* 6-50, 109-120; TsGAOR f. 586, op. 1, d. 404, *ll.* 1-46.
40. TsGIA f. 1273, op. 1, d. 443, *ll.* 7-9, 13-14; TsGAOR f. 586, op. 1, d. 404, *ll.* 16-19.
41. TsGIA f. 1273, op. 1, d. 443, *ll.* 49-50; TsGAOR f. 586, op. 1, d. 404, *ll.* 44-46.
42. TsGIA f. 1273, op. 1, d. 443, *ll.* 113-120.
43. Ibid., *l.* 497. See also Stepynin, 162.
44. TsGIA f. 1273, op. 1, d. 443, *l.* 499.
45. Ibid., *ll.* 502, 598.
46. Ibid., *ll.* 500, 502, 595.
47. Ibid., *ll.* 598-600.
48. Ibid., *ll.* 603-606, 607, 608-609.
49. Ibid., *ll.* 613-616, 626-627; Stepynin, 163.
50. TsGIA f. 1273, op. 1, d. 443, *ll.* 628-629. See also *Otchet po deloproizvodstvu Gosudarstvennago Soveta 1903/4* (Saint Petersburg, 1904), 323-325.
51. TsGIA f. 1273, op. 1, d. 443, *ll.* 635-636, 649-652.
52. Ibid., *ll.* 652-653; *Polnoe sobranie zakonov rossiiskoi imperii* (*PSZRI*), 3rd ed., 33 vols. (Saint Petersburg, 1885-1916) 26, no. 24701 (6 June 1904).
53. *PSZRI* 3rd ed., 26, no. 24701 (6 June 1904): 604-607.
54. See Redakstsionnaia kommissiia po peresmotru zakonopolozhenie o krest'ianakh, *Trudy*, 6 vols. (Saint Petersburg: Tipografiia Ministerstva vnutrennikh del, 1903-1904) 5: 450-451
55. TsGAOR f. 586, op. 1, d. 404, *l.* 79.
56. Simonova, 222.
57. *PSZRI* 3rd ed., 26, no. 24701 (6 June 1904): 605 (arts. 9, 10, 16)
58. Stepynin, 164.
59. Ibid.

UNSCRAMBLING THE JUMBLED CATALOG: FEUDALISM AND THE REVOLUTION OF 1905 IN THE WRITINGS OF N. P. PAVLOV-SILVANSKII

Thad Radzilowski

> These are times of chaos; opinions are a scramble;
> parties are a jumble; the language of new ideas has not
> been created. Nothing is more difficult than to give a
> good definition of oneself in religion, in philosophy, in
> politics....The problem of the time is to classify things
> and men. The world has jumbled its catalog.
>
> *Alphonse de Lamartine on the eve*
> *of the 1848 Revolution.*

The Revolution of 1917 so dramatically altered Russian life and consciousness and so overshadowed all that came before that it is sometimes difficult to gauge the contemporary impact of the Revolutionary events of 1905 on Russian society. Yet for many Russians the Revolution of 1905 was a watershed event that forever changed their understanding of the meaning of the Russian experience and opened up hitherto closed possibilities for the future. The writings of the Russian historian Nikolai Pavlovich Pavlov-Silvanskii, who died in 1908, give us a sense of the earth-shaking effect of 1905 on educated Russians, undistorted by the prism of subsequent revolutions. The events of that Revolutionary year were an epiphany that caused him to see Russian history and thus Russia's future in a new light. For students of Russian history, the life and works of Pavlov-Silvanskii provide an insight into the role that history played in shaping Russian national self-understanding at the beginning of this century. For a historiographer, they illuminate in a new way the complex dialogue between contemporary events and historical interpretation.

N. P. Pavlov-Silvanskii was born in 1869 at Kronstadt, the son of a naval doctor who later made his career in the civil service.[1] The family was of priestly origin and his grandfather had been a well known and respected archpriest. Pavlov-Silvanskii took his early schooling in Omsk where his father had been posted. In 1884, with his father's transfer to the capital, he enrolled in the gymnasium attached to the Historical-Philological faculty of St. Petersburg University. After overcoming initial academic difficulties because of his shyness and the inadequacy of his Siberian schooling, Pavlov-Silvanskii emerged as one of the leading students in his class and graduated with a degree in history and a recommendation for graduate study in 1892. While a graduate student he took a position as a clerk in the Internal Affairs section of the Ministry of Foreign Affairs.

Pavlov-Silvanskii's hopes for a professorial career were cut short by a tragic misunderstanding between him and Professor N. Kareev with whom he was studying Western European history. The misunderstanding, about the content of the oral examination in European history, led Kareev to fail the highly regarded and promising young scholar. Humiliated and crushed, Pavlov-Silvanskii withdrew from the University rather than retake the test.

The failure dramatically altered the course of his life. With an academic career no longer open to him, Pavlov-Silvanskii decided to continue in the government service. His intelligence and extraordinary abilities made him very successful, and he enjoyed rapid promotion in rank. In 1899, he transferred to the Government Archives as a senior clerk. He was soon promoted to assistant to the director and then by early 1906 to Collegiate Counselor. His archival work gave him a broad acquaintance and unusual proficiency with old Russian documents. Already by 1901 his reputation had won him an appointment to the prestigious Imperial Archeographic Commission.

In the course of his work he traveled a great deal in Russia and abroad and his travels to foreign archives and meetings with European scholars stimulated his interest in comparative history. In addition to medals and monetary rewards from his own government, Pavlov-Silvanskii's work brought him decorations from the Austro-Hungarian, Swedish, Turkish and French governments for his contributions to their state archives. By 1905, one of his friends noted, Pavlov-Silvanskii had become the real "moving spirit" of the state archives and had charge of most of the responsibilities for its daily operation. Rather than an assistant, he was in fact, if not in name, the "vice-director" of the state archives.[2]

Pavlov-Silvanskii published his first scholarly work, an article on the Petrine period, during the last year of his undergraduate study. During the subsequent twelve years, he produced a series of encyclopedia entries, scholarly articles and a monograph on the Petrine period, all of which focused on the reforms of the era. The most important were published between 1897-1901. Much of his writing on Peter's reign involved a debate with Miliukov's interpretation of the same period. Pavlov-Silvanskii argued for the central role of Peter in the reform process and receptivity of Russian society to the reforms. He saw Peter's activities as leading to the modernization, strengthening and, within the limits of what was possible in eighteenth century Russia, "democratization" of the country.[3]

During the first years of the twentieth century Pavlov-Silvanskii also wrote major biographical articles for the *Russkii biograficheskii slovar'* (Russian Biographical Dictionary) on the Grand Duke Konstantine Nikolaevich and the Decembrist Pavel Pestel. The article on Pestel came out of materials that he discovered during his work gathering and indexing the papers relating to the examination of the Decembrists. The article was published with official permission and heavily censored, but it marks the beginning of modern Russian scholarship on the Decembrists. It was not particularly sympathetic to Pestel, but it was fair and balanced and contained the first published summary of Pestel's *Russkaia pravda*. Pavlov-Silvanskii's account put Pestel clearly in the Jacobin tradition and placed emphasis on the importance of Enlightenment ideas in shaping his world view. However, within the limits of censorship Pavlov-Silvanskii was able to suggest that Pestel had also been radicalized by Russian conditions.[4]

The work on the Grand Duke Konstantine written in 1903, two years after the Pestel article, was a much more sympathetic treatment. The grand duke, a pivotal figure in the great reform of the eighteen-sixties, emerged in Pavlov-Silvanskii's article as a positive hero for his own period, much as Peter the Great had been for his. Pavlov-Silvanskii interpreted Konstantine as an enlightened prince who understood clearly the need for dramatic reform and devoted himself to it with a singleminded and generous concern for the common good.[5]

The most significant original work that Pavlov-Silvanskii did up to 1905 was on the history of Russian medieval institutions. What distinguished his research from the beginning was his insistence on a comparative study of Russian institutions with those in the medieval West. Although a few Russian historians of earlier generations, notably Chicherin, Kavelin and Soloviev, had made occasional comparisons, no Russian historian had hitherto attempted as detailed a comparative study as Pavlov-Silvanskii began in the 1890's. He quickly came to the conclusion that evidence pointed to the existence of feudalism in the *Udel* period. The conventional wisdom among professional historians, few of whom studied the *Udel* period, and educated laypersons of both slavophile and westerner tendencies, was that there was no feudalism in Russia's past. In their view it was precisely this fact which, for better or worse, distinguished Russia from the West.[6] Thus his first research efforts were met with considerable resistance and even outright prejudice.

N. I. Kareev, writing in 1910, noted that to speak seriously in the nineties of the existence of feudalism in Russia "was considered in itself a mark of bad taste and perhaps of bad form—a sign of historical ill breeding. It was regarded as unseemly among historians to find feudalism in Russia."[7] Sergei Platonov even advised his former student against working on the subject. He warned that if Pavlov-Silvanskii persisted in his research he could expect to be reviled by his fellow historians. Pavlov-Silvanskii did continue but, as he confided to Presniakov,

"I lived through many difficult days at the beginning of the work."[8]

Between 1892 and 1905 Pavlov-Silvanskii published a series of articles on *Kabala* slavery, *zakladnichestvo*, immunities, and the nature of feudal relations in *Udel* Russia. Leaning heavily on the comparative method, he argued that the feudalism in the West and the *Udel* order had similar or identical institutions that arose out of similar social and economic conditions and the common heritage of Slavic-German law. As in the feudal societies of the West, medieval Russian society was characterized by commendation (*zakladnichestvo*), immunities, benefices, diffusion of sovereignty, subinfeudation and a hierarchical vassal ladder.[9]

While he was working on these matters in his private research, he was commissioned to do a study of the history of the Russian nobility by a government commission researching the problems of the Russian gentry class. The research for this monograph enabled him to study all of the important documentary material pertaining to the history of the Russian nobility, which proved to be significant for his later work. The resulting monograph, *Gosudarevy sluzhilye liudi* (1898), was a very competent, if somewhat dry, survey that adhered closely to the documents. It did contain, however, an outstanding history of *mestnichestvo*.[10] All references to the similarity between Russian and West European developments were edited out prior to publication by V. K. Plehve, the commission's chair. The comparison of the Russian nobility with a vanished West European aristocracy, and the suggestion that the two had undergone similar historical evolution, implied to Plehve that the course of history had also doomed the Russian gentry. This was clearly an unacceptable implication for a commission seeking ways to save the nobility.[11]

Pavlov-Silvanskii's conclusion that Russia had medieval institutions identical to those of Western feudalism challenged the notion of a unique Russian past and created a major controversy in historical circles. Kliuchevskii, Vladimirskii-Budanov, and Sergeevich—as well as other leading Russian historians—felt compelled to grapple with his ideas. The most extended critiques were by Pavel Miliukov, in his article on feudalism in the *Entsyklopedicheskii slovar'*, and Professor F. V. Taranovskii of Warsaw University, who devoted a small monograph to Pavlov-Silvanskii's work. By 1905, despite serious criticism and the preliminary nature of some of the research, Pavlov-Silvanskii's work had achieved respectability, and his thesis on *zakladnichestvo* and immunities was widely accepted. As a result, he acquired a reputation as one of the important young historians in Russia.[12]

Like many educated Russians of his generation, Pavlov-Silvanskii had a world view shaped in adolescence and early adulthood by German materialism and French and English positivism. He was particularly influenced by the writings of Buchner, Comte, Buckle and Spencer. In 1890, Pavlov-Silvanskii became a member of the first Marxist study group organized by Peter Struve at St. Petersburg University. He never became a Marxist, but he was strongly influenced by Marx's writings. He viewed Marx primarily as the founder of a new school that he called "social materialism." This school developed the intellectual tools for a rational and systematic analysis of the economic and material bases of social institutions. Pavlov-Silvanskii never expressed an interest in the idea of "class struggle" as a motivating force in history, and he ridiculed attempts to derive "social character" or "class psychology" by the use of Marxian analysis.[13]

What interested him in Marx's writings was also what drew Pavlov-Silvanskii to the work of scholars such as sociologist Maxim Kovalevskii. One of Pavlov-Silvanskii's colleagues noted that he "studied in the sociological school in order to become a historian."[14] He himself wrote that his interest was in the "new historical science" which emphasized "economic development. . .intellectual development. . .and the social movements and government reforms tied to those developments."[15] Pavlov- Silvanskii shared with Kovalevskii and other contemporary sociologists and jurists a belief in the importance of the comparative method for the study of societies and cultures. This belief was consistent with his strong western orientation, his positivism, and his fascination with the idea of universal laws of development. It was also fed by wide reading in comparative philology and a deep interest in the sciences, especially biology. He studied and took extensive notes on the comparative botanical studies of K. A. Timiriazev.[16]

In 1901, as he was completing his first study of feudal relations, he wrote in a letter to his friend P. E. Shchegolev:

> Let us be done with comparing primitives. It is now time to begin comparing institutions of cultural epochs. Sociology is on solid ground when it leaves matriarchy...and goes on to the study of such cultural institutions as feudalism.[17]

Ultimately, Pavlov-Silvanskii's successful application of the comparative method and the startling conclusions that came of its use won him a place as one of the pioneers of the comparative method in Russian historiography, according to Soviet scholar L. V. Cherepnin.[18]

Initially, however, despite his intense interest in comparative study of Western European and Russian medieval institutions, Pavlov-Silvanskii did not challenge the accepted wisdom that Russian and European developments were essentially different. In a 1901 letter to Presniakov he denied any interest in an overall scheme of Russian history and dismissed the possibility that his work had anything to yield for a general comparison of Russian and European development. He wrote "You know that our (i.e. European and Russian) roads diverge further along. This theme has been excellently treated by Miliukov in Part I of his *Ocherki*."[19]

Until he was thirty years old, Pavlov-Silvanskii took no interest in politics. Only in 1899 did he finally decide that he "could no longer remain detached" from events around him.[20] The event which awakened his political interest was the brutal repression of the 1899 strike at St. Petersburg University. A number of friends and former teachers, such as I. M. Grevs and N. I. Kareev, lost their positions. His friend and future collaborator, Pavel Shchegolev, was one of the student leaders expelled and exiled to Volodga.[21]

Pavlov-Silvanskii's gradual political awakening, which coincided with the publications of his articles on feudal relations in Russia, did not at first affect his interpretation of the Russian past. Nor conversely did he yet show any interest in the political implications of the new history of medieval Russia which he was developing.

His friend Shchegolev remembered that at first Pavlov-Silvanskii

> did not think about the implications of his work for the interpretation of current events or as a significant contribution to the long debate between Slavophiles and Westerners. It was only the events of the twentieth century that opened his eyes to the political significance of his theories.[22]

Even as his attention to public affairs grew and Russia's crisis deepened during the first years of the twentieth century, Pavlov-Silvanskii's view of Russian history and current events remained basically optimistic and patriotic. In a popular article written in 1901 he took Russia's modern historians to task for presenting only the dark side of Russia's past. He singled out Kostomarov and Miliukov for special criticism. They failed "to see and value the bright side of our past," he complained, and this had implications for the popular understanding of the current epoch. Pavlov-Silvanskii concluded sadly: "What a strange people we are, how malevolent and hostile we are to each other. We criticize each other not only in the present but also in the past."[23]

On the eve of the 1905 revolution, Pavlov-Silvanskii began to speculate on the meaning of the Russo-Japanese war and the increasing political turmoil in Russia. In an article written in late December 1904 titled "Times of Troubles at the Beginning of Centuries, 1605-1705-1805," he optimistically pointed to the ability of Russia to survive grave difficulties and emerge strengthened. The key factor in Russia's salvation in each previous crisis had been the ability of the monarch to make timely and necessary changes. He wrote in almost reverential tones of "the important historical transformations" brought about through "the ruling will of the sovereign Emperor." He concluded,

> Our history assures us that a powerful Russian Government now as in former years of difficulty will, as a result of external and internal shocks, embark on a renewal, by taking the path of those great reforms which always ensured its successes in foreign affairs and served as an important guarantee of its steady internal development.[24]

Influenced by his studies of Peter the Great and the Grand Duke Konstantine Nikolaevich, Pavlov-Silvanskii seemed to have no doubts that the Romanovs would again save themselves by timely reforms and, in the process, advance the internal progress of Russia and restore its military prestige, national honor and international standing. These were not the judgments of a man expecting revolution or welcoming it. Whatever vision Pavlov-Silvanskii may have had of Russia's future, it did not appear to be incompatible with a strong and vigorous monarchy.

Shortly after he wrote his first assessment of Russia's crisis, Pavlov-Silvanskii began to learn new lessons from history. The events of January 9, 1905 in St. Petersburg, "shook him to the very depths of his soul," according to a close friend.[25] On that fateful day, having heard of the planned workers' demonstration, he and P. E. Shchegolev went abroad to observe. As they walked toward the Palace Square, they heard volleys of gunfire. A few minutes later, they saw cavalry attacking fleeing demonstrators and heading in their direction. Shchegolev recounted what happened then:

> Escaping from a detachment of the Guards Cavalry, sweeping down the Morskii Boulevard from the Arch, we ducked into the entrance way of a house which opened out to Moika Street. As we prepared to go out to Moika, we saw a company of infantry

draw up on the Police bridge and fire volley after volley, left and right, down the Nevsky Prospect and the Moika.

Unable to escape, the two men found refuge in the house. From the safety of their refuge, they watched with horror the ghastly drama in the street: "We watched as people and horses fell covered with blood—a coachman with his fingers shot off, an old woman wounded, crawling along the sidewalk.. .."[26]

The bloody massacre he was witnessing threw Pavlov-Silvanskii into shock and hysteria. He began to weep violently and uncontrollably. As the slaughter continued before his eyes, the weeping man, now almost mad, ran over to a wall and began to pound his head against it with great force. Through his tears, he sobbed over and over again: "What are they doing? What are they doing?" In was a long time after the shooting stopped before Nikolai Pavlovich could pull himself together.[27]

In the wake of the events of Bloody Sunday, he turned from scholarship to politics. Shchegolev, commenting on Pavlov-Silvanskii's work habits, noted that he went at his research and writing with enormous energy and passion: "A detached, cold-blooded attitude" toward his subject was alien to him.[28] That intense single-mindedness that had earlier focused his intelligence largely on Russia's past now, in 1905, led him for the first time into furious public political activity in opposition to the very government he served.

Throughout the spring of 1905, Pavlov-Silvanskii re-thought his political position as he watched the revolutionary drama unfold. By June, he had evolved from a moderate monarchist to a left wing liberal who favored a democratic republic for Russia. At that point, Pavlov-Silvanskii made his debut as a commentator on current events, writing under pseudonyms such as *Istorik* or *Istorik S*. His articles appeared throughout 1905 and 1906 in various liberal journals and newspapers such as *Rech*, *Byloe*, and *Nasha zhizn*. By the summer and fall, politics had become his pre-eminent interest. He followed the events of the day avidly, attended meetings, wrote, spoke and debated.[29]

He became a founding member of the Constitutional Democratic Party and attended all its congresses, including the one in Helsingfors held after the dissolution of the Second Duma. He was also a participant in the Zemskii Congress, which convened in Moscow in July 1905 in defiance of the police prohibition, and voted in favor of the famous resolution of the congress for a new fundamental law which would guarantee political democracy and civil liberties in the Empire.[30]

During the Duma elections of 1906, Pavlov-Silvanskii worked tirelessly for his party, especially in the Alexander Nevskii *Raion* of St. Petersburg in which he lived. One of his co-workers remembered that "Pavlov-Silvanskii acquired great popularity in the *raion*. He gave himself to the work with great enthusiasm and gloried in the party's successes."[31] His personal popularity translated into election as one of the district's electors as the Kadets swept the *raion*. Although he did not run again, he continued his involvement as a campaign worker for the party during the second Duma elections. By the third election in 1907, growing disillusionment with the government's actions, doubts about his party's course, and his return to scholarly research led Pavlov-Silvanskii to reduce the intensity of his commitment, but he remained a Kadet until his death.

The first articles he wrote after Bloody Sunday reveal his confusion about the meaning of the times. The events of the first months of the revolution had outrun his consciousness. He could not fit them into a coherent understanding of history. In June, 1905, he wrote in *Nasha zhizn*:

> We live in a strange atmosphere of uncertainty, as though we were marching and bivouacking. Working out programs of action, we try, not to master the forces of life but only to be ready in case of new and unexpected events. Thought tries in vain to penetrate the dark veil of the future and stands before it in impotence.[32]

Pavlov-Silvanskii's solution was not to abandon the study of history but to seek to understand it anew. The problem was not with history but with historians who had settled for obvious and superficial interpretations of its course. The revolutions had shown him that he and his colleagues had confused the accidental with the essential. The failure of Russian historians to correctly perceive the true course of history may have even contributed to the sad condition of Russia in 1905. As he reflected a year later:

> Our historiography taken *en masse* is far from meeting the demands placed on it by history.... History, by her every word teaches about the movement forward; the majority of our historians taught regression, not progress.[33]

Ironically, for Pavlov-Silvanskii it was the revolution itself, the very cause of the confusion, that exposed the real underpinnings of history and tore the veil of ignorance from the historian's eyes.

Pavlov-Silvanskii was, of course, not unique among historians in having to reconstruct a historical world view as a result of the shattering experience of living through revolution. In a certain sense, history and sociology as modern social sciences had been created by revolution. They had emerged as the tools which both conservatives and liberals used to explain the unprecedented change unleashed on the world in 1789. Many of the greatest historians of the nineteenth century had undergone similar traumas. Alexis de Tocqueville's brilliant analysis of the collapse of the old order in his *Ancien regime* owes much to the impact of 1848 on him.[34] The same revolution crystallized the conservative social and political views of Leopold von Ranke. Similar to the experience of Pavlov-Silvanskii fifty-seven years later, it led the great German historian to simultaneously seek the wellspring of revolutionary events in universal history and to explain their workings by concentrating on individual national histories.[35] In de Tocqueville's case, it can be argued that 1848 made such a strong impression on him because for most of his life he had been obsessed by 1789. For Pavlov-Silvanskii, the Revolution of 1905 had such profound resonances in the depths of his soul precisely because his concentration on the Petrine reform and feudalism, and his abiding interest in general laws, had always masked a deep concern to find Russia a place among the progressive nations of the West. The revolution established once and for all for him the legitimacy of Russia's claim to be part of the West.

Pavlov-Silvanskii was also not alone among his fellow Russian historians in undergoing a radical change of view during the first Russian revolution of this century. His friend, A. A. Presniakov, followed him from an apolitical acceptance of the monarchy to the *Kadet* Party. He was to end up accepting and even praising the Bolshevik Revolution.[36]

Another of Pavlov-Silvanskii's colleagues, Mikhail Pokrovskii, also had his "sincere and scientific but sharply democratic" convictions changed by the Revolution. By his own account, he began as a "bourgeois democrat and had become a Bolshevik by the time the Revolution was over."[37]

Thus Pavlov-Silvanskii's intellectual and political odyssey reflected the experience of many educated Russians of his generation. His, however, was more dramatic and more vividly chronicled than perhaps any other. He left an unusually full record of his changing thoughts in his newspaper articles; in the lectures he gave in Lesgaft's Free School, the Bestuzhev Higher Courses for Women and the St. Petersburg Higher Commercial School; and in the scholarly work he did on the Petrine period, the Decembrists, Radishchev, and most importantly the feudal period and its place in Russian history.

In a dramatic reversal, after 1905 he changed his interpretation of Peter's reign. He now denied it was a watershed era in Russian history. It became in his eyes only another step in the saddling of autocracy on the Russian people, a process which had begun with Ivan Grozny. At one point he even entertained the notion that both Ivan Grozny and Peter the Great had fashioned their autocratic rule from foreign rather than indigenous ideas—the first from Byzantium and the second from the West. In Pavlov-Silvanskii's new view, Peter merely transformed Ivan Grozny's patriarchal autocracy into imperial absolutism. He concluded this interpretation of a period he once considered positively, full of the promise of Westernization and even "democratization," with the observation that Peter's reforms had "no basic effect on our historical development." They "merely gave the building a new facade."[38]

In the first part of 1905, as Pavlov-Silvanskii was rethinking his own position, he completed the editing of Radishchev's *A Journey from St. Petersburg to Moscow* and wrote a biography of the author as an introduction. The Radishchev he described was a devotee of the ideas of the Enlightenment and a liberal reformer. A year later in his lectures he dropped this interpretation and characterized Radishchev as the first Russian Revolutionary. It was, he told his listeners, in the "archaic speech" of Radishchev "that was first heard the boldness and daring that comprises the strength of our revolution." Radishchev showed the way to the "Decembrists, the men of the sixties, the *narodnovoltsy*, the Marxists and Social Democrats and the *narodniki* and their successors, the Social Revolutionaries."[39]

One of the most important projects he undertook with Shchegolev during the Revolutionary year was to bring the history of the Decembrists to the public. His work in this field was important enough to earn him the title of "Father of Bourgeois Decembrist studies" from a Soviet historian.[40] He assisted Shchegolev in publishing the first edition of Pestel's notorious *Russkaia Pravda* in 1905. He also revised and expanded his brief 1902 biography of Pestel as an introduction to his annotated edition of the transcript of Pestel's examination before the Supreme Criminal Court which he discovered in the archives. The text first appeared in installments in *Byloe* in 1906 and then with a further revised Pestel biography as a book in 1907.[41] Pavlov-Silvanskii completed his published writings on the Decembrists with an article "Materialists of the Twenties," which was the first historical study of the secondary figures of the conspiracy.[42]

Pavlov-Silvanskii's revised interpretation of Pestel was much more sympathetic than it had been in 1902. His contemporary, the historian A. A. Kizevetter, remarked that Pavlov-Silvanskii developed "an enthusiasm for the Decembrists."[43] Now he characterized Pestel as the "first among them by virtue of his talents and his influence" and as a "person of extraordinary gifts." Pavlov-Silvanskii's final biography of Pestel stressed his passion for equality and his hatred of all aristocracies and hierarchies.[44] His final study of the Decembrists was an attack on the notion of them as Romantic revolutionaries. He put them squarely in the tradition of rationalism and materialism. The men "who sacrificed themselves on the Senate Square and at *Belaya tserkov*" were not dreamy followers of German *naturphilosophie* but "materialists" who had acquired from their French teachers a deep commitment to struggle for the common good.[45] Pavlov-Silvanskii's writings on the Decembrists are an important indicator of his changing world view. Although he was interested in the subject before the revolution, the intensity with which he approached it after January, 1905 was clearly the product of revolutionary events. He looked at the uprising of 1825 as an instructive antecedent of the Revolution of his own time. In a 1905 outline for an article on Pestel which he never completed, Pavlov-Silvanskii wrote that the Decembrists

> are extraordinarily interesting and instructive from a historical point of view. They were true warriors for the political liberation of Russia which is being accomplished before our eyes with sacrifices as bloody as their own....[46]

It is clear that the events of his own time gave him an insight into the men and events of 1825 that he did not have before. Pavlov-Silvanskii's close friend Shchegolev wrote of him that the Revolution of 1905 "widened his world view and gave him the ability to understand in a new way the ideas and reasons of the events of December 14, 1825."[47] If the Revolution had not happened, "the psychology of the heroes of December 14th would have been a closed book to him."[48]

Pavlov-Silvanskii's writing on the Decembrists had an important influence. His work was read and used by many Russian historians of his day. Both M. I. Pokrovskii and A. A. Kornilov were strongly influenced in their own writings on Pestel by Pavlov-Silvanskii's interpretation.[49] Although George

Plekhanov ultimately developed a different understanding of Pestel, he learned a great deal from Pavlov-Silvanskii. Plekhanov's copy of the 1907 essay on Pestel was full of careful and extensive marginal notes.[50] The most important aspect of the complex dialogue between past and present that Pavlov-Silvanskii carried on during the Revolutionary period was one on the meaning of the revolution for understanding the periodization of Russian history and the role that feudalism played in shaping the Russian past. It was the fruit of this dialogue that was published as *Feodalizm v drevnei Rusi* (*Feudalism in Old Russia*.) As will be seen, it had a significant influence not only on the future of Russian historiography but on the broader question of "whither Russia?"

A year after the revolution began, Pavlov-Silvanskii opened his first public lecture with an affirmation of the importance of history. The study of history, he told his audience, now "enjoyed general societal attention" because it was the key to understanding the "grand events of our time." In turn, "the times in which we are living provide us with a new illumination of the past."[51]

The events of 1905 had shown him that the myth of a Russian "patriarchal past" was an "official lie." The real history of Russia was a history of a ceaseless struggle for liberty. "Our struggle against state power" he concluded, "had its beginning in antiquity." Russia's entire history "is covered with the blood of rebellious popular movements."[52] Although often suppressed, the people's struggle "broke out periodically in sharp paroxysm" of violent revolt. From the earliest history of old Novgorod to the actions of the *Narodnaia Volia*, almost every previous century saw a new native reaffirmation of the "right of revolution" against despotism.[52]

The struggle for liberty against despotism, especially against the foreign absolutist forms which had been imported from Byzantium and the West, was carried on by the guardians of Russian customary law, namely "the *mir*, the *narod* and the *zemliia*" throughout most of Russian history. Thus, the Revolution of 1905—the most recent act of the ancient drama—marked a culmination of the development of native forces of liberty and customary constitutionalism in Russian history. He observed

> Western influence plays an insignificant role in our revolution. We see clearly in our revolution a process which is mainly the result of the conditions of our previous development.[54]

There is nothing in the revolution, he said, which is "borrowed, foreign, strange; nothing alien from the soil of our ancient history....No, the sources of this movement are found in the deepest antiquity."[55]

Yet it was also clear to him that the Russian Revolution was not just a unique local event but one of world significance, and it had powerful echoes elsewhere. "History does repeat itself," he told his audience. "Read a description of the French Revolution. On every page you are struck by the similarity of events of that Revolution in their internal essence with our present day."[56] Russia's 1905 was France's 1789 and Germany's 1848, and like them may have opened one of the great epochs of world history. He concluded

> Our days, the days of the Russian Revolution, will not pass without leaving a trace in the history and life of the Western nations and without becoming one of the great events of the world's history.[57]

The repetition in Russia of historical events essentially identical to those which had taken place earlier in the West did not, for Pavlov-Silvanskii, challenge the notion that they were the product of native sources. A few months earlier, in discussing the end of serfdom, he observed that the fact that

> an institution is replaced by another in the same order everywhere is not...a result of unthinking or chance imitation, nor the caprice of ideas but of the

iron law of the correspondence of political relationships to the economic.[58]

In his 1906 inaugural lecture, he combined a discussion of the universal laws of development with a critique of those Russians who denied the existence of those laws because they believed that Russian history was unique. In that lecture Pavlov-Silvanskii denounced those "reactionary contemporary publicists" who insisted on seeing Russian history as "a peaceful procession of crowned Tsars and loyal people" and those partisans of tsarism "who sanctify its antiquity and justify its existence by its primordial character."[59] In subsequent lectures he turned his attack specifically against his fellow historians. The errors of most Russian historians were the result of their "conservative" bent which caused them to miss the "progressive" direction in which Russian history was moving. The same cause led them to deny the similarity between Russian and Western European development. Our historians, he said, "taught us that the development of our past proceeded almost opposite that of Western history" because they held the mistaken notion that "for Russian history, there were, so to speak, no laws of development that applied."[60]

As a result of their errors "the vast majority" of Russia's historians had been taken by surprise by "the unexpected lessons taught by history" during 1905. As a result of the recent events, Pavlov-Silvanskii argued

> Reality, history, corrected the errors of historiography....We saw with great surprise that Russian History. . .at certain basic turning points developed identically with the history of the West.[60]

Pavlov-Silvanskii's lectures in 1906 bridged his early popular writings of the Revolutionary year with his later more scholarly re-interpretation of Russian history which focused primarily on feudalism. In *Feodalizm v drevnei Rusi* he omitted his comments on the Revolution, but he drew very heavily on the extensive analysis he did of Russian historiography for the opening chapter. The earlier commentary from the podium on the revolution, however, set the stage for this historiographic essay. In his lectures, he not only placed the Revolution in the context of universal history but even in the forefront of its progressive unfolding. He saw it, in essence, as identical to the French Revolution, yet located its well springs deep in the unique events and developments of Russian history. He denied a native origin to autocracy and found a nascent constitutionalism at the core of Russian customary law.

By inserting Russian history into a scheme of world historical development which made the Russian Revolution of 1905 a replay of the French Revolution of 1789, Pavlov-Silvanskii also created a guarantee of its eventual success. At the same time, his view of Russian history as a continual struggle against tyranny enabled him to reconcile his hopes for the development of a democratic, Western style constitutional order with the spontaneous rising of the masses. It assured him that his hopes were not alien to the Revolution but integral to it, and that they were about to flower into reality from deep roots Russia shared with the West. Finally, his interpretation of the revolution confirmed for him the truth of his earlier tentative assertion of the existence of feudalism in Russia's past. If Russia had had a true revolution and was moving toward a constitutional order like those in the West, then indeed it must also have had the same feudal order which had been the basis of constitutional development in the West.

Pavlov-Silvanskii's work on feudalism was done with the events of the revolution constantly impinging on his consciousness and distracting him. Doubts about the propriety of devoting his energies to scholarship when they might be better used in the battle for the future plagued him. On the occasion of the publication of *Feodalizm v drevnei Rusi*, he wrote a note expressing his anguish:

> The book comes out during the time of the Great
> Russian Revolution. . .and that Revolution strongly
> hindered me in my attempt to devote myself to this
> book and finish it. Social activity often attracted me

away from my work. It was difficult for me to work.
I had to close my eyes and stop my ears. Events
tortured me. Is this a time to be occupied with
learning?[62]

The book, which was published in 1907, was commissioned by
Pavlov-Silvanskii's old mentor, N. I. Kareev, for a series on the
History of Europe in Medieval and Modern Times by epochs and
countries which he edited with Professor I. V. Luchitskii for the
Brockgauz and Efron publishing firm. It drew heavily on all of
Pavlov-Silvanskii's earlier work on feudalism and was conceived
as a popular re-statement of his thesis in light of the new
understanding of history he had developed during the
Revolution. He assembled all of his previous articles into a
single coherent essay and added new materials he had worked up
on feudal practices and institutions in France, Germany, Poland,
Sweden and Spain to give his essay a stronger comparative
framework. He also added a long historiographic section which
discussed the way in which the question of feudalism and the
periodization of Russian history had been handled by his
predecessors and contemporaries. It was based, as indicated
above, on the lectures he gave in 1906. Finally, he concluded the
book with his own periodization of Russian history and a brief
description of the post-feudal period which he called the "State"
period. He dated this period from the founding of the
Oprichnina by Ivan IV in 1565 to the emancipation of the serfs
in 1861.[63] After the publication of the book he told his colleague
Klochkov,

> I posed the question of feudalism and indicated an
> answer; feudalism in Old Russia is now not a
> conjecture but a scientific theory with which
> Russian historical science must come to terms.[64]

Pavlov-Silvanskii's analysis led him to suggest a new periodization
of the national history. Russia's development should, he argued,
be divided into three main products:

(1) *From earliest times to the Twelfth Century—the Period of the Mir.* In this period, self governing institutions predominated. The evolution of self government moved through ever higher self governing institutions from *Rod* to *veche.* The *veche* emerged as the national self-governing institution at the culmination of this process. The development of Princes and their *druzhinas* took place only at the top and did not, until the end, affect the people's sovereignty expressed through the *Veche.* This was the period marked by the dominance of a natural economy.

(2) *From the Twelfth Century to the Mid-Sixteenth Century—the Udel or the Boiarshchina Period.* The central feature of this period was large scale Princely and Boiar land holdings, primarily as *Votchina.* The *mir* continued in existence in weakened form, largely under the control of the landlord. This was the period of feudalism. At the end of this period a national money economy which tied together the disparate parts of Russia began to emerge.

(3) *From the Sixteenth to the Mid-Nineteenth Century—the State Period.* This period can be divided into two: an initial period of Estate Monarchy and a final period of absolutism based on a class order.[65]

On the basis of this schematic breakdown of Russian history, Pavlov-Silvanskii concluded that the two most important events in Russian history prior to the nineteenth century were the sack of Kiev in 1169, which marked the end of Kievan ascendancy, the transfer of power and population to the North and the beginning of the *Udel* order, and the founding of the *oprichnina* in 1565, which signaled the destruction of the *Udel* order (and with it the power of the Boiars and Princes) and the beginning of the real unity of the Russian land. The Emancipation of 1861 was the event which Pavlov-Silvanskii felt designated the end of the Monarchical State Period. It, like the fall of Kiev and the creation of the *oprichnina*, marked the start of a new period of transition, one that would eventually lead to the development of a free civil order.[66]

The publication of *Feodalizm v drevnei Rusi* produced something of a sensation in Russian scholarly circles. In the words of Professor Leo Yaresh, it was "an event of particular importance" for Russian scholarship.[67] The Soviet historian S. V. Bakhrushkin, who was a graduate student at Moscow University in 1907, remembered that Pavlov-Silvanskii's work caused considerable excitement among the faculty and graduate students. He marked its appearance as a "moment when a significant break had taken place" in Russian historiography. He and many of his fellow graduate students were attracted to Pavlov-Silvanskii's "bold and intelligent" attack which "smashed the old historical world view and prepared the road for a Marxist understanding of the historical process."[68]

The work became a major topic of discussion among the faculty. What impressed Bakhrushkin most about the importance of the essay was that on the occasion of his first meeting with his future mentor, Dimitry Petrushevskii, the newly appointed professor gave him a long personal lecture on the correctness of Pavlov-Silvanskii's thesis.[69] S. B. Veselovskii, who was also in graduate school at the time of the publication of Pavlov-Silvanskii's work, remembered the powerful impact of the new thesis. "It enjoyed great success" according to Veselovskii. It was Pavlov-Silvanskii who first "directed the attention of young scholars" like himself to the problem of feudalism and "compelled them to see Russian history not in separation from the history of other European peoples, but in union and comparison with them."[70]

Feodalizm v drevnei Rusi inspired an unusually wide debate in scholarly journals. A few reviewers such as V. Storozhev, who found the work "a novelty," rejected Pavlov-Silvanskii's thesis out of hand while an equal number accepted it enthusiastically.[71] One of the enthusiasts, V. V. Filatov, wrote that "it is unlikely that the general position of the theory of unity [of Russian and European development] will be overthrown."[72] Most reviewers, such as Maxim Kovalevskii or the anonymous "K. M." who analyzed the work for *Istoricheskii vestnik*, concluded despite occasional serious reservations, that Pavlov-Silvanskii had made a good case.[73] "K. M." wrote that, thanks to Pavlov-Silvanskii, the idea of feudalism in Russia "has been taken out of the realm of suppositions and guesses and established as a well-documented thesis."[74]

But the work enjoyed a popularity far beyond the scholarly world. Pavlov-Silvanskii's friend I. Borozdin noted that his work was widely read and discussed by Russia's literate public and had thus "a great sociological significance." *Feodalizm v drevnei Rusi*, he wrote, "could be found not just in the offices of scholars" but in many private libraries. It "had a certain general influence."[75]

What gave Pavlov-Silvanskii's work a wide general audience was clearly not his evidence for the presence of a Russian equivalent of *morte main*, or his discussion of the extent of medieval population movements, but rather his idea that Russia was following, about a century late, the pattern of European historical development. The implications of this thesis made *Feodalizm v drevnei Rusi* a profoundly political work and, as the post-1905 repression gathered force, a powerful source of hope for many Russians.

V. Storozhev, who rejected Pavlov-Silvanskii's thesis, brought the issue clearly into the open in his review.

> I do not know why in the face of identical stages, we, in the final analysis remained in the blind alley of barbarism and slavery....If Russia's history is like the West's, why isn't it like the West? Is [Pavlov-Silvanskii] optimistically looking toward our future and wishing for a direct road to lead us into the political atmosphere of a London or Paris?[76]

A few months after Storozhev's pessimistic outburst, Pavlov-Silvanskii's colleague, V. Alekseev, read in his thesis the very hope that Storozhev mocked. Alekseev obviously spoke for many of Pavlov-Silvanskii's readers when he praised him for freeing Russian history from "the stifling tradition which bound it hand and foot" and for clearing the way for truth. More importantly, Pavlov-Silvanskii also liberated Russian society from

> the fetish of an independent, original Russian history which served as an underpinning for official patriotism and was the basis for stagnation and the prejudice against the transformation of societal and governmental relations.[77]

Pavlov-Silvanskii's message, Alekseev felt, was more important in 1908 than ever before because "dark reaction" was, at that moment, attempting to halt or at least cripple the development of a constitutional order in Russia. Pavlov-Silvanskii's view "gives us faith in the victory of a constitutional order in Russia, in the victory of law over force. It gives us the strength and vigor to battle for a new order, for a young, new Russia."[78]

A year after the publication of his popular essay on feudalism Pavlov-Silvanskii was dead at the age of 39 after a one-day bout with cholera in September, 1908 during a severe epidemic in St. Petersburg. He left a manuscript on feudal relations in medieval Russia almost two-thirds completed. This work he had hoped to submit to the University as a thesis so that he might get his advanced degree and take up a teaching career. His political activities had made his life at the archives difficult, and he was under police surveillance. The completion of the work represented for him an opportunity to escape from an increasingly oppressive situation and return to the career path he had left abruptly a decade and a half earlier.

Pavlov-Silvanskii's manuscript was edited and brought to publication by his friend Presniakov. It appeared in 1910 as *Feodalizm v udelnoi Rusi* (*Feudalism in Udel Rus*).[79] This posthumous volume provided a large body of documentation for his thesis and contained an extended analysis, based on data from his last research trip, on the relationship over time of a rural *volost* to its lay and religious overlords. He concluded before he died that he had established his thesis even more strongly than before. Presniakov ended the work with Pavlov-Silvanskii's pronouncement that

> I do not believe that my interpretation alone is true. But there are points in it whose truth I must affirm....For these establish the identical nature of the *Udel* order in Russia and Feudal Europe.[80]

Pavlov-Silvanskii's influence continued into the Soviet period. Soviet historians who had received their training before the revolution took up and developed some of the themes that Pavlov-Silvanskii originated. These included scholars such as S. B. Veselovskii and S. V. Iushkov. In fact, in his major study *Feodalnie otnosheniia v Kievskoi Rusi* (Feudal Relations in Kievan Rus), Iushkov told his readers that he set himself the task of studying feudal institutions "by continuing along the path blazed by Pavlov-Silvanskii."[81]

The most important supporter of Pavlov-Silvanskii's ideas during the early Soviet era was M. Pokrovskii. Pokrovskii had first written his well known *Russkaia istoriia s drevneishikh vremen* (Russian History from Earliest Times) shortly after Pavlov-Silvanskii's death. In it, he used Pavlov-Silvanskii's definition of feudalism and his description of the main features of a feudal order to structure his chapter on feudalism. He also accepted Pavlov-Silvanskii's views on immunities and vassalage. Pokrovskii added a greater economic content to Pavlov-Silvanskii's description of the characteristics of feudalism and downplayed the importance of their juridical nature, but the changes did not materially alter the original interpretation. Pokrovskii's work was reprinted after the Revolution and became one of the most popular and influential history texts in Russia, going through five editions between 1922 and 1933. As a result, Pavlov-Silvanskii's view of feudalism became, in essence, the Marxist view during the early period of Soviet rule.[82]

Pavlov-Silvanskii's popularity during the first decade of Soviet power, however, was primarily due to the fact that again, as in 1905, his view of the Russian past seemed to legitimize the new revolution. He had discovered a Russian feudal period that corresponded, in general if not in particulars, to the Marxist position. His support of the idea of a lawful historical process which followed the same paths everywhere was also seen as corroborative of the basic tenets of Marxism. A western scholar suggested another reason for his popularity, deriving its force from nationalism rather than Marxism:

> ...the feeling of national pride...did not allow for the admission that in Russian history there might be anything which differed from the history of other countries with pretensions to a progressive place among the nations of the world.[83]

Pokrovskii summed up clearly the political power of Pavlov-Silvanskii's work in an introduction to a new 1924 edition of his popular 1907 essay, *Feodalizm v drevnei Rusi*. Pokrovskii wrote that this work was "important and necessary to every historian of Russia, particularly Marxists" because Pavlov-Silvanskii

> from his early grave...has struck a cruel blow to the hopes of those monarchical white guardists wallowing abroad. All of their hopes are based on the idea that the fall of the Romanovs was accidental. 'Not accidental' is the answer we get from these thoroughly scholarly writings....Russia went along the same political path as Western Europe five hundred years ago....[84]

Pavlov-Silvanskii would no doubt find it disconcerting to discover that his interpretation of Russian history was being used to justify the legitimacy of a regime such as was evolving in the Soviet Union at the time his essay was reprinted. He believed that he had discovered a pattern of Russian historical development and the existence of the same institutions in the Russian past which had marked the development of a free, democratic and lawful civic order in the West.

The process of working out the new interpretation had been a complex and painful one for him. It had been forced on him by the Revolution of 1905. The Revolution required him to recognize that his understanding of Russian history gave him no basis for explaining the dramatic events he was witnessing and that his political views which both informed his historical interpretations and grew out of them were equally inadequate to provide guidance to his politics.

It took Pavlov-Silvanskii almost a year after Bloody Sunday to find his bearings. For the first six months of 1905 for Pavlov-Silvanskii, as for Lamartine in 1848, the catalog was indeed jumbled. He wrote nothing and made no public pronouncements during that period. When he finally broke his silence in June, 1905 his first articles expressed a sense of confusion, a feeling that he was living in a time out of control. His solution was to go back to restudy Russia's past in light of the new events.

By the end of the Revolutionary year his reflections on current events and history had changed his politics and led him to a new understanding of Russia's past. In politics he had moved from a moderate monarchist position to a passionate belief in democracy. His reinterpretation of Russia's past gave the revolution solid antecedents that stretched back to antiquity and a guarantee that Russia was indeed following the same path that had brought liberty and constitutionalism to other nations. He declaimed his views from the classroom podiums that the revolution opened to him and published them in the remarkable stream of reviews, feuilletons, popular and scholarly articles and historical essays that he wrote in the last three years of his life.

His reappraisal of Russia's past evoked a responsive chord in many educated Russians and gave his works, especially *Feodalizm v drevnii Rusi*, a surprisingly wide popular audience. For the men and women of his generation Pavlov-Silvanskii provided support for the idea that their aspirations for a new, humane and democratic Russia were solidly grounded in history and hence attainable. His work marked one of those rare moments in this century when the study of Russian history was a source of hope for the future rather than despair.

NOTES

1. For a brief biography see my article on N. P. Pavlov-Silvanskii in *Modern Encyclopedia of Russian and Soviet History* (1979). For a longer study of his career see Thaddeus C. Radzilowski *Feudalism, Revolution and History: The Life and Works of N. P. Pavlov-Silvanskii* (Boulder, Colorado: East European Monographs, 1992).

2. M. Klochkov, "Nikolai Pavlovich Pavlov-Silvanskii," *Istoricheskii vestnik*, no. 11 (November 1908): 639.

3. Pavlov-Silvanskii's major writings on the Petrine period are: "Propozitsii Feodora Saltykova," *Zhurnal Ministerstva narodnogo prosveshcheniia* 280 (March 1892): 228-248; "Proekt reform v zapiskach sovremennikov Petra Velikago," *Zapiski istoriko-filologicheskogo facul'teta Imp. St. Petersburgskago universiteta* 42 (1897); "Novyia izvestiia o Pososhkove," *Izvestiia otdel Russkogo iazyka i slov. Imp. akademiia nauk* 9, kn. 3 (1904): 105-148; "Ivan Tikhonovich Pososhkov," *Russkii biograficheski slovar'* 14 (1904); "Graf Piotr Andreevich Tolstoi," *Istoricheskii vestnik* (June, 1905). The last three are reprinted in N. P. Pavlov-Silvanskii, *Sochineniia* (St. Petersburg: M. M. Stasulevich, 1910) II.

4. N. P. Pavlov-Silvanskii, "Pavel Ivanovich Pestel," *Russkii biograficheskii slovar'* 13 (1901): 599-615.

5. N. P. Pavlov-Silvanskii, "Veliki Kniaz Konstantin Nikolaevich," *Russkii biograficheskii slovar'* 9 (1903): 120-155. This article is reprinted in *Sochineniia*, II.

6. For a summary of the historiography see N. P. Pavlov-Silvanskii, "Feodalnye otnosheniia v udelnoi Rusi," *Zhurnal Ministerstva narodnogo prosveshcheniia* 339, no. 1 (1902): 47-48.

7. N. I. Kareev, *V kakom smysle mozhno govorit o sushchestvovanii feodalism v Rossii?* (St. Petersburg: Tip M. Shredera, 1910), 4.

8. S. N. Valk, "Vstupitelnaia lektsiia N. P. Pavlova-Silvanskogo," in *Voprosy istoriograffi i istochnokovedenii istorii SSSR* (Moscow-Leningrad: Izd. Akademii Nauk SSSR, 1963), 618.

9. The major articles published by Pavlov-Silvankii on the *Udel* period to 1905 are: "Liudi kabal'nye i dokladnye," *Zhurnal Ministertva narodnogo prosveshcheniia* 309 (January 1895): 210-239;

"Zakladnichestvo-patronat," *Zapiski, Imp. Russkogo arkheologicheskogo obshchestva* 9, vyp. 1 & 2 (1897); "Immunitet v udelnoi Rusi," *Zhurnal Ministerstva narodnogo prosveshchenia* 331 (December, 1900): 318-365; "Feodalnyia otnosheniia v udelnoi Rusi," *Zhurnal Ministerstva narodnogo prosveshcheniia* 337 (June 1901): 1-48, 341 (January 1902): 1-32; "Novoe obiashchenie zakladnichestva," *Zhurnal Ministerstva narodnogo prosveshcheniia* 341 (October 1901): 91-100; "Simbolizm v drevnem Russkom prave," *Zhurnal Ministerstva narodnogo prosveshcheniia* 359 (June 1905): 339-365.

10. N. P. Pavlov-Silvanskii, *Gosudarevy sluzhilye liudi* (St. Petersburg: Tip. Gosudarst., 1897). This was reprinted as *Sochineniia*, I.

11. V. I. Storozhev, "N. P. Pavlov-Silvanskii o proizkhozhdenii dvorianstva," in *Otchet o zasedenii uchebnago otdela posviashchennom pamiati N. P. Pavlova-Silvanskogo. Otchet o deiatel'nosti uchebnogo otdela Obshchestva rasprostraniia teckhnicheskikh znanii za 1908 i 1909 gody* (Moscow: D. Sytin, 1910), 53-54.

12. P. N. Miliukov "Feodalizm v Rossii" *Entsyklopedicheskii slovar'* 70: 294-298; F. V. Taranovski "Feodalizm v Rossii. Kriticheskii ocherk," *Varshavskaia universitetskaia izvestiia* 4 (1902): 1-50. See also V. I. Sergeevich, "Zakladnichestvo v drevnei Rusi," *Zhurnal Ministerstvo narodnogo prosveshchenia* 337 (September 1901): 111-133; V. E. Golikov, review of *Zakladnichestvo-patronat*, by N. P. Pavlov-Silvanskii, *Zhurnal iuridicheskogo obshchestva pri St. Petersburgskom universitete* 10 (1897): 10-11; "86 Zacedanie, 23 Marta 1902," *Istoricheskoe obozrenie* 15 (1909): 62-64; M. F. Vladimirskii-Budanov, *Obzor istorii Russkogo prava*, 3rd ed. (Kiev: Tip. Imperatorskogo universiteta Sv. Vladimira, 1900), 131-132, 372-374; V. I. Kliuchevskii, *Kurs Russkoi istorii* (Moscow: Sinodalnaia tipografiia, 1904): 445-448; N. Rozhkov, "Naturalnoe khoziastvo i formy zemlevladeniia v drevnei Rossii," *Zhizn,* 9 (1900): 24.

13. N. P. Pavlov-Silvanskii, review of *Istoricheskie i sotsiologicheskie ocherki*, by N. Rozhkov, *Nasha zhizn,* 9 September 1905; Istorik [N. P. Pavlov-Silvanskii], review of *Obzor russkoi istorii s sotsiologicheskoi tochki zreniia*, by N. Rozhkov, *Nasha zhizn*, 5 August 1905.

14. A. Presniakov, "N. P. Pavlov-Silvanskii" (Nekrolog), *Zhurnal Ministerstvo narodnogo prosveshcheniia*, no. 11 (November 1908): 12.

15. N. P. Pavlov-Silvanskii, review of *Istorii Rossii v XIX veke*, *Byloe* (October 1907): 311-312.

124   *Modernization and Revolution*

16. V. A. Muravev, "Materialy N. P. Pavlova-Silvanskogo v Leningradskikh arkhivakh," in V. F. Illeristkii, ed. *Trudy Moskovskogo gosudarstvennoe istoriko-archivnogo instituta*, XIII; *Istoriografria istorii SSSR* (Moscow: Izd. vyshaia shkola, 1965), 292.

17. P. E. Shchegolev, "Pamiati N. P. Pavlova-Silvanskogo," *Minushie gody*, no. 10 (October 1908): 310.

18. L. V. Cherepnin, "K voprosu o sravitel'no-istoricheskom metode izucheniia russkogo i zapadnoevropeiskogo feodalizma v otechestvennoi istoriografii," *Srednie veka* 32 (1969): 262-265.

19. P-S (N. P. Pavlov-Silvanskii) review of *Ocherki po istorii russkoi kultury, Chast tret'ia*, by P. N. Miliukov, *Literaturnyi vestnik* 2, kn. 4 (1901): 155-156.

20. Shchegolev, 311.

21. A. N. Valk, "Istoricheskaia nauka v Leningradskom universitete za 125 let," in Leningradskii universitet, *Trudi iubilennoi sessii sektsia istoricheskoi nauk*, red. kollegiia D. L. Vainshtein i dr., otv. redaktor A. I. Molok (Leningrad, 1948): 33-38.

22. Shchegolev, 310.

23. Lesovik [N. P. Pavlov-Silvanskii], "Ob istoricheskom samounichizhenii," *Sankt Petrburgskie vedomosti*, no. 248 (1901).

24. A. N. Valk "Vstupitelnaia lektsiia N. P. Pavlova-Silvanskogo," 619. Pavlov-Silvanskii's first known participation in any political activity was in the St. Petersburg "banquet" organized by the liberal Union of Liberation (*Soyuz osvobozhdeniia*) on November 20, 1904, shortly before he wrote this article. He was among the 676 participants who signed a resolution petitioning the tsar for reforms and a parliament. The article may have been occasioned by that event. He had not yet affiliated with *Nasha zhizn*, which was founded in November 1904 and which expressed a more aggressive and militant liberalism than was evident in either the banquet resolution or his first political writings. His first *Nasha zhizn* article appeared in June 1905. On Pavlov-Silvanskii's participation in the banquet see A. D. Stepanskii, "Liberal'naia intelligensia v obshchesvennom dvizhenii Rossii na rubezhe XIX-XX vv.," *Istoricheskie zapiski*, no. 109 (1983): 90.

25. Shchegolev, 311.
26. Ibid.
27. Ibid.
28. Ibid., 310.
29. Ibid., 312.
30. Klochkov, 641.
31. Shchegolev, 312.

32. Istorik [N. P. Pavlov-Silvanskii], "Oskorblenyi patriotizm," *Nasha zhizn*, 8 June 1905.

33. Nevelev, "Pavlov-Silvanskii—Istorik Dekabristov," 66.

34. Hugh Brogan "Alexis de Tocqueville: The Making of a Historian," in W. Laquer and G. L. Mosse, eds., *Historians in Politics* (London: Sage Publications, 1974): 5-20.

35. Leonard Krueger, *Ranke: The Meaning of History* (Chicago: University of Chicago, 1977): 202-245.

36. Alfred J. Rieber, "Editor's Introduction" in A. E. Presniakov, *The Formation of the Great Russian State* (Chicago: Quadrangle, 1974): xxi-xlii; James C. Mills, "The Russian Autocracy in the Writings of A. E. Presniakov," in T. C. Radzilowski and L. J. Black, eds., "State and Autocracy in Imperial Russian and Soviet Historiography," *Laurentian University Review* 10, no. 1 (November 1977): 47-65; Valk, "Vstupitelnaia lektsiia...," 626.

37. Roman Szporluk, "M. N. Pokrovskii's Interpretation of Russian History," (Ph.D. dissertation, Stanford University, 1965), 47.

38. N. P. Pavlov-Silvanskii, *Feodalizm v drevnei Rusi* (St. Petersburg: Brokgauz and Efron, 1907), 141-144.

39. N. P. Pavlov-Silvanskii, "Zhizn Radishcheva," in N. P. Pavlov-Silvankii and P. E. Shchegolev, eds., *Puteshestvie iz Petersburga v Moskva A. N. Radishcheva* (St. Petersburg: Izd. Obshch. Pal'zy, 1905), vii-lxix; Valk, "Vstupitelnaia lektsiia...," 620-621. Except for a 1878 edition of 100 copies this was the first complete edition of Radishchev's famous work.

40. G. A. Nevelev, "N. P. Pavlov-Silvanskii—Istorik Dekabristov," *Osvoboditelnoe dvizhenie v Rossii* (Saratov, 1971), 56.

41. N. P. Pavlov-Silvanskii "Pestel' pred Verkhovym ugolovym sudom," chast I, *Byloe* 1, no. 2 (February 1906): 121-155; chast II, *Byloe* 1, no. 3 (March 1906): 206-231; chast III, *Byloe* 1, no. 4 (April 1906): 256-275; chast IV, *Byloe* 1, no. 5 (May 1906): 248-269. The introduction to the 1907 Rostov on the Don edition is reprinted as "P. I. Pestel" in *Sochineniia* 3: 206-238.

42. N. P. Pavlov-Silvanskii, "Materialisty dvadtsatykh godov," *Sochineniia* 3: 239-288.

43. A. A. Kizevetter, "Trudy N. P. Pavlova-Silvanskogo po istorii Dekabristov," *Otchet z zacedanii...*, 58. Kizevetter noted that in spite of his great enthusiasm, his work never left "the solid ground of pure scholarship."

44. N. P. Pavlov-Silvanskii, "P. I. Pestel," *Sochineniia* 2: 223-226.

45. N. P. Pavlov-Silvanskii, "Materialisty dvadtsatykh godov," 239-240.

46. Nevelev, "N. P. Pavlov-Silvanskii—Istorik Dekabristov," 60.

47. Shchegolev, 316.

48. Ibid.

49. Nevelev, "N. P. Pavlov-Silvanskii—Istorik Dekabristov," 57.

50. S. S. Landa, "G. V. Plekhanov v rabote nad istoriei dvizheniia Dekabristov," *Istoricheskie zapiski* 96 (1975): 312.

51. V. A. Murav'ev, "Lektsionnye kursy N. P. Pavlova-Silvanskogo v vysshykh volnykh uchebnykh zavedeniakh Petersburg, *Arkheologicheskii yezhegodnik za 1969 god* (Moscow: Nauka, 1971), 621. Recent revolutionary events have caused the historians of East Central Europe to echo Pavlov-Silvanskii's analysis. Polish historian Jerzy Jedlicki wrote recently "These are indeed golden times for historians....all revolutions arouse historical consciousness. A revolution implies a re-evaluation of a nation's history." Jerzy Jedlicki, "The Revolution of 1989: The Unbearable Burden of History," *Problems of Communism* 39 (July-August 1990): 39.

52. Ibid., 622.

53. Ibid., 623-624.

54. Nevelev, "N. P. Pavlov-Silvanskii—istorik Dekabristov," 61.

55. Ibid.

56. Murav'ev, "Lektsionnye kursy...," 250-251.

57. Valk, "Vstupitel'naia lektsiia...," 620.

58. N. P. Pavlov-Silvanskii, "Nachalo perelom," *Nasha zhizn*, no. 184 (29 July 1905).

59. Valk, "Vstupitelnaia lektsiia...," 622.

60. Murav'ev, "Lektsionnye kursy...," 252.

61. Nevelev, "Pavlov-Silvanskii—istorik Dekabristov," 66.

62. Murav'ev "Lektsionnye kursy...," 250.

63. *Feodalizm v drevnei Rusi, passim.*

64. Klochkov, 640.

65. *Feodalizm v drevnei Rusi*, 145-147.

66. Ibid., 147. For a full discussion of the historiographic issues raised in this essay see Thaddeus C. Radzilowski, *Feudalism, Revolution and History: The Life and Works of N. P. Pavlov-Silvanskii* (Boulder, Colorado: East European Monographs, 1992).

67. Leo Yaresh, "The Formation of the Great Russian State," in Cyril Black, ed., *Re-writing Russian History*, 2nd ed., revised (New York: Vintage, 1962): 164.

68. S. V. Bakhrushkin, "D. M. Petrushevskii i Russkie istoriki," *Srednie veka* 2 (1938): 41-43.

69. Ibid., 44-45.

70. S. B. Veselovskii, *Feodalnoe zemlevladenie v severovostochnoi Rusi* (Moscow-Leningrad: Akademiia nauk SSSR), 14-15.

71. V. V. Filatov, review of *Feodalizm v drevnei Rusi*, by N. P. Pavlov-Silvanskii, *Vestnik vospitaniia* 6, no. 3 (1908): 51-54. V. Storozhev, review of *Feodalizm v drevnei Rusi*, by N. P. Pavlov-Silvanskii, *Obrazovanie* 17, no. 3 (1908): 188-120.

72. Filatov, 53.

73. Maxim Kovalevskii, review of *Feodalizm v drevnei Rusi*, by N. P. Pavlov-Silvanskii, *Minuvshie gody* 1, no. 1 (1908): 294-298; "K. M.," review of *Feodalizm v drevnei Rusi*, by N. P. Pavlov-Silvanskii, *Istoricheskii vestnik*, no. 7 (July 1908): 307-309.

74. "K. M.," 309.

75. S. B. Veselovskii, 15.

76. V. Storozhev, 119-120.

77. V. Alekseev, "Pamiati N. P. Pavlova-Silvanskogo," *Moskovskii ezhenedelnik*, no. 46 (no. 15, 1908): 46.

78. Ibid., 47.

79. N. P. Pavlov-Silvanskii, *Feodalizm v udelnoi Rusi* (St. Petersburg: M. M. Stasiulevich, 1910).

80. Ibid., 420.

81. Quoted in A. A. Zimin and A. A. Preobrazhenskii, "Izuchenie istorii feodalizm v Rossii," in M. V. Nechkina, et. al., *Ocherki istorii istoricheskoi nauki v SSSR* (Moscow: Nauka, 1966), 3: 272.

82. M. N. Pokrovskii, *Russkaia istoriia s drevneishikh vremen* (Moscow: Idz. "Mir", 1913), 1: 64-94. One of the charges later leveled against Pokrovskii is that he was "strongly under the influence" of such bourgeois historians "as Nikolai Pavlov-Silvanskii." See S. Bakhruskin, "Feodalnyi poriadok v ponimanii M. N. Pokrovskogo," in B. D. Grekov et. al., *Protiv istoricheskoi konseptsii M. N. Pokrovskogo* (Moscow: Izd. Akademii nauk SSSR, 1939), 1: 117.

83. Konstantin Shteppa, *Russian Historians and the Soviet State* (New Brunswick, N.J.: Rutgers University Press, 1962): 256-257.

84. M. N. Pokrovskii, "Predislovie k knigi N. Pavlova-Silvanskogo, *Feodalizm v drevnei Rusi*," in *Istoricheskaia nauka i borba klassov* (Moscow: Gosudarstvennoe sotsialnoe-ekonimicheskoi izd., 1933), 107.

NEW THOUGHTS ON THE OLD REGIME AND THE REVOLUTION OF 1917 IN RUSSIA: A REVIEW OF RECENT WESTERN LITERATURE

Robert W. Thurston

A wide array of new western works exploring the background and course of the Russian Revolution has appeared in recent years, and debate about its nature has revived with *glasnost'* in the Soviet Union.[1] These developments make a general reevaluation of key issues in the Revolution appropriate. A critique of the state of the field at this moment should help clarify the debates about what happened, their political significance, and directions for further research. This essay will concentrate on recent western treatments of the background of the upheavals of 1917, especially regarding ideology, social change, the problems of the cities, and popular attitudes. A brief conclusion will comment on the implications of this new work on the prerevolutionary period for the course of 1917 itself.

This literature bears strongly on our understanding of the issue of legitimacy in the Russian Revolution, both in the overthrow of the Old Regime and in the Bolsheviks' seizure of power in October. Did the collapse of tsarism stem more from long-standing causes and unsolved problems, even after the reforms of 1905-06, or more from the immediate turmoil and difficulties of World War I? Was the Bolshevik success in 1917, in the narrow sense of gaining and holding political power, due more to some artful and devious manipulation of the masses or more to an ability to read the lower classes' desires and gain their willing support? If the latter, what exactly was the nature of that support, and what correspondence existed between Bolshevik and popular aspirations? Without question, ordinary folk made choices and followed leaders not merely on the basis of their experience in several years of war but according to personal and collective outlooks developed in the course of decades, if not centuries. As Leopold Haimson recently put it, Russia in 1917 "was a society out of joint, and the severe convulsions that beset it under the stresses of the civil war were, at least in part, but a demonstration of this fact."[2] However, we need to look carefully at the nature of this disjointedness before the Revolution, weighing its impact on the course of 1917 and the civil war against the effects of World War I.

These questions have vast implications not only for our understanding of the entire Soviet experiment, but also for appraisals of revolutions in general from 1789 to the present. Those who believe that the Russian Revolution represented a break with successful development before 1914, or that the Bolsheviks imposed themselves on an unwilling population three years later, tend to see Soviet history thereafter as doomed to descend into the mass state violence usually called Stalinism (though it must be noted that in the West there are now far-reaching challenges to traditional notions of that phenomenon).[3] In turn such opinions often lead to a blanket condemnation of revolution in general, a crucial political stance in today's world.

Older western discussions of Russia's general course by 1914 concentrated on political parties and trends. Historians analyzed the strength of the various parties on the scene after the reforms of 1905-06 and calculated the chances that liberalization would continue, resulting in a secure constitutional monarchy. With Haimson's articles of 1964-65 on urban social stability,[4] the emphasis began to shift toward more discussion of social history and developments. Much new material and a range of new analyses have appeared. Ironically in light of everyone's emphasis on the importance of autocracy, older works did not give much consistent thought to the ideology of that system of government and how it either accommodated or clashed with social change. It will be best to start with this last subject, since it affected every nuance of government policy.

The concept of autocracy seems clear enough: one person holds all political power, unlimited by any laws or institutions.

Perhaps this very clarity left most historians uninterested in profound discussion of the impact on state and society of tsarism as a system of thought. In his highly useful summation of the period, *Russia in the Age of Modernisation and Revolution, 1881-1917* (1983; see bibliography for complete citations) Hans Rogger stresses the problem of leadership in an autocracy rather than its ideological basis. It could not meet the needs of modernization because, above all, hereditary succession conflicted with the "tests of ability, popularity, and performance which are employed to select and judge the non-hereditary leader." No way was ever found

> to modify a system to whose successful operation the leadership of the monarch was essential when he not only failed to supply that leadership but was the single most important obstacle to its assumption by others. A modification of autocracy which could have solved that problem would have been tantamount to its abolition (p. 23).

These remarks are certainly apt, and they go to the heart of defects in tsarist leadership in Imperial Russia's final decades, if not much earlier as well. But leaving the question of rule at this level misses the larger problems of the Old Regime which sprang from and were imbedded in its ideology.

In *The Crisis of Russian Autocracy: Nicholas II and the 1905 Revolution* (1990), Andrew Verner has provided the most extensive discussion of tsarist ideology yet available in the West. Although he also stresses Nicholas' personal weakness, Verner argues that the autocracy's supposedly "limitless" power was ironically one of the very factors which in practice limited the monarch and the entire governmental system. First, the tsar became mired "in a swamp of anachronistic practices and senseless specificity." In an attempt to protect the monarch's prerogative to decide *everything*, as a good autocrat should, too much information and too many decisions were transmitted to the tsar. The result was that little time or energy was left over for grappling with larger issues and policies. Moreover, the system by nature was one of exceptions and special cases. Any regularity to the decision-making process at the top was not welcomed. The system required protecting

> the tsar's right of dispensation, his role of personally granting favors and deciding the fates of each of his subjects. In eliminating the need for such exemptions, any modernization of the law would have tended to automate and standardize administrative decision making, thereby circumscribing the tsar's authority and obscuring his personal role (pp. 48-9).

Nicholas' personality and vacillations made this picture even more capricious than it might otherwise have been, but the major point here is that he was very much the product and prisoner of a system developed over the course of about seven centuries.[5] This meant that Nicholas could not be a functioning constitutional monarch and that "there was no realistically conceivable way after 1906 that autocracy could have reformed and adapted itself enough to the demands of society in order to avert a revolutionary outcome" (Verner, p. 6). All discussions of whether Russia might have become a *Rechtsstaat* or "well-ordered police state" miss the point: the country's administration would remain arbitrary because that is what autocracy was all about.

Writing on tsarist ideology before Verner was Seymour Becker. His *Nobility and Privilege in Late Imperial Russia* (1985) centers in part on the concept of *soslovie* (legal estate, as in the three estates of old France) and its relationship to state policy toward the nobility. Becker writes that absolute monarchy "is the purest expression of the principle that also underlies social estates--hereditary privilege sanctioned by law" (p. 175). The concepts of estate and autocracy were thus intimately related, yet emancipation of the serfs in 1861 and the decline of the nobility's mission to perform state service meant that nobility had lost virtually all significance as a legal category by the end of the nineteenth century. Meanwhile, social change at the upper reaches proceeded rapidly, and nobles increasingly gave up their land.

Nevertheless, beginning with the reign of Alexander III in 1881, conservative gentry called repeatedly for revitalization of the estates, above all of theirs. Following its own proclivities, the government responded positively in many ways, among them by setting up the Noble Land Bank in 1885 and giving the gentry legal preference in zemstvo (organs of rural self-government) elections in 1890. The revolution of 1905 and subsequent reforms did not fundamentally change this picture, though it corresponded less and less to social and economic realities, given the continuing loss of land by the nobles. The leopard could not change its spots:

> The old regime tried to limit the risks involved in the necessary economic and social modernization that it launched in the 1860s by maintaining the formal structures of the social estates and the sense of place and deference that such a system instills in its members (p. 175).

To this one might add that it was ironically the regime's fear of revolution after the Pugachev uprising of 1773-75 that made it desire so ardently to keep society rigid—but that very rigidity made popular discontent build, helping to bring on a revolution.

A shorter discussion of tsarist ideology, but one which ties the subject to another kind of social change and to a detailed investigation of what happened in one locale, is in my own *Liberal City, Conservative State: Moscow and Russia's Urban Crisis, 1906-1914* (1987). This work also emphasizes the obstacles to meaningful reform inherent in tsarist thinking. Again the emphasis is on the concept of *soslovie*, but in a different direction. Given the regime's view of the Russian people as immature, vicious, selfish, and child-like,[6] a strict system of order and categorization was necessary to keep them from destroying each other and civilization. This perception predated emancipation and found an early expression in "Official

Nationality," the articulation of ideology produced by S. V. Uvarov in the 1830s.[7]

Sosloviia helped fill the function of social control, as they were supposed to demarcate the particular interests of each group, keep each category in a precise hierarchy headed by the tsar, provide mechanisms for the group's internal order, and alert the authorities to who people were and how to deal with them. The tsar and his officials could then in theory discover the best ways to reconcile the disparate interests of the land. Only the tsar could stand above it all, outside the *soslovie* structure; only he looked after the nation as a whole, a concept crucial to the ideology of Old Regime France as well.[8]

The *sosloviia* were ranked from peasants at the bottom to the nobility at the top, in order of status and service to the state. (Unlike the French, Russians never pretended that their clergy were uppermost.) This system served to justify the gentry's position as owners of the land and overseers of the peasantry, roles the government tried to prop up after the late 1880s. *Sosloviia* also implied that each person's standing depended on God and the tsar: God decided which estate someone would be born into, and only the tsar could alter that status. This idea underscored the regime's attempts to make each subject dependent on the throne for the basic parameters of existence: Russians were the creatures of the tsar, enhancing his role as the nation's head.

Such a theoretical structure may have worked fairly well for a medieval, overwhelmingly rural society, but, as Becker also noted, it was increasingly separated from Russian reality as the nineteenth century wore on. This trend was not only a question of the nobility's position. First, tsarist ideology was diametrically opposed to social mobility, which undermined the notions of categories and dependence on the tsar.[9] The extent to which urbanization, industrialization, education, and literacy fostered social mobility was thus the extent to which the Old Regime was threatened. In practice, only the remaining land-owning gentry found that it had a desirable position protected by the *sosloviia* system. Second, urban life *per se* had never fit comfortably into the scheme; it was always too fluid and uncontrollable. Indicative of the Old Regime's problems in coping with urban life were the facts that peasant migrants to the towns and their offspring were still classified as "peasants" by *soslovie* and that there was never a "workers" estate, despite their undoubted existence and importance. Workers were too mobile socially and geographically to be described, let alone controlled, by a system of legal categories. Thus the failure to develop coherent policy toward workers and urban life was originally and basically rooted in ideology; the tsarist regime would have had to change its very nature to deal effectively with either workers or urban affairs, and this it was not about to do.[10] Once more Haimson's ideas come to mind; in 1979 he wrote of "Russia's painful evolution from a society of *sosloviia* to one of classes."[11] But in fact there could be no question of evolution, for it would have required the Old Regime to destroy its own essence.

It was also true that the arbitrary nature of tsarism required arbitrary laws and powers on the local level. The Extraordinary Measures, a set of laws adopted after the assassination of Alexander II in 1881, granted governors, governors-general, and *gradonachal'niki* (city commandants or governors) the right to exile individuals, close public or private organizations and businesses, and prohibit any public or private gatherings. One or the other of the Measures was in effect for 152 million of 157 million subjects in 1912.[12] These laws guided tsarist officials day in and day out where things mattered to most people, on the local level. Liberals in particular found the statutes increasingly onerous.[13]

In short, the system's ideology rendered it incapable of developing policy to meet the pressing needs of modernization. Rather than a failure of leadership at the turn of the century, the basic problem was that it was impossible to modernize, defuse the resulting tensions, and remain true to autocracy at the same time.

Two studies show the difficulties the government encountered in the early twentieth century when it simultaneously attempted to placate society and control events. Edward Judge's *Plehve: Repression and Reform in Imperial Russia 1902-1904* (1983) examines the ways in which Viacheslav von Plehve, the energetic minister of the interior appointed in 1902, sought to coopt leaders of society, reform peasant life, and also maintain strict autocracy. He saw that reforms were needed, but "his police instincts also told him that to permit criticism was to invite trouble, and that to make concessions could only lead to further yielding." Therefore he persisted in repression (p. 204). The coming of the 1905 Revolution is evident in these lines alone.

If Plehve represents the classic tsarist dilemma before 1905, his story (and assassination) prefigure P. A. Stolypin's career as premier from 1906 to 1911. Francis Wcislo's *Reforming Rural Russia: State, Local Society, and National Politics, 1855-1914* (1990) reiterates and expands on several of the same themes in the different context of the "constitutional experiment." Although much was new in politics and permitted expression of opinion, Stolypin too had to rely on a combination of force, attempts to reform peasant life, and wooing educated society to the government's side. But "to consolidate government authority and its capacity to promulgate reforms, Stolypin was forced to begin removing from legitimate politics much of the 'nation' that had created it. What remained was a narrow base indeed" (p. 207). That both Plehve and Stolypin died in office by assassins' hands seems perfectly symbolic of the impossibility of breaking through such contradictions to stability. Taking Judge's and Wcislo's books together underscores the continuity of tsarist government and its problems across the 1905 upheaval.

Turning to new work on changes in Russian society, we may proceed down the hierarchy from nobles to peasants. Roberta Manning's magisterial work, *The Crisis of the Old Order in Russia: Gentry and Government* (1982) also shows the degree to which tsarist ideology was increasingly incompatible with changing conditions in one highly important sector of society, the nobility. She details the forces working against gentry landowning after 1861: dearth of capital, high debts, lack of knowledge or experience in farming, and the "long depression" in grain prices of 1876-96. Then, during and after the Revolution of 1905, many gentry engaged in panic land sales; as a result, the amount of land owned by the Russian nobility declined from about 68.8 million desiatines in 1877 to 41.8 million in 1914. Only massive subsidies from the government to zemstvo agricultural enterprises, which in turn went largely to gentry farmers, helped to slow the decline somewhat after 1906 (pp. 362, 373).

Since the franchise for zemstvo elections after 1890 specified that land-owning nobles be grouped in a separate curia, the decline in their land holdings meant severe erosion of the gentry basis of politics, such as it was to begin with, on the local and national levels. "A growing number of county zemstvos were forced to close down for lack of a quorum due to a shortage of members from the overburdened first (gentry) curia," Manning found (pp. 366-377). Various new organs arose with claims on gentry participation after the Revolution of 1905—for example the State Duma and the local commissions charged with overseeing the Stolypin land reforms—so that nobles were stretched more thinly in office than ever. In addition, the central government chose a high percentage of local officials from governors on down from "this same shrinking, overburdened group of local gentry activists, thus further weakening the local political and administrative structures of the Russian countryside" (p. 367). At the same time that urban growth and social mobility threatened the social basis of the Old Regime from one side, the decline of the landed gentry posed an equally grave problem from the other.

Seymour Becker offers another view of the Russian nobility at the end of the imperial period in *Nobility and Privilege*. He challenges Manning's findings on a number of points. Nobles did not largely flee from the land after 1861, he argues, nor did they by and large borrow money against their estates for frivolous purposes. Instead, they often left farming because it was unprofitable, taking advantage of rising land prices to acquire capital for other, more sensible pursuits. Mortgages frequently signified borrowing for investment in agriculture, and among the gentry were some quite capable farmers who had no trouble adapting to the new post-emancipation situation (pp. 6-12 and *passim*).

Manning also found that some nobles were successful and practical farmers by the 1870s; she describes this as a "turn to the land" fostered partly by economic necessity and partly by a feeling within the first estate that it was being replaced in the army and civil service by commoners. Both authors essentially agree that the nobility lost a tremendous amount of land between 1861 and 1914, that this caused serious problems for the nobility as a legal category and indeed for the whole estate system, and that the Old Regime denied reality by attempting to bolster the position of the gentry after 1881. Nicholas II phrased his vision of society this way in 1902: "I conceive of Russia as a landed estate of which the proprietor is the tsar, the administrator is the nobility, the steward is the zemstvo, and workers are the peasantry." As Becker puts it in *Nobility and Privilege*, there could be "no more vivid metaphor for Russia's traditional social order--nor a less relevant one for a society entering the twentieth century with a decade of rapid industrialization behind it" (p. 64). It must also be noted that Nicholas' view of the good society was entirely rural: urban life, industry, and workers were not even mentioned.

Even if this bucolic Russia had still existed, the nobility could not have been the administrator. Regardless of why it happened, the gentry lost land. Yet the regime turned increasingly to *landed* gentry as the political basis of both local rural government and the national parliament. Vigorous or moribund, there were simply not enough landed gentry to go around by 1914. Thus the state did not possess a viable social or political basis on the eve of World War I. As Geoffrey Hosking has shown in his *The Russian Constitutional Experiment: Government and Duma, 1907-1914* (1973), by 1912 the "regular process of legislation through the Duma [lower chamber of the national parliament] and State Council [upper chamber] was being replaced by the formation of cliques close to the Emperor, intent on impeding change and encouraged by the dissipation of authority to use their private advantages" (p. 214). Hosking believes that the constitutional experiment was "fatally weakened" even before Russia's entry into the war (p. 246).

Turning to the middle class, it is clear that it rose from having an almost negligible role before the turn of the century to great importance in the 1905 Revolution and then to dominance of the Provisional Government in 1917—before being swept completely from the stage. It is difficult to estimate how many people might have been considered middle class by 1914 or how fast the group was growing. Since the strongest demographic base for the middle class was the towns, one index related to these issues is urbanization. If in 1897 about 15% of the empire's population (in what became the USSR) lived in towns, by 1914 the figure was an estimated 17.5%. (We might compare this to the United States, where 50% urbanization was achieved by 1920.) The increase is even more striking in absolute terms, from 15,955,000 in 1897 to 24,888,000 in January 1914.[14]

Another crude indication of the numerical strength of the middle class is in the vote for the Constituent Assembly of 1917. For lack of a more precise measure, we may link the middle class to the Constitutional Democrats and other liberal parties of 1917, which together received just over 3,340,000 votes, or about 7.5% of the total cast.[15] Extending this percentage to the entire population of an estimated 145 million,[16] giving the figure of 10,875,000, may serve as a very rough guide to the size of the middle class.

The collection of articles entitled *Between Tsar and People: Educated Society and the Quest for Public Identity in Late Imperial Russia* (1991) does not address the size of the middle class or pay much attention to its relative political weight. Instead, the focus is on the nature of the middle strata and their quest for self-definition in a society traditionally devoid of sympathy for such types. Out of a rich set of ideas in the book, only a few germane to the discussion can be mentioned. A number of the authors emphasize divisions within the middle class that weakened its political effectiveness in 1917. Louise McReynolds suggests, though on the basis of one individual, that many middle-class Russians considered the West to be bankrupt and therefore would not fight for its liberalism (p. 247). Daniel Orlovsky provides a fascinating look at an unexplored group in the Revolution, lower middle-class employees. Here, too, fissures were important: these people rejected liberalism and opted for a "proletarian" or Bolshevik solution (pp. 249-268).

While these findings are of great value, they do not necessarily amount to a picture of severe social fragmentation on the eve of 1917 which then fed into the Bolshevik victory. The tsarist context, particularly ideology and the social and political weight of the nobility, profoundly conditioned everything before 1917. The storm then broke in a deeply stressful situation, wartime. Where the middle-class liberals had the chance to wield any influence on policy before 1917, in the towns, they displayed more coherence and initiative than the authors of *Between Tsar and People* credit them with.

The urban milieu, liberalism's chief location, was important above all in two ways: first, it put educated Russians and the lower classes in closer, more regular contact than usually occurred in the villages. Familiarity may not breed contempt so much as accommodation, though obviously the outcome depends on the flexibility of the social and political processes at work. Peasants still tended to view teachers and officials as outsiders, people excluded from the heart of village life and regarded with some suspicion.[17] (However, 1905 changed this picture somewhat, at least for a time, as we shall see.) While urban life certainly produced its own tensions between the classes, this could not be and was not the same as the basic we-they mentality of rural dwellers. Peasants felt that they could easily dispense with the gentry and probably with officials, too. It is not adequate to say that everyone was in the town boat together, but it was easier for poor folk to imagine that most townspeople who worked had a useful role to play. A town is made by people, so that city dwellers may not share the peasant attitude that those who do not till the land but nonetheless own it have expropriated God's natural creation. Dare we suggest that this outlook on the part of the lower classes could have applied, under certain circumstances, even to factory owners? That will be discussed below. Finally, urban dwellers do not necessarily adhere to peasant fatalism, which is based on the vicissitudes of nature.[18]

The second important point about the middle class in the towns also grew out of social proximity. Urban liberals could and did influence the masses more than rural liberals could. This process had several aspects. To begin with, the greater social mobility of the urban scene provided the poor with models for aspiration—assuming any significant degree of social rise existed. Serving as models for those lower in society meant that urban liberals could exercise some real leadership in the towns. Moreover, rubbing shoulders with the poor meant that the upper crust in the towns saw and even experienced the problems of the lower classes more intimately than did the well-to-do in the countryside. Disease spread faster in cities, for example, so that urban leaders had strong incentives to clean up the poorer quarters. Cities increasingly needed educated workers and employees, and therefore improving education was a more immediate need in towns than in the villages, where farming was often highly traditional.[19]

Urban social reform entailed programs that would leave the liberals' own position intact, such as improved transportation, medical services, and housing. To the peasants, social reform meant taking all the land, which would have reduced the gentry to nullity. Finally, and leaving the liberals aside for the moment, radicals could work among urban toilers much more easily than they could among peasants, where they were more readily rejected as outsiders by the inhabitants and more quickly identifiable by the police. But liberals were keen observers of radical influence on workers in particular before 1914, and once again they were often moved to do something about it. The Revolution of 1905 brought liberals and workers together in many Russian cities,[20] so that some moderates gained sympathy and understanding from the lower classes. In the countryside, the effect of 1905 was much more often to scare the elite into a dogged defense of its position in the wake of peasant disorders and attempts to seize all the land.[21]

Older western studies sometimes argued that the urban elite ignored the problems of the lower classes, which in turn fed the volatility of the poor.[22] But in recent years this picture has been substantially revised. The collection of articles in *The City in Late Imperial Russia* (1986) indicates that progress and elite interest in improving conditions varied greatly from town to town.[23] Riga, Moscow, and Odessa had good records, considering the financial limitations at work and the hampering interference of the central government. Kiev and St. Petersburg, by contrast, had city governments which displayed little inclination to work for the common urban good.[24] In a separate article, Michael Hamm, editor of *The City* collection, writes favorably of Kharkov's municipal affairs and reform efforts.[25] Joseph Bradley Jr.'s excellent *Muzhik and Muscovite* (1985) details increasing concern on the part of Moscow's elite by the 1890s that unruly newcomers from the countryside were not sober, stable, or productive. The fear that the *muzhik* in the city might tear it apart prompted the elite to institute a wide variety of reform programs for in-migrants, though most of these efforts concentrated on trying to remake individuals in a "respectable" mode rather than remedying underlying problems. My own work on Moscow demonstrates that its leaders, drawing on earlier traditions but spurred on by the fact that the Revolution of 1905 had peaked there in the December uprising, were deeply concerned to solve the city's abysmal difficulties. After 1905 this anxiety resulted in some efforts to attack root causes, for example in education and housing.[26]

As the attention of urban liberals focused on the defects which surrounded them, they became increasingly frustrated by the tsarist government. It concentrated reform efforts for the lower classes almost exclusively on the peasantry, reflecting its rural orientation. Prime Minister P. A. Stolypin offered a broad set of proposals for change to the Third State Duma in November 1907, but they contained almost nothing for the towns. "The essential concern of the present Government, its guiding idea," he said, "is always the agricultural question."[27] Once more, ideology left little room for attention to critical issues.

When the Old Regime did interact with the towns, it often hindered the efforts of locally chosen officials to make improvements. This was true in Odessa and Riga as well as in Moscow. On the other hand, some urban leaders were deeply frightened by the prospect of further revolution after 1905 and chose to huddle closer to the state for their own defense. Petersburg's dawdling in the process of reform can be explained in part by this tendency, and in part by the fact that well-to-do government employees supplied a sizable portion of city duma (elected council) members.[28] In Kiev the town fathers (the empire's laws barred women from municipal councils) were distracted to some extent from the tasks at hand by ethnic tensions.

What might be said in general about the position of urban liberals and the impact of their reform efforts in Russia by 1914, based on the recent literature? In 1974 William Rosenberg argued that in national politics the liberals were losing support by the eve of the war to parties of both the right and left: "the liberal center was being squeezed . . . Kadet strength even in cities and towns was seriously challenged by a strong socialist left, whose position could only improve in 1917 as workers and peasants became fully franchised."[29] Haimson found that liberals' disquietude at increasing worker activism and strikes pushed some to seek contacts with radicals, even Bolsheviks, and offer them support.[30] In *The Russian Revolution* (1990), Richard Pipes dismisses these probings as "eccentric" and tactical, suggesting that the liberals wanted once again to frighten the regime with the specter of revolution. He argues that "the very opposite trend was noticeable in Russia on the eve of the war—namely, a shift to conservativism" (p. 193).

To be sure, the Kadets went down to ignominious defeat in 1917. But it may well be wrong to read backwards from that result to infer that in the prewar period liberals were losing strength. In Moscow Kadets and other liberals did well in city and State Duma elections; only Kadets were elected to the Duma in the top two curiae (determined by amount of property owned) within the city in the 1912 election. Kadets also won in the first curia in Riga and St. Petersburg, taking seats previously held by Octobrists.[31]

It was not so much that liberals were weakening before the war as that their mood was shifting to reflect the country's growing tensions; but this trend was to the left, the opposite of Pipes' finding. The best single indication of the outlook of Russia's urban liberals on the eve of the war appeared during the Congress of Municipal Representatives, held in Kiev in 1913. Moscow's A. I. Guchkov, leader of the Octobrist Party and a key member of the city's council, addressed the gathering with fighting words: "In Moscow we do not stand for interference by the police in considering issues of municipal government." He went on to say that the slow pace of reform and deviations from the October Manifesto "threaten the country with grave convulsions and ruinous consequences." Police closed the session after this comment, but they could not prevent the assembled delegates from giving Guchkov a resounding ovation.[32]

Tsarism had proved unable to do much more for the cities than to hamper their own efforts at reform. Keenly aware of this pattern and of the regime's heavy-handedness toward workers (to be discussed below), urban leaders felt profound unease and distrust of the state on the eve of the war. In these sentiments they were generally very far politically from the landed gentry, who had cast their fate with the government. If liberals had often feared the masses by late 1905 and had sometimes turned to the state for protection, by 1913 they believed more widely that the state was their enemy: it was pushing the lower classes to another revolution, one which might well bring all of educated Russia down with it. To this story must be added the development of labor unrest and its impact on the country's moderates.

Workers were the primary motive force of 1905. They may have begun that year with strong faith in the tsar,[33] but their militancy and opposition grew rapidly thereafter. Inquiring into why this occurred and into workers' radicalism on the eve of World War I, recent western work has begun to look deeply into the proletarian world.

It will be best to start with *The Russian Worker: Life and Labor under the Tsarist Regime* (1983), edited by Victoria Bonnell, as it lays a foundation for all theorizing. The book is a collection of workers' and intellectuals' first-hand accounts of working-class life in the late nineteenth and early twentieth centuries. The workers' stories provide poignant insights into hierarchy and status within their ranks; attitudes toward management, religion, and the home villages from which they had migrated; and working and living conditions. One unusual aspect of *The Russian Worker* is that it contains two accounts of artisanal and retail occupations. Here the conditions seem even grimmer, if that is possible: shop girls were often forced to turn to prostitution in order to make ends meet, while over 58% of the tailors in one survey worked more than 14 hours a day (pp. 162, 194).

It is not new to stress that Russian workers' lack of opportunities to organize and express their grievances made them more radical, but in *Roots of Rebellion: Workers' Politics and Organizations in St. Petersburg and Moscow, 1900-1914* (also 1983), Bonnell has made the situation a good deal clearer. She details legislation, working and living conditions, and factory hands' efforts to organize after the turn of the century. The government allowed independent labor unions for the first time beginning in 1906 but almost immediately began to harass and disband them. Perhaps only 63 labor unions functioned legally in all of Russia by 1914. Even more than outright repression, government vacillation toward unions angered workers and made them more radical (pp. 372, 450).

Bonnell revises Haimson's conjecture of 1965 that it was young, inexperienced workers coming into the cities by the eve of the war who were more militant and inclined to support the Bolsheviks, the victors in key union elections by late 1913. While young unionists did incline to the Bolsheviks, so did many others. "Age and peasant outlook do not explain Bolshevik success . . . workers' radicalism came from their own experiences with employers and the state" (pp. 426-437).

The most ambitious attempt to date to portray the workers' world and the course of their radicalism is Tim McDaniel's *Autocracy, Capitalism, and Revolution in Russia* (1988). A student of Bonnell's, and like her a sociologist, McDaniel suggests that it was the fact that capitalism developed within an autocratic system which rendered the whole structure incapable of going very far to satisfy workers. Autocracy and capitalism weakened each other, so that neither "could act on the basis of a long-term interest in stability" (p. 32). The regime demanded loyalty to itself; in fact, McDaniel calls this pattern "atomization," a word usually applied only to societies termed "totalitarian." Thus tsarism offered no basis for a firm concept of contract and hence of trust between parties. It never began to convince workers that their rights could be defended in a regular, legal manner. At the same time, the government's sporadic intervention on their behalf indicated to them that the state could be a force for their interests, one which might tame the capitalists.

But this positive action also deepened the sense among factory hands that private property should be subject to strong state regulation. McDaniel therefore believes that workers absorbed some conservative notions of state activity under the Old Regime which they readily transferred in 1917 to an approval of the Bolshevik approach to industry.

Autocracy, Capitalism, and Revolution is overly cluttered with theory. It is not necessary to sketch "ideal-typical" mass and conscious workers in order to make generalizations about workers' consciousness. Nor is it clear that combining "mass society theory" with ideas from the Marxist tradition, especially Trotsky (who had contact with workers largely as an orator, and seemed to regard them by 1920-21 as fit only to be bossed), helps to build an understanding of what workers wanted. McDaniel's view that "events are important, but the overall development and structure of the labor movement are equally so" (pp. 38-39) leads to the objection that development and structure, not to mention attitudes, changed over time and depended on events. McDaniel could have noted a passage in Bonnell's *Russian Worker* where a worker, P. Timofeev, describes changing feelings about violence from supervisors. Workers had formerly tolerated such violence, but by the turn of the century "even a threat to strike a blow would stir up the whole shop" (p. 106). The structure of the working class had changed far less by 1914, compared to 1900, than its militancy and desires had. But these objections aside, *Autocracy, Capitalism, and Revolution* is a highly useful book: it details better than anything else the course and contradictions of tsarist labor policy, and it raises provocative questions about worker radicalism and its roots in the Old Regime.

Local studies of workers before the Revolution have begun to appear in recent years, so that we are building some knowledge of what their lives were like in a specific context, essential in turn to assessing their goals and politics. A challenging perspective on workers' moods is Heather Hogan's dissertation, "Labor and Management in Conflict: The St. Petersburg Metal-Working Industry, 1900-1914" (1981). The author argues that the difficulties of organizing unions played a smaller role than did other factors in rising radicalism. In the capital's metal plants, conflicts between labor and management occurred because "advanced technologies and methods of industrial organizatjon" collided with an "unreformed, largely autocratic structure of authority within the factory" (p. 2). By 1914 "the crucial factor fueling labor unrest . . . was employers' inability to respond to worker demands for equal and respectful treatment" (p. 7). Among the new conditions for workers after about 1905 was the introduction of Taylorism or "rationalization." Its emphasis on deskilling and an increased role for managers meant that employers were moving to break labor solidarity and end informal bargaining with foremen. This brought new anxiety into the plants. In addition, employers imposed new controls in the workplace, over entry to the factory, use of bathrooms, and the pace of work, which was forced upward. The Bolsheviks followed and understood these changes better than other political groups did.

Hogan argues that, given workers' prevailing lack of dignity and opportunity to be integrated into the larger society, they chose not to concentrate on broad-based organizations, namely unions. They turned instead to groups within their factories and to the radicals. Also differing with Haimson, Hogan finds that metal workers with long experience as well as "green youth" criticized their union's reformist stance after 1910 (p. 406). All of these tensions mounted so sharply by summer 1914 that the "metal workers' movement . . . had clearly transcended the parameters of labor-management conflict within the factory and had come to threaten the very stability of the autocratic regime" (p. 459). Of course, the threat would have been mild without the context sketched above and more problems to be outlined below. Despite this quibble, "Labor and Management in Conflict" is convincing, and it provides the kind of profound look at Russian workers which is necessary to a reasonably complete understanding of their stance by 1914.

In this same vein Theodore H. Friedgut has contributed *Iuzovka and Revolution. Volume I: Life and Work in Russia's Donbass, 1869-1924* (1989). This detailed and wonderfully presented book tells the story of a town created from scratch in the Ukrainian steppe by John Hughes, a Welsh ironmaster, beginning in 1870. Since there is no "h" sound in Russian,

Hughes became Iuz, and his town Iuzovka. It was a company settlement, with all the paternalism, benefits, and drawbacks that term implies. Though we must wait for the second volume of this study to explore the political results of Hughes' experiment, Friedgut has already drawn a wealth of conclusions which bear on the present and future of Imperial Russia by the eve of the war. First, he offers further information on the divisions among workers, in this case between factory hands and the region's miners, who possessed lower skills and status. Beyond that split, there were important divisions within the industrial workers, between those who had become reasonably well off by the standards of the day and those who had not, and between Russians and Ukrainians. The latter were from villages located closer to the factories and mines, and they maintained much stronger ties to their homes. On the other hand the industrial workers, largely Russians attracted to the Donbass by the "superior conditions in the steel mills," quickly became a "settled group" (p. 330).

A second major point to emerge from *Iuzovka* is that by dominating housing and keeping any independent organizations out, Hughes was able to create a community which controlled workers' lives to a remarkable extent, yet won the loyalty of a good many who labored there. The company town was not a bad place to work, considering the Russian milieu; above all it provided steady employment. Friedgut promises that in the next volume

> we will find repeatedly that in times of political and
> social crisis they [the workers] rally to the factory's
> defence, ready to do battle with anyone threatening
> it. If the New Russia factory workers show any
> group consciousness of common interests, the
> essence of that consciousness lies in this defence of
> their livelihood (p. 331).

The vast implications of these findings for 1917, at the risk of anticipating the author, will be discussed below.

Workers in the city of Moscow are studied in my *Liberal City*. The chief conclusions are several. First, 1905 made little or no difference in tsarist policy toward workers. Paternalism and sporadic intervention remained the basic approaches to labor conflicts; the city's *gradonachal'niki* invited both workers and industrialists to his office for persuasive chats. The tsarist administrators sometimes ordered corrections of sanitary violations, while even intervening occasionally in strikes on the side of workers. But such activities could not begin to satisfy workers, as they were far too erratic and incomplete. Moreover, tsarist paternalism still treated workers as children incapable of deciding matters for themselves. Finally, any positive intervention for workers was more than counterbalanced by repression, which included closing unions, forbidding their formation to begin with, and breaking up strikes. By the time of a municipal tram strike in 1913, workers identified police repression as the major factor in bringing on the stoppage. Government policy had only succeeded in inflaming the city's toilers (*Liberal City*, pp. 109-114).

Yet a good deal of enthusiasm had existed in Moscow for labor unions and a moderate path to the solution of labor troubles. Liberal evolution was clearly the choice of workers, for example among cooks. But, as the city's Bolsheviks acknowledged in October of 1906, "the government has closed the path of peaceful struggle to the proletariat." The Bolsheviks described this policy as "for the benefit of the capitalists" (p. 127). However, many local economic leaders felt otherwise.

Police practices toward labor may have been approved by most influential Muscovites in 1906, scared as they were by the violence which had just ended in the city. But prominent capitalists and other municipal leaders rejected repression after the Lena Goldfields massacre of April 1912, in which troops shot down dozens of peaceful strikers. Important Muscovites denounced the shooting as murder and a "catastrophe of state policy." Such practices only inflamed workers and drove them into the arms of the radicals. Liberals, whose outlook now spread within the city's elite, turned to support of strikes as an "extremely desirable political factor at the present moment." By 1914 the anti-government mood on this ground had grown so much in Moscow that even the Octobrist newspaper, *Golos*

Moskvy, strongly criticized central policy. In the same year the Moscow Society of Mill and Factory Owners recognized the existence of unions and approved negotiations with them, though this did not occur widely (pp. 125-127). In the wake of 1905 the city's liberals had already increased their attention to the lower classes' desires in the areas of education, housing, and municipal services; as Friedgut also makes clear, workers lived and formed attitudes in an environment much broader than just the factory floor, something future researchers might well bear in mind. It is indicative that Moscow workers struck less often and were less politically minded in stoppages than their Petersburg counterparts.

Even in the imperial capital, whose industrialists were so much more umbilically connected to the state and hence more conservative, the Lena massacre broke up employer unity versus workers. As Heather Hogan points out in "Labor and Management," owners could no longer agree on the practice of fining workers for staying away from the job on May Day, earlier a potent symbol of determination on both sides (p. 441). The growing strike movement was driving a wedge not only between workers and the state but between employers and the regime, à la 1905. In considering solutions, liberals moved further to the left, feeding the mood of opposition so clear at the Kiev municipal congress of 1913. Certainly these splits would have deepened and put the Old Regime in ever more danger, had not the war changed so much.

Almost nothing has been said thus far about the great majority of the empire's people, the peasants. To begin with, Teodor Shanin's works *The Awkward Class: Political Sociology of Peasantry in a Developing Society: Russia 1910-1925* (1972), *Russia as a 'Developing Society'* (1985), and *Russia, 1905-07: Revolution as a Moment of Truth* (1986) must be seen as essential contributions. Together they have helped to shape an agenda of Russian peasant studies not only for the period Shanin covers but before and after as well. His ideas on whether the peasantry was more a social, a cultural, or an economic entity cannot be discussed in detail here; suffice it to say that every other writer on the Russian countryside acknowledges a debt to Shanin.

Controversy over the peasants begins with the question of whether they were generally rising or declining economically by the last decades of tsarism. The classic work on the subject is Geroid Robinson's *Rural Russia under the Old Regime: A History of the Landlord-Peasant World and a Prologue to the Peasant Revolution of 1917*, originally published in 1932. He emphasized growing poverty among Russian peasants, to the point of characterizing them as generally desperate by the eve of the 1905 Revolution (pp. 99-116). This conclusion is supported by some recent work and challenged by other studies. In a useful volume of articles entitled *The World of the Russian Peasant: Post-emancipation Culture and Society* (1990 but comprised of earlier articles), edited by Ben Eklof and Stephen Frank, the Soviet scholar Boris Mironov (pp. 21 and 28) echoes Robinson. On the other hand, James Simms argues in articles published elsewhere that peasant life was improving, as measured by the number and size of bank accounts and consumption of items such as matches, kerosene, and metal goods.[34]

Another new collection of articles on the peasantry, *Peasant Economy, Culture, and Politics of European Russia, 1800-1921* (1991), edited by Esther Kingston-Mann and Timothy Mixter, a volume illustrated with stunning photographs, provides further information on the peasant economy. Kingston-Mann argues with considerable force for a revision of the view that the village commune and the strip system of cultivation were major impediments to agricultural success. Communes were much more innovative than has been recognized, while scattered strips were not necessarily a waste of space and time, especially when plowing was carried out jointly (p. 39).[35] Perhaps the most systematic inquiry into the general data on peasant well-being is in an article by Stephen Wheatcroft, also in this volume. He shows, if one can bear with all his charts, that peasants generally were doing better over time, but that in some areas and periods they were still quite badly off indeed (pp. 128-172).

A replacement for Robinson, regarding the economic issue and a host of other questions, is clearly needed. The old argument that peasants were growing steadily poorer and more desperate and that therefore they revolted in 1905 and 1917 seems sorely out of date, but as yet the scholars working on the subject have not offered a comprehensive alternate thesis.

A synthetic book on Russian peasants would have to go deeply into the extraordinarily complex issue of their attitudes and evolution after 1861, a subject about which we still know relatively little. General attitudes about society and the regime were intimately related, of course, to the issue of whether things were by and large improving or not.

Leaving that untidy problem, we may turn to several other interrelated areas which had a great impact on peasant thinking: urban influences in the village, education, and migration to work, above all by males. These trends contributed to important changes in the villages. The results, which included growing independence of women, increasing income to the villages, and falling influence of the elders, are discussed in the articles by Boris Mironov, Rose Glickman, and Barbara Engel in *World of the Russian Peasant*. Mironov suggests but does not develop the point that peasant culture into the late nineteenth century was largely an oral one, in which the elders were the guardians and dispensers of accumulated knowledge (p. 18); thus rising literacy and exposure to urban life undermined traditional ways and led to increasing tension in village existence. One would also like more from Mironov on the issue of younger peasants' expectations. As they learned to read and went to towns more often, they became exposed to different perspectives and hopes. They saw and wanted urban culture, from new haircuts through stylish clothing to higher income and books. In a word, their expectations rose. They could imagine greater development of the "I" as opposed to the "we" of the commune, to use Mironov's terminology (pp. 18-19). As time went on and the forces of change grew more powerful, he believes, the group which was more conscious of the "I"—in other words those more attuned to individualism—remained a minority, but one which was steadily gaining strength.

This description leads to one of the most fascinating and murky areas of peasant life on the eve of the revolution. To what extent were the country folk abandoning their traditional ways, especially their communal outlook? What did that degree of change mean for the growth of "bourgeois" individualism?

Would not that outlook in time have lent itself to support of liberalism rather than socialism?

In some ways, these questions seem to turn on the old debates about the meaning of the Stolypin land reforms, the laws of 1906-11 which attempted to facilitate the consolidation of separate strips and the end of the village commune. As we know, in 1917-18 the remaining peasants displayed bitter resentment against the 10% or so of their fellow villagers who had separated from the communes. The majority forced the separators back into the fold, dividing all the land on egalitarian principles in the process. But it would not be correct to conclude from those facts that peasant collectivism absolutely predominated over individualism in the prewar period. For one thing, the land redistribution of 1917 was the "black repartition," or division of *all* the land in the countryside, that the peasants had dreamed about for decades if not centuries. It probably seemed only fair at that juncture that even other peasants' holdings should be included, since peasant expansion too had occurred in a context of injustice. But that may well have been a one-time-only outlook. Second, no one disputes the notion that the traditional ways still predominated by 1917; the question has to do instead with the trend of affairs.

A great deal of insight into those traditional patterns can be found in Christine Worobec's *Peasant Russia: Family and Community in the Post-emancipation Period* (1991). We all knew that peasants were patriarchal, that their lives were conditioned by a subsistence economy, and that women suffered greatly from the combination of those two points. But Worobec takes us far beyond those bare facts to show just how, how much, and why Russian peasant existence depended on gender roles. "A rigid system of authority and command wherein individual activities were tightly controlled for the common good evolved to meet the challenges of a hostile environment," she remarks (p. 7). Essential to that system, or so peasants believed, were carefully delineated gender roles and expectations, in which women generally acquiesced because of male power and acculturation. But it is important to note, she argues, that women had some protection, status, and spheres of influence within this structure.

Because the commune and the whole structure of village life provided some social security, Worobec believes, the importance of collective activity remained high into the early twentieth century (see, for example, p. 121). One indication of this persistence is that "buying and selling for profit alone had not penetrated the peasant psyche" (p. 34). However, she is willing to admit the lure of urban life and its "trappings," which did produce "creeping individualism" (p. 33).

In examining the issue of collectivism versus individualism, two books on education and literacy among the peasants are of great interest. They are Ben Eklof's *Russian Peasant Schools: Officialdom, Village Culture, and Popular Pedagogy, 1861-1914* (1986), and Jeffrey Brooks' *When Russia Learned to Read: Literacy and Popular Literature, 1861-1917* (1985). The foci of these two works are quite different, which accounts for some of the divergences in their conclusions. Eklof looks largely at schooling and its impact on village culture. He finds that for many peasant families, "literacy was a means of protection against, rather than advancement in, a hostile world" (p. 476). Because education threatened traditional values and parental control, to the extent of encouraging literate offspring to leave the village completely, peasant parents were often leery of it. Moreover, schooling aimed to socialize peasant children in the ways of outsiders, something their elders resented bitterly and tried to combat. For these reasons even more than for economic considerations, parents often removed their children from school after they had achieved basic literacy, the amount needed for self-defense. In sum, peasants "were learning to read, but not yet learning from reading." They did not expand their world view or change their basic expectations, partly because their "reading habits were simply an extension of traditional oral readings, with a marked preference for entertainment, popular narrative, and hagiography" (p. 481).

It is exactly this last topic which is Brooks' chief concern in his superb book. By looking directly at what Russians read as literacy increased in the late nineteenth and early twentieth centuries, he is able to show that Eklof's conclusions on the impact of learning among the peasants are misleading. This point, however, does not detract from the importance of *Russian*

Peasant Schools in other regards, for instance in describing and analyzing the cultural conflicts produced by schooling. But Brooks is considerably more convincing on the implications of literacy. He too is concerned with the "tension and movement in Russian popular culture between modernity and tradition" (xviii). Yet he concludes that the lower classes indeed learned from reading. What they absorbed was perhaps of greater significance for the Old Regime than the Stolypin reforms, the State Duma, and all the other conscious efforts at change put together. Brooks finds in popular literature

> the appearance of more secular, rational, and cosmopolitan attitudes, an increased sense of individuality, and a growing belief in the ability of individuals to influence the course of their lives through their own initiative and talents. . . . The idea of freedom eventually came to resemble that expressed in Western European and American popular fiction. So did that of success, as the image of rural happiness gave way to dreams of wealth and fame in the city, and social mobility rather than prosperity within one's corporate or class group became an ideal (xviii-xix).

All of this undermined the old tradition of "passive obedience to authority" as well as "close identification" with tsar and Church. Moreover, the growth of individualism ran counter to the admonitions of both right and left. The right urged people to stay and be satisfied within the categories of their birth, while the radicals demanded submersion in a collective struggle of "toilers" or class. In their traditionally condescending way, *all* educated Russians were reluctant to "allow the market to serve cultural demands" (p. 296). If that happened, the common people would read altogether the wrong message, that of individualism, and would possibly go their own way.

Here, then, is one more instance in which tsarism was swimming against the tide of change, for it could do little to direct popular reading into the desired channels. But it is also important to see, though Brooks does not draw the lesson explicitly, that the great positive response from ordinary people to tales of individualism and social mobility has large implications for the issue of whither Russia by 1914. Not only did this trend augur badly for the Old Regime, it also raises serious questions about how deeply rooted socialist appeals were in 1917. This problem will be addressed in the conclusion.

Before that, it is important to note that all the detailed work on Russian peasants and workers before World War I indicates that they were rational, carefully calculating actors. They may have been ignorant, but they weighed the situation before them quite precisely. Pipes' *Russian Revolution*, so widely reviewed in the general press and therefore likely to be deeply influential, depicts peasants as crude and undifferentiated. In his view they responded only to raw power and were unable to distinguish between "good" and "bad" governments. "There were only strong and weak ones, and strong ones were always preferable to weak ones. (Similarly, serfs used to prefer cruel but efficient masters to kindly but ineffective ones)" (p. 118). Based not only on his own inclinations but also on the fact that he relied on a handful of comments from the elite as sources on peasant behavior, Pipes has drawn a picture of a primitive people ready for manipulation. The connection to his interpretation of the Bolsheviks as deceivers without real support is already clear. But all the recent specialized studies of the peasantry, or for that matter of the workers, offer a fundamentally different conclusion.

In fact, we now have investigations which show how the vast changes in the Russian countryside translated into coherent and rational peasant political behavior. In an article in *Peasant Economy*, Tim Mixter shows that migrant agricultural laborers around the turn of the century used their accumulated experience to advance their own cause. Cagey and sophisticated, peasants learned to use their own "turf" effectively to develop collective action and defense against greedy landowners. Thus the effects of capitalism, in this case not from the urban milieu but from large-scale farming for the market, impelled changes in peasant isolation and village-centered life (pp. 294-340).

Robert Edelman's *Proletarian Peasants: The Revolution of 1905 in Russia's Southwest* (1987) is valuable in this same regard and in describing who among peasants became politically active in 1905 and why.   Peasants in the southwest (the right-bank Ukraine) "demonstrated the ability to organize themselves coherently and make appropriate tactical choices for the attainment of realizable goals" (p. 34).   They most often based their actions on local conditions, especially regarding work and pay on the large estates.   Peasants had learned how to organize in their own communal assemblies, but were also heavily influenced from the outside by Social Democrats and Socialist Revolutionaries, Jews, returning soldiers, and those who had worked in towns.   Thus Edelman makes a major contribution to the debate between those who see peasant existence as primarily based on "timeless internal structures" and those who see it as primarily economic and thus subject to forces from the outside. Both internal and external factors are important in shaping political attitudes and actions.   Each case, he believes, must be examined on its own merits, with due attention to changes over time and the various pressures operating from without on the peasants.

In his *Russian Teachers and Peasant Revolution: The Politics of Education in 1905* (1989), Scott Seregny details the complex interaction between teachers and peasants in bringing on and shaping the course of 1905 in the countryside.   Teachers "immersed themselves in peasant politics through the peasant unions, political parties, and election campaigns to the State Duma" (p. 3).   At this crucial juncture the we-they mentality of peasants weakened, and they broke out of their traditional isolation and seeming indifference to national politics. Newspapers now passed from hand to hand until they were reduced to shreds, as peasants strained for news (p. 151).   They turned to literate villagers and to "outsiders," especially teachers, for help in interpreting events.   Peasants, moreover, became "increasingly receptive to the political demands of urban society" (p. 157).   Quickly moving beyond being mere interpreters, teachers came to serve as "cadres" in peasant-based organizations.   They found common ground with peasants on issues like "access to education, democratization of local government, civil freedoms, and constitutional reform." Teachers supported organized struggle as long as it was nonviolent; "the Peasant Union movement of 1905 represented the logical outcome of this process" (p. 211). Complementing the work of Edelman and Seregny and setting it into a broader context is an older article by Maureen Perrie on peasant activism in 1905-07, now reprinted in *World of the Russian Peasant*. Increasingly more literate, politicized, and outwardly oriented, peasants had changed profoundly under the impact of many developments by 1914.

Because of space considerations, a number of topics recently explored in the West must remain almost unmentioned here, despite the high quality of works on them. I can only list the work of William C. Fuller Jr. on tensions within the army; John Bushnell on when, how, and why soldiers rebelled in 1905; Neil Weissman on the great contradictions and problems in tsarist attempts at local reform; Manfred Hagen on public opinion, parties, and the press from 1906 to 1914; David Macey on the development of government policy toward the peasantry; Laura Engelstein on the roots and course of the 1905 Revolution in Moscow; and Abraham Ascher's general study of the 1905 upheaval, which indicts the Old Regime for callousness and widespread unnecessary violence. Undoubtedly I have missed other important works.

The remaining gaps in our knowledge of late Imperial Russia are substantial. They include a dearth of studies of workers in particular locales, so that the picture of exactly how they fared and how widely their conditions and attitudes varied could be made much clearer. This in turn would provide more insight into behavior during the Revolution and Civil War, when workers acted differently in different places. The connections between intelligentsia and lower classes might be better explored, utilizing among other sources the popular press, in the way Louise McReynolds and Daniel Brower have begun to do.[36] Individual cities could be explored in depth to get at the different sorts of tensions present before the war. Surely peasant attitudes might be elucidated more sharply, on the basis of zemstvo reports, popular literature, and detailed local studies.

To restress the point, there is a need for a summary of knowledge on the peasantry in general.

But we have learned a great amount from the western literature of recent years and are considerably further along in our knowledge of tsarist ideology, the gentry and its problems, workers and the quest for dignity, peasants' lives and aspirations, and the impact of urbanization from the city center to the village street.

What are the implications of the recent findings for our understanding of 1917 itself? Certainly the new works are virtually unanimous in depicting the failures of tsarism and its probable collapse in another revolution, even removing the war from the picture. Even as conservative a scholar as Pipes has had to admit, though with some hedging, that the tsarist regime was mired in hopeless problems and contradictions by 1914.[37]

More challenging, however, is the suggestion in some works, usually only barely developed if at all, that liberalism and not radicalism was the force of the future in Russia. Moderation's potential appeared in Moscow and other cities, in the reaction of industrialists to the Lena Goldfields shooting and the strike movement, in the desires of workers to have a legal trade union movement, in the economic forces weakening the village commune, in the growth of literacy, and in the appeal of popular reading matter stressing individualism. Perhaps the most important changes in the period 1861-1914 were the ones in everyday life, not in the laws and leading personages.

It is interesting to turn back in the light of recent work to the debate between Leopold Haimson and Arthur Mendel in 1965. Haimson maintained that two fissures were opening in Russia by 1914: one between state and society, one between educated people and the rest of the populace. Mendel countered that even Haimson's own evidence showed that educated Russians felt sympathy to striking workers and tried to draw nearer to them. He pointed to the great concern over the situation in the Kadet press, for example, and noted that political strikes were compatible with the liberals' goals. In this Mendel anticipated some of the recent studies on urban affairs. He also asked if it was necessary to refer to some "primary peasant radicalism" to explain workers' own militancy, and he suggested that conditions in the cities and urban growth were more likely causes.[38]   Hogan, Bonnell, McDaniel, and I must all agree. Mendel may also not have been far wrong in citing the effects of the war as undermining the chances for "constitutional liberalism," assuming some blowup was on the way in any event by 1914. Though Mendel now seems incorrect regarding what he saw as peasant conservatism and weak support by workers for the Bolsheviks, he was prescient on other matters. Haimson's article is rightly regarded as seminal, original, and a profound contribution to Russian studies. But Mendel's neglected reply turned out to be a keen diagnosis in its own right.

What then happened in 1917 to cause the triumph of radicalism? Some recent western examinations of workers in Petrograd, Moscow, and Saratov provide clues, though the authors shy away from the conclusions implicit in their own work. Every student of the Revolution knows that in the early stages tension clearly existed between liberals and the working class, as evidenced by the suspicion of the Petrograd Soviet toward the Provisional Government and the former's determination to monitor everything the latter did. But wasn't that outlook largely a result of tsarism and not capitalism? Just after February workers were by no means willing to take the lead themselves. What turned them in exactly that direction was the war: as it grew steadily more unpopular and exacerbated the country's economic difficulties, workers began to take over factories as a *defensive* maneuver. They were deeply afraid of losing their jobs and suspicious of the capitalists' motives in shutting the doors of their enterprises. For their part, the industrialists found it harder and harder to keep going in light of worsening problems in the supply of capital, fuel, and raw materials. It was the polarization which came out of this situation that pitted workers against liberals and soon against the Provisional Government as well, since they believed that only a radical solution could preserve their jobs.[39]

But if we could abstract the war from the situation after February 1917—that is, had the revolution broken out in peacetime—there appears to be no reason that Russian liberals could not have accomplished what the upper classes did from

Berlin to Washington and Tokyo: found a way to compromise with the workers sufficient to stave off a social revolt. Russian capitalists and their allies in the middle classes were probably no stupider on average than their counterparts in the West, and there was a clear trend toward compromise by 1914. In a peacetime situation the owners could have used their own experience, that of the West, and the strong differences within the workers' ranks to placate and divide them in the ways that happened elsewhere under capitalism.[40]

This is by no means to suggest that Lenin's party had little or no profound popular support by October 1917; after all, a socialist outcome was likely, given the antipathy of the lower classes toward the upper owing to problems with the war, the economy, and counter-revolution. And the Bolsheviks were the only branch of the socialist movement on the scene willing to work for its goals at that moment. The Mensheviks and Socialist Revolutionaries distrusted the liberals but said they had to rule now. These "moderate socialists" stood for socialism and hated capitalism, yet they said socialism had to wait until capitalism had reigned for an unspecified time and produced the contradictions Marx had predicted. They denounced the war as a butchery of the lower classes but said it had to go on. In light of this political dead end, the Bolsheviks might have won almost by default.

So the radical socialists did enjoy some serious legitimacy by the time of their seizure of power, and they could capitalize on the many unsolved tensions of tsarism by expropriating housing for the lower classes and instituting other social programs. But they lacked a profound mandate, judging by what we know of the history of prerevolutionary Russia, to maintain social levelling across the country. What they did have in their favor, and what they acted upon, as discussed best in the work of Sheila Fitzpatrick,[41] was some continuation of upward social mobility and the creation of individual opportunity. As we have seen, these trends were under way before 1914. When the Soviet state worked in these directions, it drew on historical roots and therefore enjoyed substantial legitimacy. When it moved instead to implement a radical vision of socialism, as during war communism or collectivization, it was floundering in the midst of severe crises rather than operating methodically.[42] After a spate of such activity, the new regime found that it had to return to the more durable and popular aspirations of individualism, however heretical that may sound to many students of the Soviet experiment. Close examinations of Stakhanovism, the New Class, or the "Big Deal" which won support from the elite by the 1940s[43] show that, like tsarism, early Soviet zeal for levelling could not defeat the pre-1914 tendencies.

Recent western literature has probed the last decades of Imperial Russia more deeply than ever before. The flood of literature on this period is not only large, it is generally distinguished by superior research and quality of presentation. Of course, much remains to be done. But we already have a great deal to think about from studies of the prerevolutionary years, including important clues to the nature of the 1917 Revolution, Bolshevik legitimacy, and the roots of Russian development even to the present, which since Mikhail Gorbachev's accession to power has returned in important ways to the patterns of the early twentieth century.

NOTES

1. Every work on *glasnost'* discusses new Soviet reflections on the past; see, for example, R. W. Davies, *Soviet History in the Gorbachev Revolution* (Bloomington: Indiana University Press, 1989).

2. Leopold Haimson, "The Problem of Social Identities in Early Twentieth Century Russia," *Slavic Review* 47, no. 1 (1988): 1.

3. For examples of recent literature reexamining Stalinism, see Hiroaki Kuromiya, *Stalin's Industrial Revolution: Politics and Workers, 1928-1932* (Cambridge, England: Cambridge University Press, 1988); Lewis H. Siegelbaum, *Stakhanovism and the Politics of Productivity in the USSR, 1935-1941* (New York: Cambridge University Press, 1988); Donald Filtzer (who in some ways affirms older viewpoints), *Soviet Workers and Stalinist Industrialization: The Formation of Modern Soviet Production Relations, 1928-1941* (Armonk, NY: M. E. Sharpe, 1986); Vladimir Andrle, *Workers in Stalin's Russia: Industrialization and Social Change in a Planned Economy* (New York: St. Martin's Press, 1988);

and Robert W. Thurston, "Fear and Belief in the USSR's 'Great Terror': Response to Arrest, 1935-1939," *Slavic Review* 45, no. 2 (1986).
    4. Leopold Haimson, "The Problem of Social Stability in Urban Russia, 1905-1917," *Slavic Review* 23, no. 4 (1964) and 24, no. 1 (1965). For an example of an older work focusing on parties, see Leonard Schapiro, *The Communist Party of Soviet Union*, 2d. ed. (New York: Random House, 1971).
    5. On earlier tsars' attitudes toward law see, for example, Allen McConnell, *Tsar Alexander I: Paternalistic Reformer* (New York: Thomas Crowell, 1970), and W. Bruce Lincoln, *Nicholas I: Emperor and Autocrat of All the Russias* (Bloomington: Indiana University Press, 1978).
    6. See the views of Konstantin P. Pobedonostsev, Procurator (head) of the Holy Synod, tutor to the last two tsars, and the primary spokesman for official conservatism toward the end of the Old Regime, in his *Reflections of a Russian Statesman* (Ann Arbor: University of Michigan Press, 1965), orginally published in 1896.
    7. Nicholas Riasanovsky, *Nicholas I and Official Nationality in Russia, 1825-1855* (Berkeley: University of California Press, 1969).
    8. William Sewell, Jr., *Work and Revolution in France: The Language of Labor from the Old Regime to 1848* (Cambridge, England: Cambridge University Press, 1980).
    9. Pobedonostsev, *Reflections*, 121.
    10. Robert W. Thurston, *Liberal City, Conservative State: Moscow and Russia's Urban Crisis, 1906-1914* (New York: Oxford University Press, 1987), 33-35.
    11. *The Politics of Rural Russia, 1905-1914*, ed. Leopold Haimson (Bloomington: Indiana University Press, 1979), 10.
    12. Thurston, *Liberal City*, 38, 43.
    13. Ibid., 43.
    14. Frank Lorimer, *The Population of the Soviet Union: History and Prospects* (Geneva: The League of Nations, 1946), 32.
    15. Richard Pipes, *The Russian Revolution* (New York: Alfred A. Knopf, 1990), 542.
    16. Lorimer, *Population*, 30.
    17. See Ben Eklof, *Russian Peasant Schools: Officialdom, Village Culture, and Popular Pedagogy, 1861-1914* (Berkeley: University of California Press, 1986); and Christine D. Worobec, *Peasant Russia: Family and Community in the Post-Emancipation Period* (Princeton: Princeton University Press, 1991).
    18. Worobec, *Peasant Russia*, 184.

19. I have made some of these points in *Liberal City*. On peasant farming, see any of the titles with the word "peasant" in the bibliography.

20. On contacts between workers and liberals in 1905, see, for example, Laura Engelstein, *Moscow, 1905: Working Class Organization and Political Conflict* (Stanford: Stanford University Press, 1982); and Abraham Ascher, *The Revolution of 1905: Russia in Disarray* (Stanford: Stanford University Press, 1988).

21. Manning, *Crisis of the Old Order*.

22. For example, Haimson, "Problem of Urban Social Stability."

23. *The City in Late Imperial Russia*, edited by Michael F. Hamm (Bloomington: Indiana University Press, 1986).

24. The articles are by (Riga) Anders Henriksson, (Moscow) Joseph Bradley, (Odessa) Frederick W. Skinner, (Kiev) Michael F. Hamm, and (St. Petersburg) James H. Bater.

25. Michael F. Hamm, "Khar'kov's Progressive Duma, 1910-1914: A Study in Russian Municipal Reform," *Slavic Review* 40, no. 1 (1981).

26. Thurston, *Liberal City*, 52, 73-74.

27. Ibid., 6.

28. James H. Bater, *St. Petersburg: Industrialization and Change* (Montreal: Queen's University-McGill University Press, 1976), 359.

29. William G. Rosenberg, *Liberals in the Russian Revolution: The Constitutional Democratic Party, 1917-1921* (Princeton: Princeton University Press, 1974), 30-31.

30. Haimson, "Problem of Urban Social Stability."

31. Thurston, *Liberal City*, 76-77.

32. Ibid., 186-87.

33. Ascher, *Revolution of 1905*, 21-26.

34. James Simms, "The Crisis in Russian Agriculture at the End of the Nineteenth Century: A Different View," *Slavic Review* 36, no. 3 (1977).

35. For a different interpretation, see Worobec, *Peasant Russia*, 26.

36. Daniel R. Brower, *The Russian City between Tradition and Modernity, 1850-1900* (Berkeley: University of California Press, 1990); his paper "Popular Morality and the Russian Penny Press"; and Louise McReynolds' paper "The 'Boulevard' Press and Urbanization in St. Petersburg," both delivered at the Western Slavic Association meeting, Tucson, March 1990.

37. Pipes, *Russian Revolution*, 190-92.

38. Arthur Mendel, "Peasant and Worker on the Eve of the First World War," *Slavic Review* 24, no. 1 (1965).
39. See, for example, Diane Koenker, *Moscow Workers and the 1917 Revolution* (Princeton: Princeton University Press, 1981); David Mandel, *The Petrograd Workers and the Fall of the Old Regime: From the February Revolution to the July Days, 1917* (London: Macmillan, 1983), and his *Petrograd Workers and the Soviet Seizure of Power (July 1917-June 1918)* (London: Macmillan, 1984); S. A. Smith, *Red Petrograd: Revolution in the Factories, 1917-1918* (Cambridge, England: Cambridge University Press, 1983); and Donald J. Raleigh, *Revolution on the Volga: 1917 in Saratov* (Ithaca: Cornell University Press, 1986). Raleigh emphasizes the role of social divisions in Saratov but remarks that it is "difficult to imagine the Bolsheviks' coming to power" if Russia had not been involved in the war (p. 325).
40. See the works by Friedgut, Bonnell, and Hogan in the bibliography.
41. Sheila Fitzpatrick, *Education and Social Mobility in the Soviet Union, 1921-1934* (Cambridge, England: Cambridge University Press, 1979); and her *The Russian Revolution, 1917-1932* (New York: Oxford University Press, 1982).
42. On collectivization as a response to crisis see, for example, Lynn Viola "The Campaign to Eliminate the Kulak as a Class, Winter 1929-1930: A Reevaluation of the Legislation," *Slavic Review* 45, no. 3 (1986).
43. See, respectively, Siegelbaum, *Stakhanovism*; Milovan Djilas, *The New Class, An Analysis of the Communist System* (London: Allen and Unwin, 1966); and Vera S. Dunham, *In Stalin's Time: Middleclass Values in Soviet Fiction* (Cambridge, England: Cambridge University Press, 1976).

BIBLIOGRAPHY OF WORKS CITED ON THE PREREVOLUTIONARY PERIOD

Ascher, Abraham. *The Revolution of 1905: Russia in Disarray.* Stanford: Stanford University Press, 1988.
Bater, James H. *St. Petersburg: Industrialization and Change.* Montreal: Queen's University-McGill University Press, 1976.

Becker, Seymour. *Nobility and Privilege in Late Imperial Russia.* DeKalb, IL: Northern Illinois University Press, 1985.

Bonnell, Victoria. *Roots of Rebellion: Workers, Politics, and Organizations in St. Petersburg and Moscow, 1900-1914.* Berkeley: University of California Press, 1983.

———, editor. *The Russian Worker: Life and Labor Under the Tsarist Regime.* Berkeley: University of California Press, 1983.

Bradley, Joseph. *Muzhik and Muscovite: Urbanization in Late Imperial Russia.* Berkeley: University of California Press, 1985.

Brooks, Jeffrey. *When Russia Learned to Read: Literacy and Popular Literature, 1861-1917.* Princeton, Princeton University Press, 1985.

Brower, Daniel R. *The Russian City between Tradition and Modernity, 1850-1900.* Berkeley: University of California Press, 1990.

Bushnell, John. *Mutiny amid Repression: Russian Soldiers in the Revolution of 1905-1906.* Bloomington: Indiana University Press, 1985.

Clowes, Edith W., Samuel D. Kassow, and James L. West, eds. *Between Tsar and People: Educated Society and the Quest for Public Identity in Late Imperial Russia.* Princeton: Princeton University Press, 1991.

Edelman, Robert. *Proletarian Peasants: The Revolution of 1905 in Russia's Southwest.* Ithaca, NY: Cornell University Press, 1987.

Eklof, Ben. *Russian Peasant Schools: Officialdom, Village Culture, and Popular Pedagogy, 1861-1914.* Berkeley: University of California Press, 1986.

———, and Stephen P. Frank, eds. *The World of the Russian Peasant: Post-Emancipation Culture and Society.* Boston: Unwin Hyman, 1990.

Engelstein, Laura. *Moscow, 1905: Working Class Organization and Political Conflict.* Stanford: Stanford University Press, 1982.

Friedgut, Theodore H. *Iuzovka and Revolution.* Vol. 1: *Life and Work in Russia's Donbass, 1869-1924.* Princeton: Princeton University Press, 1989.

Fuller, William C., Jr. *Civil-Military Conflict in Imperial Russia, 1881-1914.* Princeton: Princeton University Press, 1985.

Hagen, Manfred. *Die Entfaltung Politischer Oeffentlichkeit in Russland 1906-1914.* Wiesbaden: Franz Steiner, 1982.

Haimson, Leopold. "The Problem of Social Identities in Early Twentieth Century Russia," *Slavic Review* 47, no. 1 (1988).

——. "The Problem of Social Stability in Urban Russia, 1905-1917," *Slavic Review* 23, no. 4 (1964) and 24, no. 1 (1965).

——, editor. *The Politics of Rural Russia, 1905-1914.* Bloomington: Indiana University Press, 1979.

Hamm, Michael, "Khar'kov's Progressive Duma, 1910-1914: A Study in Russian Municipal Reform," *Slavic Review* 36, no. 3 (1977).

——, ed. *The City in Late Imperial Russia.* Bloomington: Indiana University Press, 1986.

Hogan, Heather J. "Labor and Management in Conflict: The St. Petersburg Metal-Working Industry, 1900-1914," Ph.D. dissertation, The University of Michigan, 1981.

Hosking, Geoffrey A. *The Russian Constitutional Experiment: Government and Duma, 1907-1914.* Cambridge, England: Cambridge University Press, 1973.

Judge, Edward H. *Plehve: Repression and Reform in Imperial Russia, 1902-1904.* Syracuse: Syracuse University Press, 1983.

Kingston-Mann, Esther, and Timothy Mixter, eds. *Peasant Economy, Culture, and Politics of European Russia, 1800-1921.* Princeton: Princeton University Press, 1991.

Macey, David A. J. *Government and Peasant in Russia, 1861-1906: The Prehistory of the Stolypin Reforms.* DeKalb, IL: Northern Illinois University Press, 1987.

Manning, Roberta T. *The Crisis of the Old Order in Russia: Gentry and Government.* Princeton: Princeton University Press, 1982.

McDaniel, Tim. *Autocracy, Capitalism, and Revolution in Russia.* Berkeley: University of California Press, 1988.

Mendel, Arthur. "Peasant and Worker on the Eve of the First World War," *Slavic Review*, 24, no. 1 (1965).

Pipes, Richard. *The Russian Revolution.* New York: Alfred A. Knopf, 1990.

Robinson, Geroid T. *Rural Russia under the Old Regime: A History of the Landlord-Peasant World and a Prologue to the Peasant Revolution of 1917.* Berkeley: University of California Press, 1969. Originally published in 1932.

Rogger, Hans. *Russia in the Age of Modernisation and Revolution, 1881-1917.* New York: Longman, 1983.

Rosenberg, William G. *Liberals in the Russian Revolution: The Constitutional Democratic Party, 1917-1921.* Princeton: Princeton University Press, 1974.

Seregny, Scott J. *Russian Teachers and Peasant Revolution: The Politics of Education in 1905.* Bloomington: Indiana University Press, 1989.

Shanin, Teodor. *The Awkward Class: Political Sociology of Peasantry in a Developing Society: Russia 1910-1925.* New York: Oxford University Press, 1972.

————. *The Roots of Otherness: Russia's Turn of the Century.* Vol. 1: *Russia as a 'Developing Society'.* Vol. 2: *Russia 1905-07: Revolution as a Moment of Truth.* New Haven: Yale University Press, 1985.

Simms, James. "The Crisis in Russian Agriculture at the End of the Nineteenth Century: A Different View," *Slavic Review* 36, no. 3 (1977).

Thurston, Robert W. *Liberal City, Conservative State: Moscow and Russia's Urban Crisis, 1906-1914.* New York: Oxford University Press, 1987.

Verner, Andrew M. *The Crisis of Russian Autocracy: Nicholas II and the 1905 Revolution.* Princeton: Princeton University Press, 1990.

Wcislo, Francis William. *Reforming Rural Russia: State, Local Society, and National Politics, 1855-1914.* Princeton: Princeton University Press, 1990.

Weissman, Neil. *Reform in Tsarist Russia: The State Bureaucracy and Local Government, 1900-1914.* New Brunswick: Rutgers University Press, 1981).

Worobec, Christine D. *Peasant Russia: Family and Community in the Post-emancipation Period.* Princeton: Princeton University Press, 1991.

RETHINKING THE ORIGINS OF
THE RASPUTIN LEGEND

Mark Kulikowski

Rasputin continues to fascinate us. Long the staple of undergraduate survey courses and innumerable publications and presentations, he remains one of the most highly recognizable figures of modern Russian history.[1] His continued popularity rests largely on the Rasputin legend, which portrays him as a mystic, libertine, evil genius, spy, political agent, and prime author of the fall of the Romanov dynasty. Given this mixture, it is clear the Rasputin legend will interest us for years to come.

While the Rasputin legend has captured the popular and scholarly imagination, various questions about it remain unanswered. The first concerns credibility. Like many legends, Rasputin's contains elements that border on the fantastic—his mystical powers, unlimited political influence, and near invincibility at the hands of his assassins. While perhaps acceptable when ascribed to historical figures of antiquity, these elements should strike a jarring note for modern audiences. Yet it is clear they do not. Undoubtedly, the constant repetition of the legend has led audiences simply to accept it as true. Yet simple repetition does not make for historical truth. In order to deal with the issue of credibility we must pose a second question. When and where did the legend as we now know it first appear? By determining its origins we can better understand how and why the legend gained the acceptance it now enjoys. The search for the origins of the Rasputin legend will be the focus of this article.

Surprisingly, given the importance afforded him by scholarly and popular audiences alike, relatively few written sources about Rasputin were published during his lifetime.

Censorship, imperial displeasure, and intermittent press interest limited what the Russian public knew about him.[2] Despite these strictures, however, several key accounts of the period helped lay the foundation for the legend, which eventually came into bloom after the fall of the monarchy in 1917.

Although Rasputin had lived sporadically in St. Petersburg since the end of 1905, it was not until 1912 that he became the subject of a major press attack. The attack was launched by Mikhail A. Novoselov, editor-publisher of the "Religious-Philosophical Library" and the author of *Grigorii Rasputin i misticheskoe rasputstvo*.[3] Responding to rumors that Rasputin was influential in Orthodox Church affairs and was seeking ordination, Novoselov sought to expose Rasputin's true character.[4] In his preface he accused the Orthodox Church and the Holy Synod of cowardice for allowing Rasputin to do "dark things" under the guise of sanctity. Novoselov went on to call Rasputin a charlatan, a heretic, a corrupter, and a lewd *khlyst*.[5] Relying on correspondence (dated 1909-1911) from priests of the Tobolsk diocese in Siberia, where Rasputin lived, the author stated that in his early years Rasputin had been a drunkard, ruffian and thief.[6] During his subsequent wanderings in Siberia in search of religious truth, Novoselov claimed, Rasputin attracted a number of female admirers with whom he had intimate relations.[7] The author, citing newspaper accounts as well as the letters, called Rasputin an "erotomaniac" who beat his women followers in order to test their faith.[8] Lastly, he characterized Rasputin's activities as "lechery based on mysticism, or mysticism based on lechery."[9] The appearance of this pamphlet caused quite a sensation. Because the author accused the Church of wrongdoing, the work was withdrawn from sale and copies were confiscated by the police.[10]

Of the allegations made against Rasputin, the most significant was the one linking him with the *khlysty*. This sect, like many others, attracted adherents in Siberia where large distances and a relatively small population meant looser control by religious authorities. However, unlike other groups tolerated by the Church, the *khlysty* were banned. Their actions were considered to be the worst sort of evil, and the Church took steps to investigate any claims of *khlyst* activity. In general, the *khlysty* believed that in order to fully understand and appreciate God's forgiveness, one had to know the power of sin. The transgression most commonly associated with them was participation in sexual orgies which usually took place outdoors around a large bonfire. The *khlysty* allegedly danced naked around the fire, sometimes beating one another to enhance their frenzy. When a signal was given, they fell to the ground and had intercourse with whoever was nearby. This random intercourse led to charges of incest as well as general licentiousness. As a result of such activities, the *khlysty* were among the most abhorred sects in Russia.[11]

By calling Rasputin a *khlyst* Novoselov clearly sought to discredit him in the eyes of the Church. Church officials, alarmed at the allegation, decided to investigate. Aleksei, Bishop of Tobolsk, sent a clergyman named Gruziia to Rasputin's village of Pokrovskoe to investigate the charges. Gruziia reported that he had visited Rasputin in his home, where he talked to him about his beliefs. He also talked to others who knew Rasputin. Gruziia concluded that there was insufficient evidence to prove any connection with the *khlysty*. He considered Rasputin to be Orthodox, very bright, "possessing the truth of Christ," and able to give good advice. He added that Rasputin had donated 5,000 rubles for the construction of a new church.[12] Although cleared by the Church, Rasputin would nonetheless remain tainted with the *khlyst* label throughout his life. This charge lived on in rumors about him and would reappear in print in 1917.

The summer of 1914 again found Rasputin in the news. While visiting his home in Pokrovskoe in June, Rasputin was badly wounded in an attempted assassination. The would-be assassin (Khionia Guseva), who saw Rasputin as the Antichrist, approached him on the street and stabbed him in the abdomen with a knife. Despite the severity of his wound, Rasputin managed to escape.[13]

The news of the attempted assassination quickly filled the newspapers of St. Petersburg and Moscow. The large number of newspapers devoting attention to the event indicates the widespread interest in the case. In the five-day period from July

1 to July 5, fifteen newspapers in St. Petersburg and six Muscovite newspapers devoted ninety three items to the attack.[14] While many of the news items were repetitious accounts, a number of newspapers used the opportunity to comment on Rasputin. These comments are significant in that they indicate the introduction of new elements into the Rasputin legend. The Moscow newspaper *Utro Rossii*, for example, characterized him as "a political villain and vile libertine."[15] *Den'*, a St. Petersburg paper, citing a foreign account, stated, "Rasputin's opinion plays a prominent role in the internal life of Russia."[16] *Russkoe slovo* commented, "Rasputin's life...has a truly secret and enigmatic character," and that he, "within a brief period of time gained enormous influence in the aristocratic circles of St. Petersburg society.[17] *Moskovskii listok* reported that "[Count] Witte asserted, in a serious conversation with representatives of foreign newspapers, that Rasputin had definite influence in some questions of foreign politics."[18]   Finally, *Peterburgskii kur'er* reported that there are "rumors that Rasputin...is not normal in sexual relations."[19]

As we have seen, press allegations of political influence, secrecy, and ties to important circles added to the general idea of Rasputin as a libertine, drunk, and thief. While all this makes for interesting reading, it proves little. We must bear in mind that what newspapers were reporting was in part based on rumor. Given the political realities of the times, newspapers were not totally free to report what they wanted or to gain the information they desired. As such, while newspapers sought to be objective, their reporting often helped spread rumors about him and, in doing so, added to his growing legend.

Slightly over a year after the attempt on his life, Rasputin was the subject of a series of articles in the newspaper *Birzhevye vedomosti*. These articles, published for four consecutive days in August 1915, were entitled "Zhitie startsa Rasputina." They began by stating that "Rasputin plays a great role in the fate of the nation."[20]   There followed a long biographical sketch, referring to him as a horsethief, drunkard, and *khlyst*, and describing his sexual adventures in a women's monastery and in the baths. The articles went on to describe his relationship with various clergy. Finally, the accounts claimed that his secretaries demanded two hundred to three hundred rubles from his "clients" for an audience with Rasputin. Overall, they hinted at Rasputin's influence with important figures in society. These articles were reprinted by other newspapers, including several in Siberia.[21]

The last major news coverage of Rasputin before the fall of the monarchy dealt with his assassination in December 1916. The press quickly picked up the story of his death and the discovery of his corpse. Brief biographical sketches appeared, giving the standard view of Rasputin as a drunk and libertine, and hinting at his political influence.[22] Accounts of earlier assassination attempts were also presented. These news items were reprinted by a number of newspapers. In general, however, news items about Rasputin's career and death were short-lived. None appeared in the press after late January. The conduct of the war and the internal problems in Russia quickly regained the public's attention. Not until after the February Revolution did Rasputin once again come into the limelight.

The February Revolution brought changes that directly affected the public's view of Rasputin. As a figure closely associated with the fallen monarchy, he was the subject of great public interest. With censorship at an end, this interest manifested itself in an outpouring of newspaper articles, pamphlets, broadsides, books, and motion pictures. This barrage of information not only satisfied the immediate public interest in Rasputin, but also played a major role in the development of the legend. Much of the legend as we know it had its origin in these works.

The majority of the newspaper accounts about Rasputin appeared in March and April 1917. They showed a great deal of interest in the details of Rasputin's assassination and in the fate of his assassins. Likewise, considerable attention was drawn to Rasputin's burial and the later disinterment and cremation of his body. As in earlier cases, standard accounts in major newspapers were reprinted verbatim in other papers. Without censorship, the newspapers were able to examine various aspects of Rasputin's life not previously permitted and to publish their findings. In most instances, the findings published were of only minor interest: photographs of Rasputin, examples of his handwriting, and so on. No matter how slight the information, it was quickly consumed by the eager press and reading public. Further claims about Rasputin also appeared in the press during this period. Some dealt with familiar themes. For example, *Petrogradskii listok* spoke of his "sexual hypnotism,"[23] and the "influence of the evil genius of our country."[24] *Petrogradskaia gazeta* characterized him as a "harmful, depraved person with lower instincts."[25]

Some accounts went further. *Petrogradskaia Gazeta* reported that Rasputin was involved with the "Black Cabinet," a group set up by the Ministry of Internal Affairs to conduct surveillance on members of the Government and the Court. The article claimed that "sometimes Grisha [Rasputin] personally had correspondence seized on his instructions, as material for entertaining study."[26] The paper went on to report that Anna Vyrubova, a friend and former lady-in-waiting to Empress Alexandra, "openly went to the baths with Rasputin and washed him."[27] *Petrogradskii listok* claimed that "dark powers" helped Rasputin gain his position at court and used him to influence Nicholas and Alexandra.[28] Just who these "dark powers" were was not disclosed, but the term was usually associated with German agents, Jews, or Russian businessmen. This sort of unsubstantiated, sensational reporting crept into newspaper accounts of the period.

Before long, political events in Russia began to push Rasputin off the pages of the daily press, and by the end of April 1917 only a few items on him were printed. Occasional cartoons, photographs, and brief portraits of Rasputin continued to appear until the summer of 1917, but it was clear by then that press interest in him had waned. While short-lived, however, the sensational newspaper accounts had added two important elements to press treatment of Rasputin. First, they seemed to signal that sensational stories about him were both acceptable and popular. Second, the stories acted as a starting point for a range of publications seeking to capitalize on Rasputin.

Chief among these sensational publications were the pamphlets of 1917. Their appearance not only indicated a continuing popular interest in Rasputin, but also marked the beginning of a new phase in the development of the legend. From the fall of the monarchy to the end of December 1917, over fifty pamphlets devoted their attention to Rasputin.[29] The majority of them were aimed at the broad popular audience, offering their readers a mixture of scandal, adventure, sensationalism, and a look "behind the scenes." The first pamphlets appeared shortly after the fall of the monarchy, with the remainder coming out at irregular intervals throughout the rest of the year.[30] Roughly half of them were published anonymously or under a pseudonym. While publishing information is incomplete, we do know that some of the pamphlets were published in large numbers. For example, A. Mel'gunov's *Samoderzhavye palachi* was published in an edition of 5,000 copies,[31] while V. Sokolov's *Temnyia sily rossiiskoi imperii* and I. Kovyl'-Bobyl's *Tsaritsa i Rasputin* were each published in editions of 50,000.[32] The sensational was stressed, with pamphlets bearing titles like *Sviatoi chert, Rasputin Grishka, zloi genii doma Romanovykh, Za kulisami russkogo dvora, Tainy tsarskogo dvora i Grishka Rasputin*, and *Krovavyi rezhim doma Romanovykh*.[33] Most of the pamphlets drew at least some of their information from items that had appeared in the press. While a small number simply reproduced press accounts verbatim, the majority used the newspaper stories as a starting point for their presentations.

Public interest in Rasputin found full expression in the pamphlets. Every phase of his life came under scrutiny. In order to supply the missing details, many writers either used their imaginations, repeated current rumors, or borrowed from one another. As a result, the allegations made about Rasputin grew in number and gained acceptance by the public. The pamphlets usually began with the standard characterization of Rasputin as the power behind the throne, the evil genius, or the real ruler of Russia.[34] This was followed by the depiction of Rasputin as a horsethief, libertine, drunkard and *khlyst*. Most of the pamphlets then made additional comments about his character. Some saw him as a malevolent figure. One stated, "Rasputin lived with a number of women...[who] withered away and died."[35] Another, commenting on his personal life, claimed that "Rasputin attracted sexual psychopaths of all ages and social positions, from streetwalkers to countesses and the Empress."[36]

A number of pamphlets dealt with an actual incident which took place at the Yar restaurant in 1915: Rasputin, having dinner with friends, became drunk and exposed himself to the women members of a gypsy group performing at the restaurant.[37] Lastly, several pamphlets presented accounts of Rasputin's life which were considered pornographic at the time.[38] These included works which contained suggestive illustrations and impolite language. Typical of the sentiments expressed in these publications is the following: "Rasputin's mother was a dog—so the majority of Russian citizens believed. Everyone, except the Tsar's family…persistently called Rasputin 'a son of a bitch'."[39]

Rasputin's activities in governmental affairs elicited a large number of comments. In this regard, his connection with the "dark powers" was noted in many of the pamphlets. A typical allegation was that the "dark powers" placed Rasputin at Court to advise the Tsar and that they dictated Rasputin's opinions on various matters.[40] Carrying this theme further, several claimed he was working for the Germans. "[Rasputin was] undoubtedly a German henchman," wrote one.[41] His role in the appointment and dismissal of various officials and his influence in Church affairs also drew notice. One pamphlet claimed that, when B.V. Stürmer wanted an appointment, "He kissed Rasputin's boot and was made a minister."[42] Another stated, "Rasputin played no small role in the dismissal of Count Kokovtsev." The pamphlet went on to assert that Kokovstev was dismissed because he had had Rasputin sent back home to Pokrovskoe in 1913.[43] Lastly, it was alleged that Rasputin, working through V.K. Sabler, the Over Procurator of the Holy Synod, had influence in Church affairs.[44]

The greatest number of allegations dealt with Rasputin's relationship with Nicholas, Alexandra, and their children. Nicholas was often portrayed as not having a will of his own and as a "pitiful and cruel pawn."[45] Empress Alexandra was frequently depicted as a wily German agent. "[Alexandra] hated all things Russian and in 1916 was prepared to help her relative Wilhelm II," a pamphlet claimed.[46] Life at court likewise came under attack. One charge was that "court life at this time [1905] was...magnificent and dissolute. Every night there occurred without failure a drunken orgy, actively participated in by the august monarch."[47]

While it was commonly acknowledged that Rasputin's presence at Court was connected with the life and health of the heir,[48] some pamphlets asserted that Rasputin and others were responsible for Alexis' illness. "Rasputin, Vyrubova, and Badmaev," several claimed, "systematically poisoned Alexis."[49] This was supposedly done to enhance Rasputin's reputation as a healer. When Alexis became ill from the poison, it would no longer be administered. Just before the boy began to recover naturally, Rasputin would be called, and then he would put on a demonstration of his healing powers. With Alexis already getting better, Rasputin could claim a miraculous cure had taken place. Rasputin's actions were extended to the other Romanov children as well. It was alleged that "[Rasputin] openly...went to their bedrooms to 'bless them' just before bedtime and to do what he wanted."[50]

Other charges about him were made as well. Many of the pamphlets stated that Rasputin had sexual relations with Empress Alexandra. One claimed that Rasputin boasted, "When I am at the Tsar's [place] I spend the whole day in the bedroom with the Empress."[51] One pamphlet even went so far to suggest Rasputin may have been Alexis' real father.[52]

Finally, most of the pamphlets directed a great deal of attention to Rasputin's burial. They presented a picture of the grieving Nicholas, Alexandra, and Vyrubova, and the details of the funeral arrangements. These imaginary presentations were drawn directly from the newspapers.[53]

A further indication of Rasputin's notoriety can be seen in the broadsides of the period. At least eight dealing with him appeared in 1917.[54] Each broadside had a distinct title and carried an extensive printed account of Rasputin's life and activities. They repeated many of the same charges that appeared in the pamphlets. Although fewer in number, the broadsides were published throughout European Russia. They acted as another source of popular information about Rasputin.

Book length works on Rasputin also appeared in 1917. Chief among these was a book by Iliodor entitled *Tainy doma Romanovykh*,[55] which, drawing on an earlier account attributed to Iliodor, *Sviatoi chert*,[56] was one of the longer to deal with Rasputin. Like the pamphlets, it presented the standard view of Rasputin; what made it significant was its author. Iliodor, a member of the clergy, had been Rasputin's friend for a number of years. He had later ended his friendship with Rasputin and had become one of his most vociferous opponents. The book recorded a number of unsubstantiated conversations with Rasputin. These conversations, which purported to show that Nicholas and Alexandra thought that Rasputin was Christ and treated him as such, were widely reprinted. The author's friendship with Rasputin gave the book a measure of authenticity and added further substance to the legend. A lengthy work in a similar vein by Kadmin, and a political novel focussing on Rasputin, also were published.[57]

Finally, motion pictures probably aided as well in the creation of the Rasputin legend. After the fall of the monarchy, film makers rushed to produce motion pictures on the Old Regime. Sensational films about Rasputin were planned or produced. While we do not have a great deal of information about the films,[58] which had titles like *Zhizn' i smert' Grishki Rasputina*, *Tainstvennoe ubiistvo v Petrograde*, and *Sviatoi chort, ili Rasputin v adu*, it is clear they sought broad popular appeal. In addition to motion pictures, Rasputin was the subject of at least one public lecture, and his image appeared on playing cards and postcards of the period.[59]

The degree to which the Russian public believed all this information is unknown. Clearly, all these media stressed the same themes over and over. Furthermore, the material was widely dispersed geographically. Pamphlets were published in Petrograd, Moscow, Arkhangel'sk, Feodosiia, Kazan', and Kiev, while broadsides appeared in Moscow, Elabuga, Khar'kov, Kiev, and Rostov na Donu. A librarian of the period suggested that these works were widely known. Complaining about the lack of good books, she claimed that there were "leaflets in 100,000 factories (sic) about Grisha Rasputin."[60] In his memoirs, Viktor

Shklovsky also supported this view. He recalled that, "Later, the revolutionary pamphlets—all those 'Adventures of Griskha'—and the success of this type of literature proved to me that, for large numbers of the common people, Rasputin had become a peculiar sort of folk hero—something like Vanka the Steward."[61] All this suggests that by the end of 1917 the Rasputin legend was widely known and largely in place.

Just what was the legend of 1917? Briefly summarized, it is as follows: Grigorii Rasputin was a Siberian peasant who in his early years drank heavily, stole horses, and generally led a dissolute life. For roughly a decade he wandered around Siberia and European Russia in search of religious truth. During this period he became a *khlyst*, but also gained a reputation as a man of God. Becoming known in Church and aristocratic circles, he came to St. Petersburg in 1905 and met Nicholas and Alexandra. As he gained influence through his ability to help their son Alexis with his healing powers, he tried to reconcile an increasingly libertine lifestyle with genuine religious sentiment. Owing to his own schemes and the weakness of Nicholas and Alexandra, he became a trusted advisor. Although seriously wounded in 1914, he recovered and with Alexandra took virtual control of the government in 1915. Through his actions, guided in part by the "dark powers," he oversaw the appointment and dismissal of ministers and in general caused great harm. His influence continued until December of 1916, when he was assassinated by members of the nobility and the Duma. This legend, with some minor changes, remains intact to the present day.

In evaluating the reasons for the legend's longevity, it is necessary to consider a number of points. Quite clearly, as this article has demonstrated, much of the Rasputin legend as we know it had its origin in the popular publications of 1917. However, two earlier sources undoubtedly contributed. The first was the rumor mill resulting from the general secrecy surrounding the court of Nicholas II and Rasputin's role in it. Without some knowledge of Alexis' illness and Rasputin's role in healing him, the Russian public was at a loss to explain how a person of such dubious character remained in favor at court.

This situation provided a fertile field for rumors which grew considerably as time went on, and became the source for subsequent press coverage. The second source was Rasputin himself. Living among the rich and powerful, he enjoyed boasting, not always truthfully, about his activities. His boasts further fueled the rumor mill and contributed to the atmosphere which precipitated his assassination. These sources helped create the legend. Given the enormous political upheaval Russia underwent starting in 1917, the legend provided a simple explanation for much of what had occurred earlier. With the passage of time and the pressure of current events the legend was not challenged and became, through frequent retellings, fixed in people's minds. Even the most incredible elements added to the legend's longevity. They made the story interesting and linked the listener, however tenuously, to a world of intrigue, plots, secrecy, mysticism and murder. Given these ingredients, the life expectancy of the legend was unlimited.

The world of scholarship has no room for fantasy. And yet, despite its largely sensational, unsubstantiated, and rumor-filled origins, the legend lives on in contemporary scholarship. A major reason for this has been the failure of scholars to question the legend's roots. Virtually all serious research on Rasputin since 1917 has considered the legend true, and has sought to fit the facts to it.[62] This has led, at best, to very minor adjustments and to the idea that there is nothing new to say, which unfortunately means that writing on Rasputin has been left largely to popular authors who simply retell the old story. Still unanswered are some fundamental questions not only about Rasputin, but about our understanding of the end of the monarchy in Russia. Given the recent call to rethink major questions of Russian history, perhaps we can no longer afford to accept Rasputin as he appears to be.

NOTES

I would like to thank the editors of this volume, Professor James Y. Simms and Professor Edward Judge, for their advice and patience.

My sincere thanks to Professors Alton S. Donnelly, Thadd Hall, Sidney Harcave, Michael Neufeld, and Edwin Rutkowski. I would also like to warmly acknowledge the support of the Office of International Programs, State University of New York, the National Endowment for the Humanities, the staffs of the Hoover Institution on War, Revolution and Peace, the Library of Congress, Slavic Library, University of Illinois, Urbana-Champaign, Slavonic Division, New York Public Library, Lenin Library, State Public Historical Library, Library of the Academy of Sciences of the USSR, the Central State Historical Archive (Leningrad) and the Central State Archive of the October Revolution (Moscow). Any and all errors are my responsibility.

1. Interest in Rasputin and his contemporaries remains high. Recent books in English range from the substantial, like Joseph Fuhrmann's *Rasputin: A Life* (New York: Praeger, 1990) and Christopher Dobson's *Prince Felix Yusupov: The Man Who Murdered Rasputin* (London: Harrap, 1989) to superficial treatments like Douglas Myles' *Rasputin: Satyr, Saint or Satan?* (New York: McGraw-Hill, 1990) and Jane Oakley's *Rasputin: Rascal Master* (New York: St. Martin's, 1989). Soviet interest is likewise high, but has been largely limited to reprinting primary sources. Recent newspaper and journal articles include R.F. Miller, "Sviatoi chort," *Trud*, 22 October 1989, 4; N.A. Teffi, "Rasputin," *Moskovskii komsomolets*, 7 January 1990, 3; 14 January 1990, 3; 21 January 1990, 3; 28 January 1990, 3; 4 February 1990, 3; A. Krylov, "Pravda o mal'enkom printse," *Moskovskii komsomolets*, 18 April 1990, 4; F.F. Iusupov, "Konets Rasputina," *Detektiv i politika*, 1989, no. 3: 233-321; S.P. Mel'gunov, "Poslednii izbrannik," *Nauka i religiia*, 1989, no. 5: 24-25; M. Rodzianko, "Krushenie imperii," *Slovo: V mire knig*, 1990, no. 2: 66-69; A. Simanovich, "Rasskazyvaet sekretar' Rasputina," *Slovo: V mire knig*, 1989, no. 5: 55-62; no. 6: 76-79; no. 9: 69-70; no. 10: 78-82; 1990, no. 2: 79-81, no. 4: 81-84; no. 8: 70-82; A Vyrubova, "Voennye gody v Tsarskom Sele," *Slovo: V mire knig*, 1989, no. 9: 71-75; 1990, no. 1: 45-48. Book length reprints also have recently appeared. They include N.N. Evreinov, *Taina Rasputina* (Moscow: Moskovskaia pravda, 1990; Kiev: Kievkniga, 1990; and Georgian language edition, Tbilisi: Merani, 1990); Maurice Paleologue, *Rasputin: Vospominaniia* (Moscow: SP "Interkinotsentr," 1990); F.F. Iusupov, *Konets Rasputina* (Moscow: IPO Profizdat. Agenstvo "Komp'iuterPress," 1990) and his *Gibel' Rasputina: Vospominaniia* (Moscow: n.p., 1990); A. Simanovich, *Rasputin i evrei*

(Moscow: Sovetskii pisatel', n.d.); N.A. Teffi, *Rasputin* (Moscow: VIKMA, 1990); and A. Vyrubova, *Rasputin* (Moscow: Panorama, 1990). Two volumes of source material have also been published. They are A. Chekhovskoi, ed., *Rasputin: Vospominaniia sovremennikov* (Moscow: VTsPKhL, 1990) and A.V. Kochetov, comp., *Sviatoi chert: Taina Grigoriia Rasputina* (Moscow: Izdatel'stvo "Knizhnaia palata," 1991). Vladimir Purishkevich's account of Rasputin's assassination is probably the most reprinted text. See his *Iz dnevnika V.M. Purishkevicha: Ubiistvo Rasputina* (Moscow: SP "Interprint," 1990; Moscow: Sov.-Brit. sovmestnoe predpriiatie "Slovo," 1990); *Dnevnik: "Kak Ia ubil Rasputina"* (Moscow: Sovetskii Pisatel', 1990); and "Ubiistvo Rasputina," *Nauka i religiia*, 1989, no. 5: 32-36. His work is also included in the works by Chekhovskoi and Kochetov (above) and is serialized in the journal *Kuban'* (1990 no. 1: 62-72, no. 2: 65-74, no. 3: 78-90). Recent Soviet secondary sources discussing Rasputin include A. Ia. Avrekh, *Tsarizm nakanune sverzhdeniia* (Moscow: Nauka, 1989) and I. V. Alekseeva, *Agoniia serdechnogo soglasiia* (Leningrad: Lenizdat, 1990).

2. A.V. Bel'gard, "Pechat' i Rasputin," *Mosty* 9 (1962): 345.

3. Mikhail A. Novoselov, *Grigorii Rasputin i misticheskoe rasputstvo* (Moscow: Pechatnia A. I. Snegireva, 1912), 96 p. The copy of this pamphlet held in the rare book room of the Lenin Library is incomplete, with pages 50-64 missing. A typewritten version exists in the B. I. Nicolaevsky Collection (Series no. 74, folder no. 1) at the Hoover Institution on War, Revolution and Peace. See also Novoselov's "Golos pravoslavnogo mirianina," *Golos Moskvy*, 24 January (6 February) 1912, 4.

4. For a discussion of this event, see Joseph Fuhrmann, *Rasputin: A Life* (New York: Praeger, 1990), 81-92.

5. Novoselov, iv.

6. Novoselov, 13.

7. Novoselov, 15.

8. Novoselov, 46-47.

9. Novoselov, 49.

10. Mikhail V. Rodzianko, *The Reign of Rasputin: An Empire's Collapse* (London: A. M. Philpot, 1927), 31.

11. A. S. Prugavin, *Bunt protiv prirody. O khlystakh i khlystovshchine* (Moscow: Zadruga, 1917).

12. Central State Archive of the October Revolution (TsGAOR) f. 612 (G.E. Rasputin), op. 1, d, 13, *ll.* 1-2; and Central

State Historical Archive (TsGIA), f. 797 (Office of the Over Procurator of the Holy Synod, 2nd Department), op. 82, d. 77, *ll*. 9-10.
13. Rodzianko, 104-105; Fuhrmann, 106-109.
14. Based on clippings found in TsGAOR f. 612 (G.E. Rasputin), op. 1, d. 37, *ll*. 1-97.
15. *Utro Rossii*, 20 June (3 July) 1914. TsGAOR f. 612, op. 1, d. 37, *l. 5*.
16. *Den'*, 20 June (3 July) 1914. TsGAOR f. 612, op. 1, d. 37, *l*. 2.
17. "Pokushenie na ubiistvo Grigoriia Rasputina," *Russkoe slovo*, 18 June (1 July) 1914. TsGAOR f. 612, op. 1, d. 37, *l*. 86.
18. "Eshche o pokushenii na zhizn' Grigoriia Rasputina," *Moskovskii listok*, 19 June (2 July) 1914. TsGAOR f. 612, op. 1, d. 37, *l*. 65.
19. A. V., "Polovoi psikhoz," *Peterburgskii kur'er*, 20 June (3 July) 1914. TsGAOR f. 612, op. 1, d. 37 *l*. 3.
20. "Zhitie startsa Rasputina," *Birzhevye vedomosti*, 2-5 August (15-18 August) 1914. TsGAOR f. 612, op. 1, d. 39, *ll*. 2-3.
21. TsGAOR f. 612, o. 1, d. 22, *ll*, 81, 89. It is interesting to note that at almost the same time in which the articles were appearing in *Birzhevye vedomosti*, Rasputin reacted to an article in *Sibirskaia torgovaia gazeta* which referred to him as a horsethief. Rasputin telegraphed the editor to complain. "Quickly tell me where and when and whose horse I stole, as printed in the paper," he demanded. "I await your answer in three days. If you don't answer, I know to whom to complain" (TsGAOR f. 612, op. 1, d. 57, *l*, 20). The editor, Krylov, did not respond to the telegram. Instead, he reprinted it in the paper and called Rasputin a half educated *muzhik* ("Gniev startsa," *Sibirskaia torgovaia gazeta*, 29 July (11 August) 1915. TsGAOR f. 612, op. 1, d. 22, *l*. 74.
22. For example, see "Ubiistvo Grigoriia Rasputina," *Russkie vedomosti*, 20 December 1916 (2 January 1917), 4; and "Smert' Rasputina," *Vechernee vremia*, 21 December 1916 (3 January 1917). TsGAOR f. 612, op. 1, d. 39.
23. "Psikhiatr o Rasputine," *Petrogradskii listok*, 21 March (3 April) 1917, 1.
24. "Rasputinskiia zhertvy," *Petrogradskii listok*, 27 March (9 April) 1917, 2.
25. "Iz vospominanii psikhografologa, kharakteristika...Rasputina...," *Petrogradskaia gazeta*, 26 March (8 April) 1917, 3.

26. "Uzhasy starogo rezhima," *Petrogradskaia gazeta*, 9 (22 March) 1917, 2.

27. "Anna Vyrubova i Gr. Rasputin," *Petrogradskaia gazeta*, 25 March (7 April) 1917, 13.

28. "Temnyia sily u trona," *Petrogradskii listok*, 25 March (7 April) 1917, 2.

29. The exact number of pamphlets published about Rasputin is unknown. With the end of censorship and the flood of new publications, *Knizhnaia letopis'*, the weekly bibliographic publication of the *Knizhnaia palata*, was able to register only a fraction of what was appearing in print.

30. It is difficult to determine whether the dates indicated in *Knizhnaia letopis'* are accurate dates of publication, or simply indicate when the publications were received. The period from March to December 1917 remains one of the main bibliographic problems in modern Russian history.

31. Aleksei Mel'gunov, *Samoderzhavnye palachi* (Moscow: Svobodnoe slovo, 1917) 102 p. Edition size cited in *Knizhnaia letopis'*, 1917, no. 24: 4.

32. V. Sokolov, *Temnyia sily rossiiskoi imperii* (Moscow: Tipografiia T-va I. D. Sytina, 1917) 32 p. Edition size cited in *Knizhnaia letopis'*, 1917, no. 29-30: 8. I. Kovyl'-Bobyl', *Tsaritsa i Rasputin* (Petrograd: Svobodnoe izdatel'stvo, 1917) 48 p. Edition size cited in *Knizhnaia letopis'*, 1917, no. 15-16: 6.

33. *Sviatoi chert, Rasputin Grishka, zloi genii doma Romanovykh* (Moscow: Tipografiia P. V. Biel'tsova, 1917); O. Speranskii, *Za kulisami russkogo dvora* (Moscow: Moskovskoe izdatel'stvo, n.d.); *Krovavyi rezhim doma Romanovykh; nekotorye cherty iz zhizni Nikolaia II, Aleksandry Feodorovny i Grigoriia Rasputina* (Feodosiia: Torgovyi soiuz, 1917).

34. For example, M. Vasilevskii, *Grigorii Rasputin* (Moscow: Izd. T-va N. V. Vasil'eva, 1917). The author states (p. 3): "The influence of the evil genius of Russia, Rasputin, was enormous. In the final period...Tsardom was the Tsardom of Rasputin."

35. P. Kovalevskii, *Grishka Rasputin* (Moscow: Moskovskoe izdatel'stvo, 1917), 7-8.

36. Al'bionov, *Zhitie nepodobnogo startsa Grigoriia Rasputina* (Petrograd: Sever, 1917), 4.

37. For example, A. Mikhailov, *Temnyia sily* (Moscow: Zadruga, 1917), p. 13. For the official report on the Yar incident, see TsGAOR f. 612, op. 1, d. 22, *ll.* 56-59.

38. Al'bionov, *Zhitie nepodobnogo startsa Grigoriia Rasputina* (Petrograd: Sever, 1917) 7 p. This pamphlet was marked "only for adults." Also, Khersonskii, *Akafist Grishkie Rasputinie* (Petrograd: Uspekh, 1917) 4 p.

39. Al'bionov, 2.

40. *Tainy tsarskosel'skogo dvortsa* (Petrograd: Petrogradskii listok, 1917), 3.

41. A. Demidov, *Izmienniki Rossii* (Moscow: Moskovskoe izdatel'stvo, 1917), 18.

42. *Grigorii Rasputin. "Temnyia sily starogo rezhima."* (Feodosiia: Torgovyi soiuz, 1917), 2-3.

43. *Zhizn' i pokhozhdenie Grigoriia Rasputina* (Kiev: Tipo-Litografiia M. E. Zaiezdnogo, 1917), 9.

44. *Sviatoi chert. Rasputin Grishka, zloi genii doma Romanovykh* (Moscow: Tip. P. V. Biel'tsova, 1917), 12.

45. A. Demidov, *Izmienniki Rossii* (Moscow: Moskovskoe izdatel'stvo, 1917), 4.

46. Demidov, 4.

47. O. Speranskii, *Za kulisami russkogo dvora* (Moscow: Moskovskoe izdatel'stvo, 1917), 7.

48. *Tainy tsarskogo dvora i Grishka Rasputin* (Moscow: Tip. P. V. Biel'tsova, 1917), 4.

49. For example, M. Vasilevskii, *Grigorii Rasputin* (Moscow: Izd. T-va N. V. Vasil'eva, 1917), 5.

50. *Novaia knizhka o "sviatom chertie Grishkie"* (Moscow: Tip. E. D. Peterson, 1917), 3.

51. *Novaia knizhka*, 3.

52. Akim Valdykin, *Taina rozhdeniia b. nasliednika i pridvornaia kamaril'ia* (Petrograd: Pobeda, 1917), 7-8.

53. *Posliednie dni Rasputina* (Kiev: Tipo-Litografiia M. E. Zaiezdnogo, 1917), 45; *Kazn' Grishki Rasputina* (Petrograd: Izd. A. A. Kaspari, 1917), 15.

54. The eight known broadsides dealing with Rasputin are *Zhizn' i pokhozhdeniia aferista Grigoriia Rasputina. Pozor Doma Romanovykh* (Khar'kov: Kommercheskaia tip., 1917), TsGAOR f. 612, op. 1, d. 42, *l.* 2; *Starets Grishka s Nikolaem dosidielisia za chaem* (Rostov na Donu: n.p., 1917). TsGAOR f. 612, op. 1, d. 58, *l.* 1; *Kto otkryl glaza narodu o Rasputine* (Kiev: Izd. E.A. Ignatova, 1917), cited in *Knizhnaia letopis'*, 1917, no. 26: 3; *Sila vliianiia Rasputina na zhenshchin* (Kiev: n.p., 1917), cited in *Knizhnaia letopis'*, 1917, no. 26: 6; *Sviatoi chort* (Moscow: n.p., 1917), cited in *Knizhnaia letopis'* 1917,

no. 24: 7; *Alisa i Grishka s Nikolaem dosidielisia za chaem* (Khar'kov: n.p., 1917), cited in *Knizhnaia Letopis'*, 1917, no. 24: 1; and *Orgii Rasputina* (Khar'kov: n.p., 1917, cited in *Knizhnaia letopis'*, 1917, no. 20-21: 7. The broadside *Pozornyi Dom Romanovykh i akafist Grigoriia Rasputina* was published in Moscow (Izd-vo N. N. Sharapov) and in Elabuga (Tip. I. N. Kibardina) in 1917. A copy of the Moscow edition is in TsGAOR f. 612, op. 1, d. 42, *l.*1, while the Elabuga edition is cited in *Knizhnaia letopis'*, 1917 no. 20-21: 8.

55. Iliodor, *Tainy doma Romanovykh* (Moscow: Pechatnik, 1917) 156 p.

56. *Sviatoi chert, Rasputin Grishka, zloi genii doma Romanovykh* (Moscow: Tip. P.V. Biel'tsova, 1917) 14 p.

57. Kadmin, *Padenie dinastii, temnyia sily i revoliutsii* (Moscow: Tip. G.V. Vasil'eva, 1917) 148 p., N. N. Breshko-Breshkovskii, *Pozor dinastii* (Petrograd: Novyi satirikon, 1917) 195 p.

58. In regard to the film titles mentioned here, see *Kinezhurnal*, 1917, no. 3-4: iii and no. 5-6: 99. Unfortunately, Soviet secondary sources do not offer much information about the Rasputin films of the period. See V. Rosolovskaia, *Russkaia kinematografiia v 1917 godu: Materialy k istorii* (Moscow-Leningrad: Iskusstvo, 1937), 75-76, 139; Iu. S. Kalashnikov, ed., *Ocherki istorii sovetskogo kino* (Moscow: Iskusstvo, 1956), 1: 20; N. Iezuitov, "Kinoiskusstvo dorevoliutsionnoi Rossii," *Voprosy kinoiskusstvo*, 2 (1957): 303-304; and S.S. Ginzburg, *Kinematografiia dorevoliutsionnoi Rossii* (Moscow: Iskusstvo, 1963), 352-353. See also Richard Taylor, *The Politics of the Soviet Cinema 1917-1929* (Cambridge: Cambridge University Press, 1979), 22-23; and Jay Leyda, *Kino: A History of Russian and Soviet Film* 3rd ed. (Princeton: Princeton University Press, 1983), 98-99.

59. See V. P. Lapshin, *Khudozhestvennaia zhizn' Moskvy i Petrograda v 1917 godu* (Moscow: Sovetskii khudozhnik, 1983), 88, 103.

60. "Prizyv bibliotekarei," *Biulleteni literatury i zhizni*, 1917, no. 9-10, 62. These comments were reprinted from *Russkoe volia*, 1917, no. 125.

61. Viktor Shklovsky, *A Sentimental Journey, Memoirs, 1917-1922* (Ithaca: Cornell University Press, 1984), 8-9.

62. For two works which question what we know about Rasputin see Martin Kilcoyne, "The political influence of Rasputin," Ph.D. dissertation, University of Washington, 1961; and my "Rasputin and the fall of the Romanovs," Ph.D. dissertation, State University of New York at Binghamton, 1982. Much of the work presented here originally appeared in my dissertation.

MOSCOW, 1917:
WORKERS' REVOLUTION, WORKER CONTROL

Diane P. Koenker

The 1917 revolution came to Moscow in a burst of joyous enthusiasm. No sooner had the suppressed news of revolutionary strikes in Petrograd reached Russia's second city than crowds of workers, students, clerks, and soldiers surged into the city. Stopping along the way to pull reluctant onlookers into the revolutionary crowd and to strip resisting gendarmes of their weapons, the crowd triumphantly made its way to the city center, where it celebrated the end of oppressive tsarism and hailed the possibilities of a new political and social order.

Eight months later, the revolution took a new turn. This time, however, the mood was grim and somber. The October revolution represented the closing of certain of the possibilities immanent in February: the ten days that shook the world also eliminated the prospect that free Russia could transcend class politics and that a new political order could solve social and economic problems left as the legacy of tsarism. By October 1917 the Russian revolution was on the defensive: for many workers in the streets in October, the Soviet seizure of power represented the only way to save the revolution from disintegration. Hence, joyous crowds were absent, as workers and students faced each other armed with rifles and revolvers instead of joining in a triumphal march along city boulevards. Whereas the representative photograph of the February revolution in Moscow was a scene of a huge crowd gathered outside the gates of the old city, in October the mood of resignation was captured by a Red Guard unit posed menacingly, with rifles pointed, on its commandeered automobile.[1]   There were two revolutionary Moscows in 1917. One had a broad, optimistic, and amorphous agenda for revolutionary change, and included workers, soldiers, shopkeepers, intellectuals, bureaucrats and entrepreneurs. The second had a narrow agenda defined in part by the failures of the "all-democratic" revolution to achieve any of the items on the broad agenda, and in part by the conflicts set in motion during 1917 by competing efforts to define the revolution. The narrow revolution excluded much of Moscow society: it represented   workers,   soldiers   and   socialist intellectuals.   My concern in this article is the first revolution only, with the possibilities of revolutionary change set in motion by the February overthrow of the monarchy.   My particular focus is on one of the groups in Moscow which claimed to be an agency of change, the working class.

I am especially interested in the possibilities created in February for the assertion of workers' claims for greater autonomy, respect, and power within the workplace. There are of course other aspects of revolutionary activism, of the definition of revolutionary goals: politics, ideology, and institutions.   I have dealt with some of these issues before, but it seems important to address one significant aspect of Moscow's February revolution that has not until now received careful scrutiny: the set of phenomena characterized as worker control. But in order to explore these phenomena, it is necessary first to outline in brief the essential characteristics of Moscow as a revolutionary workers' city.

Moscow 1917

Moscow in 1917 existed in a traditionally agrarian society with relatively recent industrial development. Cities like Moscow and St. Petersburg had become pockets of capitalism, and in these centers capitalist relations came to dominate social life. Some historians of Russia have stressed the peculiar nature of Russian economic development, in which industrial workers labored full time in cities but maintained their families in their native villages, permitting a retreat to the countryside in times of industrial stress. Such workers were not fully proletarianized, not fully dependent on wage labor.[2] This may have been true in 1897, but the dual identity of Russian workers was changing during the years of rapid capitalist development in the early twentieth century. By 1914, it is indeed fair to speak of an urban proletariat in Moscow, St. Petersburg, Kharkov, and other large cities, a society of workers dependent for their livelihood on wage labor. Russian industrial capitalists were perhaps newer at the game than their West European counterparts, but, due to the advantages of backwardness, they shared a common level of technology with the West and by and large demonstrated attitudes toward labor very similar to those of capitalists in the West. They ranged from those who chose naked exploitation, to paternalist managers, to "corporate liberals" who sought to shape an enlightened state policy toward industry and labor.

A second point is the nature of the state. The February revolution in Russia dramatically transformed state power. Tsarist Russia, despite fatal weaknesses, remained a centralized repressive monarchy until the collapse of the autocracy on March 2. It was not very effective at policy making in the final years of its existence, but the organs of repression remained at full strength. This all changed after February. The secret police and army were no longer available for preserving domestic tranquility and the new volunteer militia could hardly cope with ordinary crime, let alone challenges to the prerogatives of the ruling class. Workers could not be arrested or drafted for participating in labor protest. This left the new democracy free to demand reforms and to mobilize to support its interests. But the new state apparatus, a Provisional Government tentatively trying to guide the ship of state toward a constitutional assembly, was unable to satisfy the competing claims of the revolutionaries for war and peace, socialism and capitalism. Alexander Kerensky insisted in retrospect that the Provisional Government had enacted important and stabilizing social reforms, but in fact reform measures were preparatory, tentative, and contradictory. Whether in the area of land reform, work rights in the factory, or regulation of the home front's food supply, the Provisional Government was unable to develop, let alone implement, an effective policy. Increasingly during the course of 1917, the role of the state diminished; it became a minor player in the battle between workers and capitalists in the city and between peasants and landlords in the country. When the Bolsheviks assumed leadership of Soviet power in October, a process of new state building began immediately, complete with a sense of direction (official ideology) and power to enforce that sense.

A final point to be addressed here is the role of ideology, particularly with respect to revolutionary models. In February 1917, there was no successful socialist revolution to emulate. Russian workers in 1917, as others in the capitalist world, had an assortment of doctrines from which to choose: capitalism (still revolutionary in tsarist Russia), socialism, internationalism, patriotism, centralism, syndicalism, anarchism. In terms of political parties, workers were most likely in 1917 to support one of three socialist groups that had operated above or under ground since the late nineteenth century: the Marxists, divided into Bolshevik and Menshevik Social Democratic wings, and the agrarian socialist Socialist Revolutionary party, which enjoyed a great deal of worker support. In competing for workers' allegiance, each of these parties had only ideas to offer, not accomplishments. In 1917, ideology was only in the making, and even Bolshevism, not to mention its Stalinist and Trotskyist variants, was not as powerful an ideological or mobilizational factor as it would become in Russia or Europe in the 1920s and 1930s.

Moscow in 1917: City and Society

With these points in mind, let me turn now to an examination of the revolution in Moscow, to the dynamic interplay between the revolutionary city and its working class. Moscow in 1917 was a city of nearly two million inhabitants. According to a detailed census of 1912, upper and middle classes (gentry, professionals, industrialists, and their families) comprised 20 percent of the population. Small entrepreneurs and their families accounted for 7.3 percent of the total. Of the remaining groups, factory workers and their families accounted for 15 percent of the total urban population, artisans and their families

16 percent, and employees and service workers (white collar, transport, domestic service workers) and their families represented 33 percent of the population.[3] The effect of World War I on the Moscow economy tended to increase the size of the factory work force at the expense of the artisanal and especially the service sectors. Thus, the number of factory workers by 1917 had doubled, from 165,000 in 1912 (counted without dependents) to about 360,000 in 1917.[4] In short, Moscow was a socially heterogeneous city and one whose work force was balanced among factory, artisanal, and service and transport workers.

Moscow's revolutionary experience was marked from the outset of the February revolution by moderation on the part of its political leaders from all parties, and by a spirit of cooperation. In part, as I have argued, this was due to the heterogeneous social composition of the city and of the working class. Metalists, who were extremely militant in Petrograd and throughout Europe, did not dominate the Moscow labor force the way they did in Petrograd. In any case, Moscow's February revolution was a relatively bloodless affair and was characterized by an absence of class tension, as industrialists and workers congratulated each other on the fall of the old regime. The Moscow Soviet quickly declared its support of dual power and tentatively endorsed a defensive revolutionary war: more important, at the outset of the revolution, the Soviet worked together with organs of the Provisional Government to construct a new political order for the city.

Economic and political crisis combined to increase the tension in the city among classes and among parties. Consequently, even though defenders of the Provisional Government assumed Moscow to be quiet enough to hold its State Conference at the Bolshoi Theater there in mid-August, leaders of the revolution were met instead by a general strike of workers protesting the policies and plans of the Kerensky government. Class hostility among workers in Moscow intensified with the Kornilov uprising, and this hostility was translated in September into a Bolshevik party majority both in the Soviet of Workers' Deputies (elected by workers only) and in elections in municipal district dumas (elected by the entire adult population). By October, a wide spectrum of Moscow's workers supported a transfer of power to a government of soviets, although it is important to remember that this support did not necessarily also imply support either for an armed seizure of power or for a Bolshevik monopoly of power. Moscow's Bolshevik leaders in particular were among the critics of the party's arrogation of this power. To the end, then, Moscow remained relatively moderate in its response to revolution.

From within this matrix of Moscow's unique combination of historical, social, and economic factors emerged processes that linked Moscow's workers to broader trends both in Russia and in the West. Freed from the tutelage of the tsarist system of repression and paternalism, Moscow's workers in 1917 began to organize themselves, and to extend the limits of their control over life in the factory and life in the neighborhoods. In the remaining pages of this article, I wish to explore the nature of this struggle to extend limits by examining the experience of "workers' control" in the months between February and October, 1917.

"Contested Terrain": The Struggle for Workplace Control

Much of the discussion of workers' control in the Russian revolution concerns the dichotomy between the autonomous, democratic activities of factory committees before October and the imposition of hierarchical structure on this movement by Bolshevik institutions after October.[5] Depending on whether one takes a democratic or productivist perspective, the fate of workers' control in 1918 and after can be seen as either a betrayal or fulfillment of workers' basic aspirations revealed during 1917. But in this discussion, defining the nature of "control" in 1917 itself often remains outside the agenda.

More central to the revolutionary process of 1917 is the meaning of workers' control to the participants in the revolution at the time. The Russian word for control, *kontrol'*, comes from the French and is more benign than the English homonym: it connotes "checking" and "supervision" rather than direction and management. Control therefore included activities ranging from monitoring factory warehouses for fuel reserves, to auditing factory accounts, to taking responsibility for auxiliary factory activities like food supply or housing. It also included workers' committees taking over factory administrations and throwing the bosses out. This latter activity has been widely identified as standard "workers' control" in the Western historical literature. "Workers conceived of control as ownership," according to Frederick Kaplan. John Keep claims that delegates to Petrograd factory committee conferences understood the slogan of worker control to mean "a real transfer of power within the enterprise to the men's chosen representatives, who were to exercise the functions of management in the interests of their electors."[6]

More recent scholarship has refuted this view. When workers took over the direction of factories (itself a rare occurrence), they did so defensively, because the alternative was almost always the closing of the enterprise and the loss of work altogether. Whether this was therefore an economic movement, as William Rosenberg has written, or a political one, as Steve Smith argues, this extreme form of control must be seen in the specific context of the experience of 1917.

Some Soviet historians go further than their Western counterparts in their understanding of workers' control. For some, worker control includes all activities of the factory committees, including negotiation of higher wages and organization of food supply and housing.[7] S. A. Smith advocates the acceptance of Z. V. Stepanov's definition of control, which limits the term to control at the point of production.[8] Control concerns not wages and hours but regulation of the labor process and the social organization of production. The problem, as Smith concedes, is that in 1917 theory and precise definition fail to describe adequately the phenomena of control, whether workers were monitoring the activities of management or actively competing for power at the point of production.

This is so, I would argue, for two reasons. First, one must accept that the workplace is, in Richard Edwards' phrase, always "contested terrain." The interests of labor and management at the point of production do not coincide. Management wants efficiency (and, in the capitalist economy, profits resulting therefrom). Workers have no interest in producing someone else's surplus; any effort beyond the threshold of boredom or without the inner satisfaction of creative work is not in their interests. Management can try to stimulate productivity with pecuniary incentives, but historically it has had to supplement economic incentives with other forms of control: rules on the organization of work, work pace, conditions, rights, and relations among employees.[9]   Cressey and MacInnes go further. "Capitalists must harness workers' creative powers, and therefore rely on eliciting a degree of cooperation as well as using coercive methods. Workers, as well as trying to resist subordination, have an interest in the viability of the units of capital that employ them."[10]   For this reason a "balance of power" is struck. Managers accept certain rules of shop floor organization more or less favorable to what workers consider an acceptable level of effort. Conflict occurs over the amount of compensation for this effort. In other words, conflict takes the form of economic struggle; strikes are most often fought over wages and other pecuniary issues.[11] Historically, however, managers have sought to realign the balance of workplace power in their favor, to extract more from their labor force; the results include new forms of technological control, such as rationalization and the assembly line, new rules and penalties for their violation, and intimidation of workers by selective dismissals.[12] At such times, the resistance of workers takes the form not of economic struggle but of the struggle for control, to reestablish an understanding about an acceptable level of effort on the shop floor. As Richard Edwards notes, both components of the slogan, "A fair day's work for a fair day's pay," are contestable items.[13]

Secondly, and of particular importance in the comparative study of revolutions and revolutionary cities, the 1917 revolution exploded the former limits of the "terrain of consent." As William Rosenberg and I have argued elsewhere, the February revolution did not so much introduce new rules of the game into workplace relations as shatter the old rules without offering a new system to replace them.[14] Even if workers and managers tentatively accepted the rules of a bourgeois-democratic system of shop floor relations after February, the limits and extent of this system were far from clear. Even in democratic industrial relations systems, as I have argued, the workplace and its rules are contested terrain. In 1917, precisely because of the political and social revolution, the "norms of control" were especially plastic. They were therefore especially prone to be established through experiment, through negotiation, and through conflict.

Workers' Control in Moscow, 1917

One of the most radical forms of workers' sallies across the accepted frontier of control in Russia occurred so immediately and so universally after the February revolution that it generated surprisingly little managerial resistance. From the first days of the February revolution, workers at the factory level took advantage of their political power and the new spirit of democracy to insist on the dismissal of managerial personnel whose past behavior had been inimical to their interests. Such actions were widespread in Petrograd, where hundreds of administrators, foremen, technicians, engineers, and other representatives of the old factory order were summarily expelled from their posts.[15]

Similar action occurred elsewhere in the provinces and in Moscow. Here the record is less complete than for Petrograd, or else the actions were not as common or as thorough. Unlike the wholesale purges of Petrograd factories, in Moscow only the ouster of isolated individuals received notice in the press or in Factory Inspector reports.[16] Workers at the cable factory "Optovik" demanded the dismissal of a foreman who had fired workers for their participation in the days of the February revolution.[17] At the Prokhorovka cotton manufacture, the factory committee decided to fire three administrative personnel, with no reason given.[18] Metal workers at the Dobrov-Nabgolts machine construction plant insisted that the director, co-owner Nabgolts, resign, despite twenty years of service in the factory. Perhaps this was a settling of scores for Nabgolts' actions in the 1905 revolution, when he fired activist workers for their participation in the October general strike.[19] Motives for firing were varied, when given at all. At a telephone factory, workers wanted to fire two engineers because they were totally unqualified. At the Gulavi boiler factory the owner was evicted because he was German. At the Elevator Construction factory, workers charged "improper behavior" and a general meeting voted to fire a foreman on July 17.[20]

Elsewhere, the workers' decision to oust an administrator followed from a disagreement over wages or other demands. Most such incidents occurred, as they did in Petrograd, in the first three months after the revolution, although one or two instances continued to be reported in Moscow each month thereafter. From the records at my disposal, I have concluded that conflicts concerning administrative personnel arose in some forty cases, about half of them during April and May. Only eight of these conflicts led to strikes; in the others workers gained their objectives either through moral suasion, force or the threat of force,[21] or the outside intervention of soviets or conciliation boards.

Another incremental change in the balance of power in the factory was reflected in the campaign for the eight hour day. This was a grand political slogan dating back officially to the First International and current among workers even before that. It had been high on the list of workers' demands in Russia in 1905. But, however politicized, the eight hour work day had to be implemented in the factories, and in demanding it workers signaled their intention to claim control over the length of their work day.[22] The issue was contested in many different ways. In Petrograd, the association of factory and mill owners agreed on March 10 to the universal introduction of the eight-hour work day in factories along with recognition of factory committees and the establishment of arbitration boards. This was a three-pronged agreement designed to preserve labor peace, but one which substantially shifted the balance of workplace power.[23] In Moscow manufacturers were more reluctant to yield on the eight hour day, so in scores of factories, workers demanded the issue be settled politically, either by a decree of the Provisional Government or by the Moscow Soviet. Some workers went further and unilaterally implemented the shorter day in their factories. This, I would argue, was another assertion of control, another battle won by workers. Still, as with the administrative evictions, workers seized control of the factory clock in relatively few plants. Whereas during the months between March and October some 73 factories publicly declared support for the shorter day, and workers in 27 plants made the eight hour day a strike issue, only in twelve did workers actually claim the shorter day without the agreement of their management, *iavochnym poriadkom*.[24] All of these latter instances occurred in the first three weeks after the February revolution, before the Moscow Soviet was able to enforce its decree on the shorter work day. Most of the twelve plants employed skilled metal workers, workers accustomed to controlling the pace of their work, and most were located in the most concentrated industrial district of Moscow, the Zamoskvorech'e district just south of the Moscow River.

Coming so early in the revolutionary year, these two kinds of actions in which workers claimed authority over certain prerogatives formerly held by management suggest that some workers, at any rate, had been inclined to challenge management over the limits of control even before the fall of tsarism. The collapse of the old regime gave these skilled confident workers the freedom to assert their claims in the workplace without fear that the government would lend its repressive powers to factory authority. These claims need not be seen as responses to revolutionary politics and revolutionary challenges; they emanated, I would argue, from a longer term sense of workers' place in the factory and of the "natural rights" of workers. Management felt especially vulnerable in the early weeks of the revolution, perhaps out of guilt, perhaps because state power could no longer enforce its interests, and so it conceded this territory with remarkably little struggle.

As politics became more heated, however, the struggle to define workplace control sharpened. Workers sought to negotiate new norms of control; the Soviets and the Provisional Government also sought to influence these norms; and management began to resist further encroachment on what it saw as the natural rights of property ownership. This struggle became somewhat routinized in the form of strikes and labor conflicts during the spring of 1917. Workers made demands, management accepted or rejected them, workers then faced a choice of whether to give up their claims or to strike in support of their demands. Strikes became an increasingly popular method of struggle as the weeks of the revolutionary order unfolded; in Moscow, more strikes began in May than in any other month of the revolution.

The strike was a weapon normally less challenging to management's sense of propriety than the unilateral actions of the early spring, and the predominantly wage-related content of strikes in Moscow reinforces the impression that strikes in 1917 were part of an institutionalized, orderly system of industrial relations. Nonetheless, the content of strikes also suggests the extent to which workers remained interested in challenging managerial prerogatives and pushing back the limits of control.

During the eight months between March and October, some 70 percent of all strikes in Moscow included claims about wages: higher pay, either by time or by piece, bonuses, and minimum wages. But in addition, many of the 247 strikes in the period included demands about other issues.[25] One set of issues concerned workers' dignity. In thirty strikes, Moscow workers demanded reforms in the personal relations between management and workers or between customers and workers: politeness in the workshop, an end to tipping in restaurants and taverns. Another set of issues concerned managerial rights more directly. In nearly half (45 percent) of all strikes, workers made demands which in the context of labor relations at the time clearly challenged the prerogatives of management. Such demands included issues nominally about wages, as for example, when workers demanded the old ten hours level of pay for eight hours of work. They included issues of work conditions: changes in hours, the provision of a dining room for workers, and the right of waitresses to sit down during slack periods in restaurants. For example, the demand for a paid vacation for all workers with six to twelve months seniority in a plant challenged the prevailing right of management to grant vacations as special awards to a selected few loyal employees. Such demands also included issues more traditionally associated with job control: recognition of unions or of factory committees, allowing factory committees to hire and fire workers, changes in job descriptions and work rules.

Such demands, whose intent was to extend the limits of control over these productive activities, appeared most frequently in Moscow at moments of "revolutionary situations," both in the aftermath of the fall of the old regime and in the weeks of political crisis leading to the October revolution. Two-thirds of all strikes in March, for example, concerned these issues (many of them over the eight-hour work day). Thereafter, such demands declined in proportion to strikes as a whole, until September. In that month, half of the strikes involved issues of factory control, broadly defined, and in October, the share of such strikes climbed again to two-thirds of the total. Most of these strikes also involved economic issues, but it is impossible and probably incorrect to identify "primary" and "secondary" demands, as the factory inspectors tried to do before February. In short, these figures indicate that worker pressure for increased autonomy was an important factor in labor conflict in 1917, and one especially intense during moments of the greatest political instability.

Far fewer cases of actual worker control, as in self-management, were reported in 1917. The known cases are of two types, cooperative and hostile worker management. "Cooperative" cases of management are not normally revealed in the published record, and it is not possible to determine how frequently they occurred. In these instances, management willingly devolved some of its authority to workers' committees. At the Prokhorovka textile manufacture, for example, a city within a city that furnished jobs, housing and recreational facilities for its workers, the factory committee assumed responsibility for policing the dormitories and for eliminating theft of textiles from the factory floor.[26] In numerous plants, workers were given authority to run factory canteens or factory shops.[27] By and large, these shifts in the locus of authority were not contentious. In at least one factory, workers and management cooperated amicably in actual factory operations. At the Provodnik rubber plant, a technologically advanced plant evacuated from Riga to Moscow during the war, "the commission for workers' control appeared for the administration not a hindrance, but a help. Through the commission passed all daily affairs, including the permission for finished goods to leave the factory premises." The factory administration actually enlisted the workers' aid in seeking raw materials, because the workers had more influence with the Moscow Soviet, which had a hand in allocation. As a result of this partnership, claims a skilled worker from this period, productivity was higher after the February revolution than before.[28]

To be sure, more aggressive and unilateral acts of worker management also occurred in Moscow during 1917. Wood workers at the Benno-Rontaller button factory seized their factory on October 12, operated it under the direction of the factory committee, and after the October revolution turned the director over to a revolutionary tribunal on the charge of sabotage.[29] On October 11, workers at the Shmulevich electrical fittings plant seized the factory and reported to the owner their intention to sell off the plant's inventory.[30] At the Guzhon metallurgical plant, conflicts between technical personnel and workers—who were demanding that some of them be fired—led to a strike of the white-collar staff. When the plant owners closed the factory, workers remained inside and ran the plant through their factory committee.[31] Ultimately, the government was prevailed upon to sequester and to operate the factory itself.

Such instances were in fact rare. I have uncovered only twelve cases in which workers actually seized control of their own plants. In one case, the workers took over from their ousted German owner (see above). Almost all the other cases involved strikes or other disputes that had already shut down production. Workers took over the factory in order to keep the plant running, to protect their livelihoods. For example, three such cases emerged from a protracted strike of 110,000 workers in hundreds of shops and factories in the Moscow leather industry. Having negotiated in what they felt was good faith since mid-July, workers at the Dement, Rus, and Shevrokhrom factories decided in mid-October to force the issue. They seized the factory keys, occupied the plants, and announced they would operate them on their own if the owners did not settle within one day. The takeover was not intended to be permanent, but rather a more extreme form of collective pressure, albeit one that exceeded the "acceptable" norms of collective bargaining in 1917. But it is significant that the chief issue of contention in this long strike, the one on which management adamantly refused to yield, was control over hiring and firing.

As S. A. Smith and David Mandel have shown for Petrograd, this extreme form of workers' control was defensive, a last resort in struggles over other issues rather than an act of principled anarchy. To contemporaries, of course, the logic of this behavior was not so apparent. "Anarchy in the Factories" read the headline over the story about the Benno-Rontaller takeover in the conservative *Utro Rossii.*[32] William Chamberlin, following the tone of the liberal and conservative press, wrote in his history that "the wresting of Russia's industrial enterprises out of the hands of their owners was the third major event of a socially revolutionary upheaval that was also marked by the breakup of the army and by the seizure of the landed estates by peasants." Russia's workers, he claimed, welcomed "the first opportunity to pull down the temple of private property."[33]

Conclusions: Property, Democracy, and the Frontier of Control

Did workers in 1917 reject the notion of private property? I would argue that workers in 1917 were much less wedded to this notion than their opponents, the Russian bourgeoisie. Outright seizures of property were rare. But extremely frequent in 1917 were demands—in strikes and political resolutions—for state or soviet ownership or management of property. The evidence from published sources and from workers' behavior suggests that workers perceived property as a public trust, as a social good. If private entrepreneurs operated their trust in a manner beneficial to the society as a whole, workers accepted this reality and struggled within this relationship to preserve their domain of autonomy. Hence the frequency of issues about control of the eight-hour work day. When individuals in private enterprises betrayed the public trust, or were seen to have betrayed this trust over long years of tsarist authority, workers singled out the offenders and drove them from their posts. And in extreme cases, as at Guzhon or Benno-Rontaller or Shmulevich, workers acted to remove the plant from the control of those who would not continue to operate it, and turned it over to those who would: the Provisional Government, the Soviet, or, usually as a last resort, themselves.

Such attitudes may conflict with more traditional bourgeois notions of private property, but they do not appear incongruent with the long history of Russian state control—supervision and management—of industry and of the economy in general. The notion of the sanctity of private property was not nearly as well developed in Russia in the twentieth century as in England, France, Germany, and the United States, so it is hardly surprising that, given the collapse of the old order in February 1917, the very nature of property became one of the contested issues. It is precisely that absence of old norms and the struggle to establish new ones, whether in political, social, or economic life, that made 1917 a revolutionary year, and Moscow a revolutionary city.

It is also because of this absence of norms that workers' control in Russia has been so difficult to comprehend. The issue is not whether workers preferred authority or autonomy, or whether they were driven by economic need or political ideas. The struggles workers engaged in during 1917 were of the same general nature that workers everywhere were accustomed to waging; they grew out of the contradictory relations of production described at the outset of this discussion. These relations were inherently contradictory, and such struggles would continue to engage workers even after the establishment of Soviet power and a socialist order.

NOTES

1. See L. Volkov-Lannit, *Istoriia pishetsia ob"ektivom* (Moscow, 1971), 158, 185.

2. R. E. Johnson, *Peasant and Proletarian: The Working Class of Moscow in the Late Nineteenth Century* (New Brunswick, N.J., 1979), offers a history and new contribution to this discussion.

3. *Statisticheskii ezhegodnik goroda Moskvy i Moskovskoi gubernii*, vyp. 2 (Moscow, 1927), 68-74.

4. This is by my count; an official statistical publication gives 206,000 workers in 1917. See *Fabrichno-zavodskaia promyshlennost' goroda Moskvy i Moskovskoi gubernii*, (Moscow, 1928), 1.

5. Paul Avrich, "The Russian Factory Committees in 1917," *Jahrbuecher fuer Geschichte Osteuropas* 11 (1963): 161-182; Frederick I. Kaplan, *Bolshevik Ideology and the Ethics of Soviet Labor* (New York, 1969); Chris Goodey, "Factory Committees and the Dictatorship of the Proletariat (1918)," *Critique* 3 (1974); M. Brinton, "Factory Committees and the Dictatorship of the Proletariat," *Critique*, 4 (1975); William G. Rosenberg, "Workers and Workers' Control in the Russian Revolution," *History Workshop*, 5 (1977): 89-97; S.A. Smith, "Craft Consciousness, Class Consciousness: Petrograd, 1917," *History Workshop*, 11 (1981); Carmen Siriani, *Workers' Control and Socialist Democracy: The Soviet Experience* (London, 1982); S.A. Smith, *Red Petrograd: Revolution in the Factories, 1917-1918* (Cambridge, 1983).

6. J. L. H. Keep, *The Russian Revolution: A Study in Mass Mobilization* (New York, 1976), 89, and Kaplan, *Bolshevik Ideology*, 128-29, quoted in Smith, *Red Petrograd*, 141.

7. T. A. Ignatenko, *Sovetskaia istoriografiia rabochego kontrolia i natsionalizatsii promyshlennosti v SSSR, 1917-67 gg.* (Moscow, 1971); V. I. Selitskii, *Massy v bor'be za rabochii kontrol' (mart-iiun' 1917 g.)* (Moscow, 1971); M.L. Itkin, "Tsentry fabrichno-zavodskikh komitetov v 1917 g.," *Voprosy istorii* 2 (1974): 21-35; L. I. Balashova, "Rabochii kontrol' nad raspredeleniiam v period podgotovki sotsialisticheskoi revolitusii," *Voprosy istorii* 5 (1973): 47-58.

8. Z. V. Stepanov, *Rabochie Petrograda v period podgotovki i provedeniia oktiabr'skogo vooruzhennogo vosstaniia* (Moscow, 1965).

9. Richard Edwards, *Contested Terrain: The Transformation of the Workplace in the Twentieth Century* (New York, 1979), 12-13.

10. Peter Cressey and John MacInnes, "Voting for Ford: Industrial Democracy and the Control of Labor," *Capital and Class*, no. 11 (1980), 5-33, as cited in P.K. Edwards, *Conflict at Work: A Materialist Analysis of Workplace Relations* (Oxford, 1986), 42.

11. Carter L. Goodrich, *The Frontier of Control: A Study of British Workshop Relations* (New York, 1920): 51-54.

12. See Michelle Perrot, "Three Ages of Industrial Discipline in Nineteenth-Century France," in John M. Merriman, ed., *Consciousness and Class Experience in Nineteenth-Century Europe* (New York, 1980)

13. Richard Edwards, *Contested Terrain*, 15.

14. William G. Rosenberg and Diane P. Koenker, "The Limits of Formal Protest: Worker Activism and Social Polarization in Petrograd and Moscow, March to October 1917," *American Historical Review* 2 (1987): 296-326.

15. Smith, *Red Petrograd*, 56-57; Heather Hogan, "Conciliation Boards in Revolutionary Petrograd: Aspects of the Crisis of Labor-Management Relations in 1917," *Russian History* 9 (1982): 49-66.

16. The sources for the Petrograd dismissals include archival records of factory committees and of conciliation boards; these records are not available for Moscow, and it is conceivable that such actions were just as common. This would explain why in neither city was there much notice paid in the daily press to the dismissals.

17. *Gazeta Kopeika*, 28 March 1917; *Vpered*, 24 March 1917; *Izvestiia Moskovskogo Soveta Rabochikh Deputatov*, 24 March 1917.

18. *Torgovo-Promyshlennaia Gazeta*, 27 April 1917; Tsentral'nyi gosudarstvennyi istoricheskii arkhiv (TsGIA), f. 23, op. 27, d. 360, p. 42. Curiously no mention is made of this action in the minutes for the day in question of the factory committee, published in 1931 ("Protokoly fabrichno-zavodskogo komiteta Prokhorovskoi Trekhgornoi manufaktury" *Istoriia proletariata SSSR*, 8 (1931): 112-13.

19. TsGIA, f. 23, op. 27, d. 360, p. 43; on 1905, Laura Engelstein, *Moscow, 1905* (Stanford, 1982): 93.

20. TsGIA, f. 23, op. 27, d. 360, p. 43; *Revoliutsionnoe dvizhenie Rossii v mae-iiune 1917 g.* (Moscow, 1959), 283; Gosudarstvennyi arkhiv Moskovskoi oblasti (GAMO), f. 196, op. 1, d. 18, *l*.5.

21. The standard Russian application of force was to seize the individual, put him in a wheelbarrow (sometimes covered with a sack, sometimes smeared with machine oil), and dump him outside the factory, in a puddle, dung heap, or nearby pond. I have uncovered one

case of similar practice in Hamburg. Richard Comfort, *Revolutionary Hamburg* (Stanford, 1966).

22. The demand also signified a claim over the nonworking portion of their day; earlier management objections to the eight hour work day had included the opinion that the free hours would only be idled away and workers were better off inside the factory. Defenders of the eight hour work day in 1917 took pains to describe the positive uses workers would make of their extra time. M. Roe Smith, "Becoming Engineers," unpublished paper on American entrepreneurs in the early 19th century; I. Sukhodeev, *Svobodnye chasy rabochego (gimnastika i igry na svezhem vozdukhe, kniga, isskustvo, sel'skoe khoziaistvo, ekskursii, semeinyi krug)* (Moscow, 1917).

23. Smith, *Red Petrograd*, 66.

24. These calculations come from Diane Koenker, "Moscow Workers in 1917" (Ph.D. dissertation, University of Michigan, 1976): 168.

25. The sources for this discussion are the strikes included in the data base for a study of strikes across Russia in 1917, which have been analyzed in Diane P. Koenker and William G. Rosenberg, *Strikes and Revolution in Russia, 1917* (Princeton, 1989). For purposes of this study, a strike is defined as a work stoppage with common goals, and such a strike may involve one or more enterprises. (The Factory Inspectorate definition of a strike is a single enterprise on strike, whether coordinated with others or not. This difference must be kept in mind when comparing our figures with those incomplete statistics furnished for 1917 by the Factory Inspectorate.) This source base is not identical to that used for chapter 8 of my earlier monograph, *Moscow Workers*.

26. "Protokoly fabrichno-zavodskogo komiteta Prokhorovskoi Trekhgornoi manufaktury," *Istoriia proletariata SSSR* 8 (1931): 105-171; 9 (1932): 154-178.

27. Balashova, "Rabochii kontrol' nad raspredeleniiam," 47-58.

28. Eduard Dune, "Zapiski krasnogvardeitsa," unpublished manuscript, Nicolaevsky archive, Hoover Institution, Stanford, California, 32-33.

29. *Uprochenie sovetskoi vlasti v Moskve i moskovskoi gubernii. Dokumenty i materialy* (Moscow, 1958): 212-13; *Utro Rossii*, 22 October 1917; *Delo Naroda*, 15 October 1917.

30. *Trudovaia Kopeika*, 12 October 1917.

31. *Ekonomicheskoe polozhenie Rossii nakanune velikoi oktiabr'skoi revoliutsii* (Moscow, 1957), 1: 436 ff.

32. *Utro Rossii*, 22 October 1917.
33. William H. Chamberlin, *The Russian Revolution*, vol. 1 (New York, 1935): 275.